CONFRONTING THE CRISIS:
WAR, POLITICS AND CULTURE
IN THE EIGHTIES

The proceedings of the Essex Sociology
of Literature Conference, July 1983.

edited by

Francis Barker
Peter Hulme
Margaret Iversen
Diana Loxley

University of Essex
Colchester
1984

PREFACE

This volume contains the proceedings of the 1983 Essex Sociology of
Literature conference, the seventh since the series began in 1976.
The 1982 conference, published as *The Politics of Theory*, reviewed
the theoretical developments over those seven years and re-emphasised
the central presupposition of the conferences, that it was necessary
to hold in sustained focus the relationship between politics and theory
in face of the post-structuralist tendency to depoliticise. *Confronting
the Crisis* then undertook to utilise the theoretical skills developed
over the preceding period in the explicitly political analysis of the
present conjuncture and its immediate provenance. Details of the
earlier conferences can be found inside the back cover.

With one exception all the essays included here were delivered as papers
at the conference. David Morrison and Howard Tumber were unable at the
last minute to attend the conference; we welcome the opportunity to
publish their contribution to an important debate.

For their help with organizing and running the conference we would like
to thank Noreen Proudman, Celia Hirst and Barbara Disney.

The editors
University of Essex
May 1984

CONTENTS

RIGHT APPROACHES: SOURCES OF THE NEW CONSERVATISM	Boyd Tonkin	1
IMAGES OF THE SIXTEENTH AND SEVENTEENTH CENTURIES As a History of the Present	Simon Barker	15
THE POLITICS OF MEANING	Catherine Belsey	27
ON NUCLEAR TERMS IN THE UK	Gordon Brotherston	39
THE FALL AND RISE OF LABOURISM	Ian H. Birchall	53
THE FALKLANDS/MALVINAS WAR - 1982: A PERSPECTIVE FROM THE REPUBLIC OF IRELAND	John Arden	62
SOME NOTES ON MEDIA COVERAGE OF THE FALKLANDS Or: "The Soviet Union Could Teach Us a Few Lessons"	Anthony Barnett	74
THE FALKLANDS WAR: TRIUMPH OF AN IDEOLOGY	Christopher Hampton	90
THE GOVERNMENT AND INFORMATION IN TIME OF WAR: THE FALKLANDS AND THE MEDIA	David Morrison & Howard Tumber	100
TELEVISION NEWS AND THE LABOUR MOVEMENT	Antony Easthope	111
THE VERBAL ARSENAL OF BLACK WOMEN WRITERS IN AMERICA	Melissa Walker	118
LITERATURE AND SOCIETY IN CRISIS The Case of Israel	Nurith Gertz	131
CRISIS, INSTITUTIONS AND THE UNCONSCIOUS	David Punter	140
"WHY I WROTE A BOOK ON THE YORKSHIRE RIPPER"	Nicole Ward Jouve	153

RIGHT APPROACHES: SOURCES OF THE NEW CONSERVATISM

Boyd Tonkin

Within the speech and writing of academic radicalism, a rhetoric which allies the notions of "crisis" and "confrontation" has the effect of turning attention outwards, from text to referent. Invoking an image of material threat and disturbance, the language connotes a violent encounter between the instruments of understanding - method, analysis, discourse - and some present or impending historical calamity. The crisis this paper attempts to confront concerns the presence and power of right-wing positions in current British cultural and political debate. However, the approach adopted assumes that no valid distinction can be maintained between a crisis "out there", in a distant realm of events and ideologies, and a confrontation "in here", staged within a safe discursive space of critique and interpretation. For the retreats and divisions this conference addresses lie inside as well as outside the means it employs, and one persistent symptom of "crisis" in British intellectual dissent is its unease in meeting, or even recognising, overt and militant conservatism on a theoretical plane.

Political hegemony requires and generates a network of ideological defences. "Thatcherism", in its daily enforcement of values and principles which vastly exceed the scope of free market economics, rests on and refers to a growing body of recent intellectual work. Through the 1970s the emergence within academies and media of a New Right eager for a name and an identity accelerated, a process which in Britain succeeded by a few years the cult of the "nouveaux philosophes" in France and matched the growth of American neo-conservatism. Election victories in 1979 and 1983, and the presence in the Conservative administration of ministers willing to patronise congenial ideologues, have led to a spate of descriptive accounts striving to define and connect the diverse origins, personnel, and institutional formations of this ostensibly fresh and fertile clerisy. (1) Inevitably these journalistic sketches are marked by an urge to personalise and classify. A scene thick with huddled and secretive sects appears, lit by the reflected glory of executive power. In another medium, David Edgar's play *Maydays* dramatises the perplexity of its ex-revolutionary hero as his rightward migration leads to a conservatism split between the liberty of the market and the grandeur of the nation, increasingly willing to argue "not for the roll-back of the state but for the reassertion of its full authority". (2) Here, an emphasis on the social and psychic roots of political apostasy squeezes the rightist theory Martin Glass encounters into ready-made moulds of spoken doctrine, its outlines simplified in the service of theatrical clarity. Only in the sphere of economics has the drastic effect on public policy of monetary and fiscal neo-liberalism generated anything like a thorough analytic response to its theoretical premises. (3) Among British radicals, the cultural and philosophical pretensions of the new conservatism, so glaringly at variance with its economic faith, have been greeted by gossip, caricature and (at the time of the Falklands War) a kind of mesmerised defeatism. Yet a radical critique is perhaps more vulnerable to cunning competition than to crude hostility, and its self-defence must begin where rivals move closest to its own themes and practices.

Given the scope and context of this paper, I think it necessary to limit its interrogation of conservative theoretical positions to those fields in which successive Essex conferences have for a decade worked to re-formulate the object of knowledge; aesthetics; theories of the subject and of the text; the history and sociology of culture. In these areas of inquiry a small but growing rightist presence overlaps with arguments and interests dominated in the academic interchanges of the sixties and seventies by Marxist, feminist or left-liberal approaches. But it remains a resurgent conservatism of a peculiar, even marginal, kind. Its immersion in the politics of culture, gender or language frequently stems from an authoritarian and traditionalist definition of conservative aims, at odds with the libertarian appeal of favoured party propagandists such as Paul Johnson and Ferdinand Mount (who drafted the Conservative manifesto at the 1983 general election). This severely illiberal creed has become associated through its own and others' publicity with the recently-launched *Salisbury Review*; with various alumni of Peterhouse, Cambridge and the London School of Economics; with the members of the Conservative Philosophy Group. Its most assertive statements have come in the work of historians such as Edward Norman and Maurice Cowling, philosophers such as Roger Scruton and Anthony Quinton, and the aesthetic theorists John Casey and David Watkin. Diluted, this conservatism of discipline, hierarchy and nationhood surfaces in a sympathetic press: in *The Times*, *The Spectator*, *Private Eye*. Its distaste for the "free market" and for monetarism, pure or trimmed, is considerable; but, with a twist of reactionary dialectic, a right-minded government gets respectful support, or obedient silence.

Conservative doctrine of this stamp, with its economistic and individualistic cognates, represents far more than a casual by-product of electoral success and social supremacy. For its practitioners, it amounts to a systematic effort to reverse a presumed liberal hegemony in British education and society established before and after 1945, and sustained at least until 1979. Hence its unavoidable entanglement with the past and present work of this Conference, as a regressive version of the challenge to ideological consensus taken as axiomatic on the academic left since 1968, 1956, or whenever the founding moment of dissent is placed. The historical myth that underpins much current right-wing thought is summarised by Maurice Cowling in his autobiographical account of an intellectual career blown along by a "reactionary wind" strong enough to resist:

> the progressive, psychoanalytical, para-marxist egalitarianism which had constituted the undergraduate movement of the thirties and which, when emasculated into average wisdom by association with victory over Hitler, was to exercise predominant influence on English public thought until the late 1960s. (4)

In this, and similar, passages, it is probably most useful as an aid to interpretation to suspend, for the moment, possible objections to the content, and instead attend to the tone: the air of rebellion and heterodoxy; the assumption of dissidence. We confront a conservatism both evangelical and minoritarian in its idiom and

and attitudes. As a reading of post-war British intellectual history, the force accorded by Cowling and others to liberal and egalitarian modes of thought in the realm of doctrine and policy may seem, after five years of unchecked reaction, either a tendentious debating trick or a grotesque example of self-serving false consciousness. However innocent or crafty it may be, this mood of militancy and martyrdom has proved exceptionally difficult for radical critics to resist.

What counts as "theory" in the recent discourse of the humanities has seldom been developed in order to question or withstand overtly reactionary argument. A roll-call of its major constituents will reveal that their competence, and occasional authority, has been established since 1968 in the form of a critique of liberalism; as ideology and myth; as creed and as code. Sometimes the dim sense of a shared target has offered the only cement able to bind an eclectic mixture of post-Freudian and Lacanian psychoanalysis, modern and post-modern aesthetics, structural linguistics, Marxist historiography, and radical phenomenology. Its chosen antagonists have been human nature and common experience; or the claims of transparency and universality in language and subjectivity. Perhaps forgetting Barthes' dictum that "myth hides nothing", its local operations have preferred a rhetoric of detection and discovery, avid to disclose and to denounce, to exhibit contradictions and to prise apart spurious totalities. Its goal, and its reward, has been difference. Presuming on the humanism and empiricism of the opposition, "theory" in its British guise can easily find itself embarrassed or tongue-tied in the face of manifest reaction. For, whether by inadvertence or opportunism, the conservative theoretical case is often presented in a voice which resembles an echo, parody, or inverted image of radical and revolutionary positions. A question which must be confronted concerns the ways in which the language of reaction appears at times to mould itself to the forms of Western academic radicalism, even to educe its repressed or rejected content, just as conservative ideology in its turn can be seen to possess a revolutionary "other", a secret sharer or shadow-side.

Before looking at some examples of anti-liberal, pseudo-radical conservative theory and polemic, it must be noted that these doctrines are compelled to define themselves not only in relation to their enemies on the left, but also as a refusal of right-wing libertarianism and individualism. That monetarism and the principles of the "free market", however inflected with the authority of F.A. Hayek or Milton Friedman, revert in a British context to a version of Manchester-school liberalism, has long been acknowledged, not least by Tory paternalists such as Sir Iain Gilmour. For Roger Scruton, "there is no logical identity between conservatism and capitalism", and he recalls the historical period, which endured to some degree until the 1930s, when "the English Tory party stood against the 'market' economy, not in the interests of national wealth, but in the interests of a social order which it felt quite rightly to be threatened by it." (5) It would be no more than commonplace observation to mark the distance of such an attitude from the Hobbesian clamour of the market theorists:

> "In the absence of government men would have certain ambitions (such as the acquisition of wealth for themselves) which are natural to their humanity. They still have those ambitions when they come to live

under governments. It is no part of a government's
function to disapprove of those ambitions, or to seek
to change or frustrate them, for it owes its existence to them." (6)

What must also be recognised, however, is the continuity of
belief that unites paternalist and entrepreneur - most clearly, the
doctrine of inequality and the conservative habits of faith in, and
obedience to, persons and institutions, which act as a powerful dis-
incentive to intellectual secession.

Internecine dispute over the nature and function of the market
stands as an example of the area of debate in which the conservatism
of party propaganda and everyday ideology finds itself crossed and
confounded by upholders of tradition and authority: discussion of the
meaning of "freedom". More in connection with economic conduct than
with other forms of social, sexual and cultural choice, conservative
publicity adopts a language of universal rights; of unfettered liberty and of abstract, transcendant subjectivity. These concepts and
their application tend to be advanced most stridently by what might
be called the Apostate Tendency of Tory ideologists, former social
democrats such as Paul Johnson, Hugh Thomas and Alun Chalfont. In-
heriting the Cold War liberalism of the 1950s, associated with Hannah
Arendt, Arthur Koestler and the revisionist readings of George Orwell
inescapable in 1984, the friends of liberty have over recent years
shown a prudent willingness to make their peace with the state and its
works, especially since the governmental call for a principled defence
of nuclear weaponry. The casuistry and contortion involved, vividly
dramatised in Edgar's *Maydays*, has left libertarian apologists of the
nuclear state fluent in Newspeak, while the philosophical basis of
their erstwhile individualism has been somewhat obscured. There are
few British precedents for a philosophical, rather than economic,
libertarianism, the work and influence of John Stuart Mill having
proved notoriously resistant to right-wing appropriation. During the
1970s American political philosophy furnished more malleable material,
particularly in the minimal-state, maximal rights theory of Robert
Nozick. Taken in earnest, Nozick's libertarianism would have difficulty in accommodating itself to any shape or coercive agency, political or economic. In consequence, the candour and subtlety of anti-
state argument in *Anarchy, State and Utopia*, best understood as a book-
length quarrel with John Rawl's monumental *A Theory of Justice*, had to
be drastically laundered before it could be used as part of a language
of rights which had no words for economic or domestic oppression.
Benignly anarchic, tempered by an interventionist guilty conscience to
deal with extant inequalities, Nozick's position reads more like a
philosophical epitaph to the spirit of Woodstock than an ethical defence
of established power:

"Treating us with respect by respecting our rights, (the
minimal state) allows us, individually or with whom we
choose, to choose our life and to realise our ends and
our conception of ourselves, insofar as we can, aided by
the voluntary co-operation of other individuals possessing the same dignity. How *dare* any state or group of
individuals do more. Or less. (7)

Serious libertarianism, with its recognition that states are not the sole agencies of unjust coercion, and that dignity and autonomy are never simply given, is a firework liable to explode in the hands of its conservative users. One route away from the dilemmas of untrammelled freedom, taken by Ferdinand Mount in *The Subversive Family*, is to exalt the authority of the European family, with its dependent women and subject children, against that of the national state. Defending the inviolable privacy of family life, and thus the power of the father within it, Mount disputes the mutuality of family and state, the exploration of which has been a staple theme of political thought, radical and conservative, since Aristotle. (8) Not surprisingly, Mount's tenure as a policy adviser to the Prime Minister was limited. Most conservative ideology remains organicist in its social vision and global in its reach, unwilling to concede the political neutrality of private experience. Such a cast of thought renders libertarian positions fragile and marginal, while bringing its upholders into contact and conflict with the arguments of their radical counterparts.

The species of New Right thought that thus has most to say about the theoretical assault on consensual notions of identity, culture and communication tends to celebrate hierarchy rather than liberty, and to valorise communal and national solidarity rather than individual self-definition. "It is not freedom that Conservatives want", affirms Cowling, "what they want is the sort of freedom that will maintain existing inequalities or restore lost ones in so far as any political action can do this." (9) Authoritarian dogmatics of this kind owes its origin to the crystallisation of traditionalist belief, Christian and pessimistic in its tone and bearing, that followed the French Revolution. Edmund Burke and Joseph de Maistre are distant progenitors; T.S. Eliot, Michael Oakeshott and R.G. Collingwood more recent British sources. (10) That such a project remains politically and academically possible in Britain is largely due to its exemption, in the mid-twentieth century, from the taint of Fascism. Cowling points to the existence of an unbroken line of reactionary ideologues deriving from Burke and his associates, a succession broken in Europe by the disgrace of collaboration and seldom restored thereafter. Free from these historical shadows, close to the party in power, intellectual reaction in this country has been able to move with easy confidence from academia to media. In discussing the sudden fame of the right-wing, but deeply individualist, "nouveaux philosophes" in France, Régis Debray ascribed their celebrity to an "ideological scoop" within broadcasting and the press. (11) Certainly, the economy of media fashion explains much of the current buoyancy of illiberal ideology, but critics on the left are often baffled by the zest of an aristocratic and anti-populist creed in seeking publicity, and relishing its attendant simplifications. Part of the reason for this cheerful embrace of slogan and cliche, in newspaper column and television chat-show, seems to lie in the absence in rightist discourse of radicals' anxieties over ordinary language and experience. Theirs is not a counter-intuitive or counter-empirical project. While left opponents shrink from triviality and banality, the ideologists of reaction happily raid the national bank of received wisdom and common sense. In such a language, the claims of originality and validity cease to matter. For a conservative, whether the Articles of the Church of England are actually true, or whether the symbolism surrounding the monarchy refers to any existing system of feudal tenure and obligation, is less important than the rhetorical and ritual efficacity of these practices. Whatever happens, the show must go on. In the supreme value it accords to custom, repitition, and the manifest content of ideology, the intellectual work of the right most clearly shows its separation from the delving and probing scepticism of radical analysis. According to Roger Scruton's formulation of this preference,

> "In matters of human significance, it is always the surface, and what can be brought to the surface, that counts." (12)

A practical result of this cult of appearance and surface is a reluctance to bother with the investigative detail of radical critique. Swollen with platitude, conservative ideology thus veers towards pleonasm, the re-statement of what is already known, in the same moment as it denounces the visible "consensus" of liberalism. The paradox generated can be found in the most casual and the most considered of New Right texts, but has so far attracted little notice or commentary.

I want now to specify some of the nodal points of speculation and discussion at which an oppositional position is likely to find itself shadowed or mocked by a conservative stance, however internally-divided and self-contradictory the latter may appear. Theoretical activity among British conservatives has often taken the form of jumping through doors opened by radicals in the facade of academic orthodoxy. To strengthen the metaphor, it has been parasitic upon a radical host. (13) Maurice Cowling historicises this process:

> "The Marxism that was adopted by the young in the late 1960s and early 1970s, by opening up the closed minds of the 1950s, or by showing how closed they were, suggested that sympathetic consideration (of principled conservatism) was now a possibility." (14)

What might be called the end of the "end of ideology" in the sixties is located as the breakthrough, when a collapse of confidence in instrumental rationalism permitted the entry into debate of dissident and sectional beliefs. Given this shared point of origin, the rightist disdain for liberal and secular humanism can look to an unwitting audience like a version or derivative of the radical case. The example of subjectivity, and of the conceptualisation of human "nature" or "essence", offers a crucial example. Conservative theory has been traditionally scathing in its treatment of the humanist attempt to argue from, or for, a transcendent subject, free of determination, the natural possessor of rights, qualities and dignities. Public ideologies of "human rights" have formed a prime target, the critique of their unpolitical idealism no more than a gentle nursery slope for reactionary debunkers. Their objections have varied little from those of Hobbes in *Leviathan:* that the notion of a "free subject" is like that of a "round quadrangle", not an error but an absurdity, "without meaning". But recent conservative response to the floating and abstract subject of liberal rights theory has sometimes drawn explicitly on support from materialist sources. For John Casey:

> "As much as a Marxist, a conservative characteristically sees human nature as defined by human activities in the world, rather than as fixed, timeless and universal." (15)

In its diction, this quotation discloses the reactionary's quandary. "Human nature" must somehow be retained, against the materialist tenets whose aid has proved tactically necessary, yet it must be disendowed, stripped of the power to elevate selfhood over obligation and dependency.

Yet conservatives are never willing, as radicals occasionally are, to assume that to demonstrate the preconstitution of subjectivity somehow marks a terminus of inquiry. Against the empty self of liberal anthropology, the New Right tends to set a subject composed of a plenitude of needs, variously modified by history and culture, but always expressive of a certain helplessness, or will to subordination. The first half of this argument may appropriate a radical vocabulary, particularly that of the young Marx : the "species life" of the 1844 *Economical and Philosophical Manuscripts* provides a favourite text. But Roger Scruton illustrates the final, bizarre outcome of this confiscation:

> "The conservative, like the radical, recognises that the civil order reflects not the desires of man, but the self of man. Neither will hesitate to propose or defend a system which frustrates or diverts even the most innocent of human choices, if he sees those choices in conflict with the order that breeds fulfilment." (16)

What this "order that breeds fulfilment" may be is evidently not for its members or citizens to judge, still less to create through conscious choice and action. "Alienation" in Scruton's version is severed from capitalist productive relations, and returned to its Hegelian roots, an immemorial plight rather than a historical condition. Yet this unhappy and unformed human essence confers on its owner neither natural rights nor the potential for self-determination. It bequeathes merely a set of appetites and aversions, a profound dependence on others and a profound need for constraint, best satisfied by the stern guidance of family and national state. Where this image of the self as inherited and trained, rather than given or discovered, seems to rhyme with the figures of a radical critique, is in the recognition of the ubiquity of power and the interdependence of its levels of enforcement. Following Burke's metaphor of the family as the "little platoon" whose combinations make the state, Scruton presents the relations of parents and children as a bond in which there can be "no granting of love, that is not also, in the first instance, an exercise of established power." An awareness of dependence in the child anticipates the "similar recognition of constraint, helplessness, and subjection to external will that herald's the citizen's realization of his membership of society; in this recognition love of one's country is born." (17) Conservative dogma may not admit the concept of patriarchy, but it knows the thing.

Yet this open defence of the rapport linking domestic and political subjecthood deepens, rather than lightens, the problems of a radical riposte. Once again, the tuning of feminist and socialist thought towards the defective nostrums of privacy, liberty and individuality entails a neglect of manifestly reactionary propositions. When conservatives affirm the correspondence of personal and public experience, of the life of individuals and the life of institutions, their words may resemble an inverted statement of radical axioms. Where radicals would use such correspondence to unmask oppression, conservatives display and celebrate submission. One side in particular of rightist thinking about family life and human affection will effortlessly resist liberal demur, but probably succumb to a bold and lucid radical challenge. Conservative apologists are deeply attached to the notion of piety, and to the related concept of the transcendental bond. "Piety" in this usage is close to the Roman *pietas*, and has no specifically religious meaning. It denotes the love, duty, honour or solidarity due to a person or institution, not out of rational calculation, but because it binds the individual with thick, unchosen cords of dependency and need. Parents, state and nation, the gods: reverence belongs to these because their relationship with the subject exists independently of agency and election. John Casey recommends "a sense of piety towards the surface of institutions" as an essential conservative trait, and confirms that it is the institution itself, not its symbolic or representative nature, that deserves respect. (18) Scruton cites Japenese society as an instance of a community rich in such "transcendent bonds", despite the absence of a personal deity in its religious life.

Now there exists a liberal, deflating rhetoric of demystification, the residue of the Voltairean Enlightenment, which labours to prove that behind the cloak of piety, father, priest and emperor are, indeed, naked. Radicals often share this language, and the Falklands War provoked some belated exposure of the pieties of patriotism. (19) Yet this idiom often seems inappropriate to its task, for it takes rationalist tools to a problem largely immune to their working. A reactionary response to evidence of ideological misrecognition, false consciousness, and so forth, is quite likely to be: so what? since such acts of intellectual impiety leave untouched, or so the case runs, the deepest ethical springs of human conduct. Another pillar of Enlightenment, David Hume, was led to a sceptical Toryism from his exemplary demonstration of the impossibility of rational belief. Conservative dogma remains precisely that. Careless of evidence and correction, it is a shamelessly eristic speech: the aim is victory, not truth. This, I presume, is what Cowling has in mind when he blithely concedes that, "Marxism is not so much untrue as, for certain purposes and in limited respects, true and unimportant." (20) Faced with such an elastic enemy, opponents on the left might be tempted to give up in despair. Yet there remains a loophole in the right's exaltation of piety, and derogation of reason, one which an agile radicalism might exploit more than it has done.

Affection for "the surface of institutions", and for the intuitive and involuntary bonds they impose, leaves the content and identity of these institutions beyond the scope of rational definition. Here the doctrine is disabled by its own implicit mysticism. The alternative focuses of loyalty and commitment proposed by radicals, based on gender, racial or class alignment, sexual orientation, or (in the peace movement) simple undivided humanity, can not be dismissed by conservatives as "unreal" or "untrue", since the concept of piety on which they predicate allegiance and solidarity is an expressive one, an utterance of the self and its origins, deeper and stronger than external prescription, or conscious choice. A conviction that individuals do not select their identity, and are not the makers of their selfhood, is another reversible weapon in the arsenal of reaction. Scruton's predictable anti-feminism, for instance, disputes women's claims to equality, but at the cost of permitting an unlimited affirmation of sexual difference, a "great ontological divide", responsible for our sense of "a masculine and a feminine in everything". (21) On the other side of that "great ontological divide" may happen things which the conservative theorist cannot allow himself to define or to judge. One consequence of the New Right's retreat from universal classifications to a concern with concrete and particular forms of being, is that it enables its "others" to be in some sense unknowable, subject to control, perhaps, but never to integration. Forms of community and affiliation drawn from other commands than those of familial (that is, paternal) or national authority, the conservative may only strive to defeat or subdue.

Unlike liberalism, a reaction that worships the promptings of communal piety has no grounds for dismissing such allegiances as misguided or illusory. It may work to destroy the subjective and enacted solidarity of its black, female, proletarian, or pacifist foes, but the logic of its own case forbids contempt. Any examination of the place of affective bonds in the creation of political order invokes the erotics of power. By insistence on visible agency and the embodiment of authority, and on the role of need and desire in the dynamics of loyalty and subjection, conservative ideology eroticises the body of the state in a manner sometimes reminiscent of radical analysis. Recent work of Foucault, of Lyotard and of Deleuze and Guattari, has familiarised academic theorists in the humanities with notions of power "from below", of libidinal economy, and of the psychoanalytic reading of political domination and submission. (22) "Desire" has become such an inescapable watchword on the left, and a sado-masochistic account of subjection can prove so appealing in times of failure and fragmentation, that "radical" thought in Britain has consistently overlooked the origin of this work in Nietzschean irrationalism, alien and hostile to any collective project of human liberation. Reaction, likewise, has its erotics of obedience, founded on the personalisation of power at every level, and taking its intellectual sustenance from Burke's revulsion at the abstract imperium of light and reason ushered in by the French Revolution:

> "Nothing is left which engages the affections on the part of the commonwealth. On the principles of this mechanic philosophy, our institutions can never be embodied, if I may use the expression, in persons; so as to create in us love, veneration, admiration, or attachment.... There ought to be a system of manners in every nation which a well-formed mind would be disposed to relish. To make us love our country, our country ought to be lovely." (23)

In Burke's case it is, notoriously, the femininity of the monarchy, in the person of Marie Antoinette, which inspires or should inspire "generous loyalty", "proud submission", and "dignified obedience". (24) Mary Wollstonecraft thought Burke might have made a "violent revolutionist", and although this is not the place to hunt for subversive undertones in the *Reflections*, the passionate fealty it voices often appears displaced or overdetermined. The fathomless love of the subject for the incarnate state introduces a tone which conservative theory, with its liking for a cold forensic idiom, is chary of developing. However, all conservative theories of obligation share with Burke's usage a belief in the irrelevance of utility and reason as criteria for personal and public affections. Burkean notions of loyalty conceive of the activity of government, like relationship between individuals, as an end in itself, not a means to an end. An effective radical challenge to this position must therefore expose the results and implications of the idea of power as reciprocal ritual, rather than revive a liberal utilitarianism whose stock has fallen irrevocably on both right and left.

Here we meet the analogy of government and friendship, employed repeatedly in conservative argument to justify a stable and unchanging pattern of authority and obedience. Michael Oakeshott's work seems particularly influential in this respect, though similar propositions can be found in Kant's *Groundwork of the Metaphysic of Morals*, and in classical and Renaissance defences of friendship. For Oakeshott,

> "Friends are not concerned with what might be made of one another, but only with the enjoyment of one another; and the condition of this enjoyment is a ready acceptance of what is and an absence of any desire to change and improve." (25)

Leaving to one side the passivity and complacency of this "steady-state" model of human affection, it should be noted that the extension of this principle to the public realm means that, at every juncture, this non-contractual and purposeless power must be expressed in persons and forces which are always available to the subject. If government is to be like friendship, or like fatherhood, then it is obliged to remain visible and tangible, clear of any bureaucratic anonymity which might turn ends back into means. The remoteness of this theoretical scheme from any empirical evidence of how conservative governments operate in modern conditions hardly needs to be laboured. What does require the attention of opponents, is the logical outcome for public policy of a spectacular and sacramental theory of power. Issues of punishment and retribution provide a case in point. Conservatives tend to believe, as did Hegel, that the criminal has a right to punishment, a right acquired by virtue of his crime. In accordance with a faith in affective and unmediated forms of power, this right should not be granted in the alienated guises of imprisonment, or the confiscation of property. There must be visible agency and palpable retribution. Both corporal and capital punishment are unavoidably endorsed, sanctioned by the full rigour of the *lex talionis:*

> "The healthiest form of punishment will be immediate, intelligible, even violent, conceived by the citizen as a natural retaliation, which takes away the sting of resentment and removes the necessity for private revenge." (26)

Oddly enough, it was Burke who said of another kind of political theorist: "In the groves of their academy, at the end of every visto, you see nothing but the gallows." (27) This conservative taste for the chastisement or extinction of the criminal's body amounts to no more than the necessary obverse of a cult of ceremonial desire. Once violated, the domestic and intimate bonds which unite state and person can only be restored through the physical enactment of outrage and vengeance. In response to this gleeful ferocity, a radical critique might be best advised merely to signal the logical ends: mutilation, public execution, and the rest; a potentially endless catalogue of judicial terror, mitigated neither by a notion of deterrence and rehabilitation, nor by a residual belief in the dignity of the legal subject. Given the social organicism of New Right positions, individuals cannot be the sole possessors of their persons, acts or intentions; and the savagery of these penal preferences indicates where a theoretical anti-humanist may lead, when purged of the dialectics of liberation.

Many of the doctrines discussed in this paper can be seen as examples of what Walter Benjamin, writing of Nazism, called the "aestheticisation" of politics. The authoritarian conservatives cited here are not Fascists, and owe their ideological cachet to an ability to dissociate themselves from the mid-century slide of European reactionaries between nostalgic withdrawal and barbaric revenge. But they share a fetishism of the surface and of appearances, and a belief in the immanence of meaning in unmediated contemplation, which tends to

transform social and cultural experience into a permanent exhibition
of self-validating rituals and artefacts. The constancy of this motif
in New Right texts, and its assumption of immunity from analytic challenge or rebuttal, makes it a suitable terminal point for this paper.
Fundamental to the conservative approach is a refusal of the epistemological model which sets surface against depth, the outer against the
inner, the latent against the manifest. It suspends the hermeneutical
impulse identified by Foucault and others as a dominant presence in
modern European rationality. Speaking of the debility of the concepts
of "unconscious" and "superstructure" in the criticism of architecture,
Scruton asserts that, "The Marxist, like the Freudian, is systematically misled by a metaphor of 'depth'". (29) Conservative theory, however, condemns not so much the method as the purpose of "symptomatic
reading" in the humanities, and of inquiry into the historical and
ideological character of representations. It does so, not by specific
rejection of the truths thus disclosed but by the insistence that the
disclosure is based on false dualities; that the material uncovered is
irrelevant to a common moral or aesthetic sense; or even that such
demystification will prove injurious to the order of the community and
the contentment of its citizens (though this is a theme reserved more
for the chat-show than for the academic treatise). For Burke, one of
the terrors of revolution was that: "All the decent drapery of life is
to be rudely torn off." (30) Defending the Platonic 'Noble Lie",
Scruton gives an overt account of reaction's mythopoeic need, "to
propagate the ideology which sustains the social order whether or not
there is a reality that corresponds to it. For even if there is no
reality, the politician can in any case do no better than provide new
myths for old." (31)

Ingenious theorists of the right, however, are much more likely
in the present climate of ideas to adopt a version of post-structuralist rhetoric, and affirm that no body lies beneath the drapery; no
kernel in the nut, no centre to the onion. They will claim that the
stable continuance of cultures and communities rests on an attachment
to the surface of practices and institutions so rooted in human need as
to lie beyond curiosity and beyond disillusion. This is far from
being an unprecedented intellectual gambit. To take one modern example:
in the years after the First World War, a generation of reactionary
modernists defied the hermeneutic menace of psychoanalysis, relativist
sociology, and linguistic analysis. All, they thought, were solvents
of faith and order. For Wyndham Lewis, in theory and artistic practice,
the most interesting part of any creature was not its innards but its
shell. In a celebrated essay on Ben Jonson, T.S. Eliot defends the
satirical moralist's "art of the surface" against the Romantic call for
organic and totalising truth. One feature of the modernist comedy of
manners, in the work of Lewis or of Evelyn Waugh, is its loathing of the
claims of interpretation: a hatred of the muddy depths of motive and
history. Their successors retain an attitude to the politics of art,
and the art of politics, that is "dramatistic" and spectacular, but
neither symbolic nor commemorative, since the acts of government and
representation it praises have no force or signification beyond or behind their performance.

In the matter of architecture, for instance, the conservative
attitude is understandably keen to support the classical orders as an
embodiment of selfhood and community. If we recall the ideological
correlates of classicism, from Augustan Rome to Lutyens's New Delhi and
Speer's Nuremberg, their enthusiasm seems appropriate. But conservatives

seem willing to take as models buildings and styles that radical or
modernist critics will identify as mock-classical, as pastiche, or as
superficial imitation. Here again, a delight in appearance and usage
scorns the hermeneutic intelligence. (32) Classicism, like the ideology of state, becomes an order based on necessary illusion, continuous
in expression but shifting in function, able to gratify different needs
at different times. An aesthetic of display, a mystagogic dogma, and
a politics of domination coincide. Charles Jencks, fasionable postmodern theorist and architect of grandiose, classicising corporate headquarters, assures clients and admirers that this new monumentalism is
"a reflection of a return to a public order".

The conservative critic's pleasure in a hollow classical facade,
covering nothing and concealing nothing, offers an image which might
serve as a final caveat. Theoretical work on the left remains much concerned with demystification: it labours to dismantle, decreate, deconstruct. Unless allied to the expression of concrete alternative
practices, this storming of liberal or humanist strongholds may merely
strengthen the resolve of the intellectual right to build, and to
celebrate, the saving illusions which guarantee the subjection of
persons and of peoples. In the 1950s a generation of British political
and cultural thought, much of it conservatively-inclined, was influenced by the study of Wittgenstein; especially the later work of the
Philosophical Investigations. I suspect that the traces left in the
minds of those involved differed not all that much from the residue
deposited at present by, say, a cursory acquaintance with some of the
available translations of Derrida. The movement in Wittgenstein's later
thought, from a notion of language and meaning rooted in a profound
nominalism, to one concerned above all with the linguistic foundations
of social praxis and "forms of life" - from propositions as "pictures",
to language as "game" - appeared to give some encouragement to a social
quietism whose formal expression should be preservative, if not conservative. It must be stressed that these were indirect and roundabout
extrapolations, and in no strict sense "interpretations" of Wittgenstein.
Conservative moralists, such as John Casey and Anthony Quinton, seem on
occasions to make inferences drawn, if not from Wittgenstein, at least
from a British Wittgensteinian "tradition". One may detect the use of
Wittgenstein's repudiation of the Cartesian first-person case, in which
a knowledge of the self founds a knowledge of the world; of his assertion of the priority of act and appearance in verbal and cultural expression; and of his belief in the anteriority of a public language, as
the precondition of any understanding of, or speech about, the self.
These positions may be stretched to support the claim that any subversion or dissolution of shared and given forms of life, can only be induced by, and in any case entails, a disintegration of the subject: a
subject whose being in language is created and sustained only by, and
in, these external forms. Thus the integrity of the person, and the
intelligibility of a culture to its members, are conjoined. This
stance neatly mirrors (that is, reflects and transposes) the quest for
a "revolutionary subjectivity" found in such digests of radical thought
as Coward and Ellis's *Language and Materialism*, a text innocent of the
name and work of Wittgenstein. (33) In the absence of any demonstrable
theoretical alternative, research into the conditional and contingent
nature of personality and communication may result in a desperate fidelity
to the extant "forms of life", however unjust, unequal and dominative
these may be. Radical theorists should reflect on the sad history of the
Parisian journal *Tel Quel*: the history of a dangerous liaison between
vanguardism and dandyism, in which the *flâneur* always outlives the revolutionary.

FOOTNOTES

1. See, for example, Martin Walker, 'The unthinkable men behind Mrs. Thatcher', *The Guardian*, 1 March 1983, p.17, and Godfrey Hodgson, 'Now is the time for all right-thinking men...', *Sunday Times Magazine*, 4 March 1984, pp.44-52. Less conspiratorial is David Edgar, 'Bitter Harvest', *New Socialist* 13 (1983), pp.19-24.

2. David Edgar, *Maydays* (London, 1983), p.56.

3. See Nick Bosanquet, *After the New Right* (London, 1983).

4. Maurice Cowling, *Religion and Public Doctrine in Modern England* (London, 1980), p.xvi.

5. Roger Scruton, *The Meaning of Conservatism* (Harmondsworth, 1980), pp.94-95.

6. Keith Joseph and Andrew Sumption, *Equality* (London, 1979), pp.100-101.

7. Robert Nozick, *Anarchy, State and Utopia* (Oxford, 1974), pp.333-334.

8. Ferdinand Mount, *The Subversive Family:An alternative history of love and marriage* (London, 1982).

9. Maurice Cowling, 'The Present Position', in *Conservative Essays* (ed. Cowling), (London, 1978), pp.9-10.

10. Cowling, *Religion and Public Doctrine in Modern England*, although idiosyncratic and inclined to dismiss many conservative influences as 'Whiggish', is as systematic an account of its origins as this school is likely to give.

11. Régis Debray, *Teachers, Writers, Celebrities :the intellectuals of modern France* (London, 1981).

12. Roger Scruton, 'Humane Education', in *The Politics of Culture* (London, 1981), p.224.

13. See, among other works, Laurence Lerner (ed.), *Reconstructing Literature* (Oxford, 1983), a response to Marxist, feminist and post-structuralist literary analysis whose title mimics Peter Widdowson (ed.), *Re-reading English* (London, 1982).

14. Cowling, *Religion and Public Doctrine in Modern England*, p.xxi.

15. John Casey, 'Tradition and Authority', in *Conservative Essays*, *op.cit.*,p.96.

16. Roger Scruton, *The Meaning of Conservatism*, p.120.

17. Scruton, *op.cit.*,p.32.

18. Casey, *op.cit.*, *passim*.

19. Anthony Barnett, *Iron Britannia* (London, 1983), remains the most searching and persuasive epilogue.

20. Cowling, *op.cit.*,p.xvi.

21. Roger Scruton, 'The case against feminism', *The Observer*, 22 May 1983, p.27.

22. Michel Foucault, *The History of Sexuality, vol.1* (Harmondsworth, 1980); Jean-Francis Lyotard, *Economie Libidinale* and *La Condition Postmoderne* (Paris, 1974;1979); Gilles Deleuze and Felix Guattari,

Anti-Oedipus: Capitalism and Schizophrenia (London, 1984); Felix Guattari, *Molecular Revolution:Psychiatry and Politics* (Harmondsworth, 1984).

23. Edmund Burke, *Reflections on the Revolution in France* (Harmondsworth, 1968), pp.171-172.

24. Burke, *op.cit.*, p.170.

25. Michael Oakeshott, 'On Being Conservative', in *Rationalism in Politics* (London, 1962), p.177.

26. Scruton, *The Meaning of Conservatism*, p.82.

27. Burke, *op.cit.*, pp.171-172.

28. For the connections between mystical racism, cultural aristocracy and incipient Fascism in Germany, see Fritz Stern, *The Politics of Cultural Despair* (Berkeley, 1974).

29. Roger Scruton, *The Aesthetics of Architecture* (London, 1979) p.154.

30. Burke, *op.cit.* p.171.

31. Scruton, *The Meaning of Conservatism*, pp.139-140.

32. See Scruton, *The Aesthetics of Architecture*, especially chapters 6,7 and 10.

33. Rosalind Coward and John Ellis, *Language and Materialism* (London 1977).

IMAGES OF THE SIXTEENTH AND SEVENTEENTH CENTURIES
As a History of the Present

Simon Barker

In this paper I want to discuss a particular "history of the present" which is constructed through representations of the sixteenth and seventeenth centuries as a "Golden Age" of "civilization". (1) I want to argue that to some extent at least, these representations underpin the ideology characterized by the now familiar slogan "the resolute approach". But I think it is important that the notions of determined government, self-reliance, and "no alternative" evinced by this slogan should not be overemphasized as defining the actual behaviour of the present Conservative Government.

I would argue that there is little fundamental difference between Thatcher's regime and previous governments, both Tory and Labour. The "resolute approach" is a myth. If Thatcher was "resolute" in "holding out" against the Health workers, and in sending the Task Force to the South Atlantic, then a succession of Labour cabinets have been no less resolute in their deployment of troops against workers in the British Isles. Quite apart from Ireland there are numerous examples of such resolution, ranging from Attlee's use of the army against the dock workers in 1945, to Callaghan's introduction of military scab labour during the firemen's dispute of 1977-8. In fact the success of Thatcherism partly depends upon a factor of consent which is largely secured by the existence within the labour movement of a bureaucracy of full-time trade union officials and Labour Party politicians committed to the reconciliation of labour and capital. Thatcher's "resolute approach" is extremely severe in its evocation of national pride, restraint and a curious kind of puritanism; yet stripped of its "resolution" the "approach" is all too familiar. The slogan is simply a new standard to raise above a set of policies which have been justified in terms of "the national interest" by every shade of government since the establishment of bourgeois democracy, and especially in times of recession in the capitalist mode of production. At the present time, in the face of an extremely reactionary government, mass unemployment and the prospect of wage cuts, there exists a distinct lack of confidence amongst those sections of the social formation which have most interest in resisting the state. During such a downturn the kind of history which I want to describe is most effectively pursuasive, helping to neutralize what little resistance there is.

The "history of the present" which represents the sixteenth and seventeenth centuries in a particular way is important for two reasons. Firstly, it is highly pervasive; its power is distributed across a wide range of institutions in order to offer a variety of people a notion of a smooth historical continuum. The effect is to make the present crisis appear within "our" control, so long as "we" react according to the evidence of "our" history. Opposition to the order of things is neutralized through the participation of people in such seemingly disparate practices as watching television, reading books and newspapers, and, crucially, I shall want to suggest, studying literature. The history offered through these practices must offer hope - an ideal reward for our submission to images of the present inscribed in the representations of the past.

Secondly, this history is important because it most powerfully conveys exactly that sense of "the national interest" and "resolution" which frames a variety of popular consents to a form of government which includes amongst its policies such nationalistic planning as immigration control, limits on importation, and nuclear "defence", as well as acts of international aggression such as the sinking of the *General Belgrano*.

The paper is in three sections. In the first I want to examine a small selection of contemporary texts which construct an ideology of the present through specific representations of the sixteenth and seventeenth centuries. I hope these will indicate just *how* pervasive the discourse is. In many ways the representations I shall describe are more powerful, and certainly less equivocal (perhaps because of their comparative historical "distance" from popular experience) than those of a Victorian world which were summoned and fought over during the 1983 General Election.

Secondly I want to address the educational institution, and English studies in particular, in order to show how powerfully linked it is to the wider context through which these images are presented. Indeed it might be argued that however "sound" one's re-reading of English may be, to regard the educational institution and its critical practice in isolation from a wider context itself constitutes something of a neutrality.

Lastly I shall want to suggest some ways of resisting these histories by the production of a knowledge of the sixteenth- and seventeenth-century epoch as a period of crisis and rapid change. Such a knowledge offers a disruption of the smooth continuum of history and the naturalness of consent. If things have changed in the past, they can change again. If nationalism is a bourgeois ideology fostered by myths of the past, then it can be demythologized in the name of internationalism.

To start at the top, so to speak, I want first to discuss the Queen's *Message to the Commonwealth* which was broadcast on Christmas Day 1982. With the possible exception of the World Cup Final, which is relayed throughout the Eastern Bloc, no other broadcast is available to such a massive and literally global audience. It is a classic use of history in order to reinforce contemporary values. As Her Majesty is anxious to point out, she is speaking from the Library at Windsor Castle, "a room once occupied by Queen Elizabeth I". This is a significant situation since the theme of the message is (as ever) the unity of the Commonwealth, and "it was the voyages of discovery by the great seamen of Queen Elizabeth's day which laid the foundation of modern trade ... [and] ... discovery and trade in their turn laid the foundation of the present day Commonwealth". Moreover, "the members of the Commonwealth which evolved from Britain's seafaring history have acquired an affinity through sharing a common philosophy of individual freedom, democratic government and the rule of law". Since these values were disseminated, apparently individually, by "such names as Drake, Anson, Frobisher, Cook, Vancouver and Philip", they must be eternal values because they also inspired "our sailors, soldiers and airmen to go to the rescue of the Falkland Islanders eight thousand miles across the ocean; and to reveal the professional skills and courage that could be called on in the defence of basic freedoms".

In the face of all this history the "difficulties" experienced in the Commonwealth during the twentieth century, due to its component nations becoming multi-racial and multi-religious, are of little importance and may be overcome partly through a "sense of tolerance" and also, it seems, through evens such as the Commonwealth Games which "stand out as a demonstration of the better side of human nature". In the closing sentences of the speech this spirit of harmony and tolerance is linked through a quotation from the seventeenth-century poet John Donne ("No man is an island ...") to the message of Christ who

> ... attached supreme importance to the individual ... amazed the world in which he lived by making it clear that the unfortunate and the underprivileged had an equal place in the Kingdom of Heaven with the rich and powerful ... but ... also taught that man must do his best to live in harmony with man.

As a "history of the present", the Christmas *Message* depends upon a negation of history itself. It is not simply that what is said is not true, but that all the values of the Elizabethan epoch are recognizable because they are vital, and demonstrative because they produce a material practice in the form of the South Atlantic war effort. Furthermore, their substance is an individual responsibility. The great seamen of the past can be named, as can the poet who encapsulated their enduring experience. Similarly, Britain can be named individually as a nation, the centre and eternal distributor of all this peace and tolerance. By contrast, the Commonwealth is simply a conglomerate. It may be "an association of free and independent nations" - but it is not *English*. It was discovered, but can discover nothing for itself. Since the Commonwealth is both multi-racial and multi-religious, it has a distinct potential for "argument, disagreement and violence". Its only hope lies in the "better side of human nature" carried to its many shores by an endless flotilla of Elizabethan values.

Whilst on the subject of great Tudor seafarers, one who did not get quite as far as his contemporaries was Sir George Carew, the unfortunate commander of Henry VIII's flagship, the *Mary Rose*. The *Mary Rose* sank in Portsmouth harbour before it could play a part in the war between England and France (1543-1551) for which it was built. Having survived plans to blow it up during the nineteenth century (when it was significant to Portsmouth seafarers as an undersea hazard), the vessel was raised to the surface within hours of the so-called Falklands Victory Parade. Like the parade itself, the emergence of the hulk was witnessed by a television audience of millions. What is interesting about the *Mary Rose* is the host of texts which conjoin the sixteenth and twentieth centuries in order to represent a distinct kind of co-existence in terms of "Englishness"; from what might seem a rather inauspicious start, the second coming of the *Mary Rose* has seen it laden with a significance based upon transhistorical and nationalistic values. Television viewers were invited by a series of commentators and "experts" not only to marvel at the technology of the recovery, but also to take comfort from the peculiarly English eccentricity of the whole event and the sense of national pride and heritage which seeped from between the Tudor timbers. Similarly, most of the texts which narrate the raising (or rescue?) of the ship, which might colloquially be described as "coffee table" volumes, invite a sense of historical continuum which, in ideological purpose, is quite as powerful as the Falklands Parade itself. I want to offer two quotations from the second edition of a book produced by the leader of the *Mary Rose* project, Margaret Rule; her text is the most comprehensive and technical of the popular volumes. Amongst the acknowledgements is this:

> What can I say of the inspiration and involvement of His
> Royal Highness Prince Charles, Prince of Wales, President
> of the Mary Rose Trust, scuba diver, archeologist, and
> heir to the throne of the United Kingdom of Great Britain
> and Northern Ireland? Our confidence in and loyalty to
> our president can only equal that of Henry VIII's Admiral
> to his king who wrote 'I submit all this to the order of
> your most noble Grace who, I pray God preserve from all
> adversity and send you as much victory of your enemys as
> ever had any of your noble ancestry'. (2)

This invites the reader to recognize a timeless and *individual* worth which is shared between Charles and his distant ancestor. Nothing has really changed because time changes nothing. Like Henry, Charles is the "Renaissance Man", a rounded and accomplished individual invested with a multiplicity of talents and boundless confidence in every project upon which he gazes.

Charles himself, in a foreword to the same book, describes the usefulness of the *Mary Rose* excavation with disarming clarity:

> The result of all this hard work and expertise is that
> future generations, we hope, will be able to glimpse a
> small part of Britain's maritime heritage; will be able to
> see history 'come alive' and to step, as it were, into the
> shoes of a Tudor seaman in the reign of Henry VIII. The
> only real way of understanding and coping with the present
> is, I believe, through an adequate knowledge and interpre-
> tation of the past. From that point of view we are able,
> at once, to transform a contemporary naval disaster into a
> victory in terms of human awareness. (3)

Allowing the reader to cope with the present is, in fact, precisely the work of such texts. Amongst the numerous volumes which succeeded to the South Atlantic war is one which was published in 1983 entitled *The True Glory*, which folds the recent fighting into a general account of Britain's maritime military past and includes the *Mary Rose* debacle in some detail. Again, the practice of modern warfare is made intelligible because the reader is encouraged into an "awareness" of the values which over-reach time itself. And just as the *Mary Rose* volumes are liberally sprinkled with quotations from Shakespeare, who best records the enduring experience of these values, this volume's title is validated because it derives from the letters of Sir Francis Drake. The foreword explains that:

> Now that the age of materialism shows signs of drawing to a
> close, with earlier and more noble values being in part
> restored, I hope that this partial record of British seamen,
> their successes, their failures, their characters, their
> reliability and their steadfastness in the face of great odds
> may inspire in those with a feeling for the sea a possible
> drawing together or at least an increased understanding of a
> story remarkable by any criterion. This I venture to call
> *The True Glory* after the prayer concocted from Drake's letters
> home whilst blockading Cadiz in 1587. This prayer, which
> General Montgomery pinned up in his caravan throughout the
> desert campaign of the Second World War serves well as the
> keynote to all that follows ... 'Oh! Lord God, when thou
> givest to thy servants to endeavour any great matter, grant

us to know that it is not the beginning but the continuing
of the same until it be thoroughly finished which yieldeth
the True Glory' [sic] (4)

What we are dealing with in these kinds of texts is a set of
peculiarly English values such as steadfastness, loyalty, character, and
so on, which might perhaps be synthesized as a "resolute approach". On
the one hand these values are almost tangible because we can observe
their manifestation in the actual battles which the histories narrate
in their partial way. But at the same time such values rise above
materialism, that cancer which is held at bay only by a treatment which
involves recognition of the truly timeless values of human existence.
And in order to assimilate these values, those of us unfortunate enough
not to make history, but only to read of it, must be attuned to human
awareness, have a "feeling for the sea" perhaps, and understand and
interpret correctly.

Great literature, it seems, can help. It certainly stands as a
substantial component in the overall presentation of the sixteenth and
seventeenth centuries as a "Golden·Age". The canon of great works, and
especially those secured by that most potent signifier of Englishness,
"William Shakespeare", is aimed across a range of institutions whose
business is not primarily the analysis and interpretation of the words
on the page. That work is done for them elsewhere. The discourses
which are presented through the kinds of institutions which I am thinking of simply require a consent to the notion that their representation
of the period must be correct and complete, since it can be endorsed by
evidence of a high level of cultural productivity. The pages of
Hansard, for example, fairly bristle with allusions to the former epoch,
particularly when "Englishness" is threatened by a "national emergency".
Shakespearean language provides a suitable medium through which to
articulate the gravity of the present moment, against which "we" are
armed, as a nation, with the imminent rediscovery of "our" Elizabethan
selves. The utterances of various government "think tank" personnel,
which are frequently handed to the press as releases, also tend towards
allusions to the Elizabethan period. The urgent requirement for
investment in new technology, for example, can easily be associated with
a new "renaissance", however odd the parallel may appear in terms of
"history". (5)

There are numerous other examples. In the issue dated 25th
December 1982, *The Economist* ran what it described as an eight-page
"spoof" of the Falkland Islands dispute; the diplomacy and military
engagement were represented entirely through quotations from Shakespeare
which were put into the mouths of the Argentinian and British leaders.
The point about this was not the unpleasant flippancy which was applied
to an event which had cost the lives of well over a thousand people, but
the assumptions about Shakespeare which were so readily engaged in the
pursuit of Christmas cheer. (6)

The host of television and film productions which arose during
the early seventies are also worth some consideration; these centred
the sixteenth and seventeenth centuries on the lives of a chain of
"glamorous" individuals, beginning with Henry VIII and his six wives,
and moving towards the later Stuarts via a recuperated Oliver Cromwell,
whose regicidal tendencies were more than adequately mitigated by the
voice-over which concluded the 1970 screen production. The interregnum,
it seems, was a "hiccup" in the course of English history which served
to secure our present freedom and democracy; the word is restoration
not revolution. (7)

Such productions are entirely appropriate both to the ideology of Thatcherism and to the educational institutions' representation of history. As far as the former is concerned, Thatcher's message to student voters, which was sent to the National Union of Students newspaper *National Student* (and also published in a number of constituate member journals), is almost wholly concerned with an image of the present in terms of a mythologized past:

> ... the choice before the nation is stark. Either to continue our present steadfast progress towards recovery, or to follow policies more extreme and more damaging than those ever put forward by any previous opposition. I believe that Britain has recovered confidence and self-respect. We have regained the regard and admiration of other nations. We are seen today as a people with integrity, resolve, and the will to succeed ... our history is the story of a free people - a great chain of people stretching back into the past and forward into the future. All are linked by a common belief in freedom, and in Britain's greatness. All are aware of their own responsibility to contribute to both, none more so than young people. Our past is witness to their enduring courage, honesty and flair, and to their ability to change and create. Our future will be shaped by those same qualities. (8)

As far as institutions of higher education are concerned, the young people who read Mrs Thatcher's election address start their courses having already been most deliberately drawn into a particular conjunction of literature and history. Almost without exception, history books produced for children evaluate the sixteenth and seventeenth centuries in terms of the profusion of great literary works and then link this to colonial expansion. The literary works, after all, hold the key to "what it felt like" to be involved in such adventuring, the same critical mode developed by the Queen in her *Message to the Commonwealth*. The first four quotations below are taken from the current editions of Ladybird Books, whilst the fifth is from a text aimed at slightly older children.

> Shakespeare had arrived in London at an exciting time when the Golden Age of Elizabeth was at its peak. It was just before the Great Armada set sail from Spain. The English seamen were adventuring everywhere - Hawkins, Raleigh, Drake. Drake had "singed the King of Spain's beard" when he raided Cadiz with his fire-ships destroying many ships and stores being prepared for the Armada. The Great Armada itself was destroyed in 1588. England seemed on the crest of a wave of success and achievement. No wonder there was a feeling of intense pride and patriotism among the robust and vigorous people. (9)

> Queen Elizabeth reigned over England for forty five years. When she came to the throne England was poor. When she died, England was rich, prosperous, united and happy. Her reign saw the beginnings of what came to be the British Empire. The fighting sailors of her reign, and the great victory over the Spanish Armada made England one of the greatest of the countries in Europe. (10)

> The reign of Elizabeth has been called the Golden Age of English Literature. This means that as well as the great sailors and explorers there were living at that time men

who wrote some of the most wonderful poems and plays in
our language ... (11)

The Queen liked Shakespeare's plays so much that he was
frequently commanded to bring his company to the palace.
It is wonderful to think that many of the plays we see
today were first acted before the Queen herself. (12)

... the seamen were by no means the only men who contributed to the greatness of the Age of Elizabeth. The
astonishing outburst of English Literature at this time
would alone make Elizabeth's reign the greatest in our
annals. The two movements are not unconnected; poets and
men of action both expressed, in their different ways, the
spirit of adventure of the time ... Shakespeare is supremely
great as a philosopher. The sayings which he puts into the
mouths of his characters have passed into the very substance of our thought and language. (13)

In many texts of this kind the narrative offers the reader some historical "distance" in its description of England's glorious seafaring
past - "the seamen *were* by no means ...". When it comes to Shakespeare,
this distance disappears and the present tense confirms the parallel of
cultural "spirit" and "adventure".

It is hardly surprising that students, and especially students of
literature, should recognize themselves in this history and that such a
recognition should effectively neutralize their practices both in terms
of struggle within the institutions and in the wider context. For it
is within these institutions, and particularly within departments of
English, that this history is distilled, using the raw material of a
canon which is rigorously defended for any number of reasons, but in the
end best produces a knowledge of the timeless values and truths which
can be recognized in the texts I have outlined. It is not so much a
conspiracy as an effect of the sublime status which criticism has
achieved in relation to other branches of the humanities.

The political power of criticism lies in the considerable distance which exists between itself and vulgar political discourse. Very
few critics of Tudor and Stuart drama are politically active; and I can
think of only one production of a Shakespearean play which has caused
riots in the streets. Similarly, I have not heard of any critics prepared to volunteer for active service in the Malvinas. Yet it is
exactly their work upon the texts which fosters the kind of history
available to the ideological apparatus of the state in general. The
link between criticism and the wider context may be glimpsed during
those periods of crisis when an *overt* use of "literary" texts may occur
in order to secure a sense of national identity. It seems to me that
the history of the present constructed through representations of the
sixteenth and seventeenth centuries over the last decade bears some
relation to a general decay in the "body" of British society. Notions
of a regainable organic world have grown as a *general* palliative (though
not the cure, as I suggested earlier), for a sickness which took hold
in the West from the mid-sixties onwards as the post-war boom withered
away. In Britain, concrete struggles took place against sexual and
racial inequalities, the war in Vietnam, the military occupation of the
north of Ireland, the Industrial Relations Bill, and to some extent,
against trade union bureaucracy. The late seventies saw mass organization on the streets against fascism, and more recently, some protest
against the bomb. It was these activities which succeeded the more
ephemeral and now largely mythologized "spirit of the sixties"; and if

they did not cohere into a mass revolutionary practice, they at least disrupted the "one nation" ideology which has regained a hold during the last few years.

As a general palliative, criticism may produce its histories and its knowledges of human nature and organization over a long period. This was the case with the *Scrutiny* group of critics whose project has been closely associated with the threat to "Englishness" posed by revolution in Europe and the growth of Marxism in the British labour movement and intelligentsia during the twenties and thirties. To a large extent the present-day purveyors of the sixteenth and seventeenth centuries as an organic and homogeneous social order are in debt to the *Scrutiny* group. These critics worked hard on Shakespeare's texts in order to produce a knowledge of his times in terms of this ideal, as well as to define their own discipline as the protector of this vision in the face of the moral and cultural bankruptcy which haunted Europe during the inter-war years. And the long-term success of the *Scrutiny* group can be measured by the way that their resulting works of criticism have given both shape and purpose to curricula around the world.

Yet as I suggested, there are moments of relatively *overt* participation by criticism in matters of national concern. This is especially true when "national identity" is sufficiently susceptible to external threat or internal instability for the guise of apoliticality to be jettisoned almost entirely. The best known examples of this extrusion were the war-time productions of Shakespeare's history plays for stage, radio and film, including Laurence Olivier's *Henry V*. As Derek Longhurst has remarked, the years 1939-45 also saw the publication of some of the most persistent works of criticism by E. M. W. Tillyard, whose work, although registering a marked departure from the *Scrutiny* group through a concern with "extra-textual" material, nonetheless regarded Shakespeare as the supreme advocate of an ordered but hierarchical world. (14) In these critics' publications, the groundwork was done for exactly the ideology of heroic patriotism in which the war-time productions were framed.

It is interesting to note that almost forty years of Shakespeare criticism and some very radical appropriations of Shakespearean texts in the theatre have done little to eclipse the potential the canon holds for re-insertion into just such a framework of ideas. In the book *Authors Take Sides on the Falklands* an opinion was sought from the critic G. R. Wilson Knight concerning the war in the South Atlantic. Wilson Knight had been most active during the Second World War when his rather closet life-style as an academic gave new meaning to the term "reserved occupation". Years of textual analysis were finally invested in a number of stage productions which confirmed Shakespeare's unique contribution to the British war effort. And since the values discovered in Shakespeare's texts are self-evident and timeless, Wilson Knight's own contribution to the debate on the South Atlantic War is given as though entirely motivated by Shakespeare's eternal prompting:

> Britain's response to the Falklands crisis was ratified by all three parties in Parliament, and I accordingly would not presume to register any complaint. However I feel that behind the astounding speed, energy, resource, expense and brilliant organization employed in what seems, taking a long view, a hazardous cause, there may be reasons unknown to me and the general public. As for the future, I can only assess our prospects by stating my own convictions. I have for long accepted the validity of our country's historic contribution, seeing the British Empire as a precursor,

or prototype, of world order. I have relied always on the
Shakespearean vision as set forth in my war-time production
This Sceptred Isle at the Westminster Theatre in 1941 (described in *Shakespearean Production*, 1964). This theme I
also discuss in various writings collected under the title
The Sovereign Flower in 1958. Our key throughout is Cranmer's
royal prophecy at the conclusion of Shakespeare's last play,
Henry VIII, Shakespeare's final words to his countrymen.
This I still hold to be our one authoritative statement, every
word deeply significant as forecast of the world-order at
which we should aim. Though democratic, it involves not just
democracy alone, but democracy in strict subservience to the
crown as a symbol linking love to power and the social order
to the divine. For world-order, this symbol, or some adequate
equivalent, must be supposed. (15)

The extraordinary feature of Wilson Knight's contribution lies beyond his unreserved acceptance of Parliament's decision (which was tellingly shared by some sections of the left), or even his anachronistic asser- tions concerning the British Empire; what is at stake here is the *future* inscribed in the Shakespearean text for all time as a prophecy which reaches over the mere discussions and voting of Parliament and the United Nations. The power of Shakespeare's contribution to the his- tory of the present and a practice for the future lies in the greater truth of Shakespeare *vis-à-vis* an "expanding British tradition". It would be easy to be sceptical of Wilson Knight's tenacious commitment to "the word" of Shakespeare; yet quite apart from the fact that the tenor of his remarks is exactly that of his criticism, which remains a powerful current in the field of Shakespearean studies, he is by no means alone in his celebration of the Shakespearean "word" as bearing a conspicuous relevance to the present state of the nation. His contri- bution to *Authors Take Sides on the Falklands* is dated 9th June 1982.

Exactly a year later on 9th June 1983 the Royal Shakespeare Company gave its first performance of a new production of *Henry VIII* at the Memorial Theatre in Stratford-upon-Avon. Apart from all the general comments that can be made about the Stratford enterprise, such as its role as a signifier of "Englishness", its concern with the mutuality of "culture" and big business, and the curious fictioning of a biography for Shakespeare himself, the notable feature of this production, as well as its timing, was the programme which was published to accompany it. The programme displays an overriding preoccupation with the play's textuality. Extracts from the Penguin edition are reproduced together with a selection of other printed material ranging from Holinshed, the source, to part of an article in *Woman's Own* concerning the fortunes of Anne Boleyn. The effect is to determine for the play a rightful place within that distinctive body of writing which is English Literature. Offering the play as such a special kind of writing is, of course, wholly inappropriate to seventeenth century notions of writing. It is unlikely that any of Shakespeare's plays in folio form would have enjoyed the kind of privilege afforded by the R.S.C. above and beyond a spectrum of other forms of writing. By impressing the assumption of the *text* as origin for performance, the Stratford programme secures the fixed category of Literature whilst suggesting the flexibility of other kinds of writing which append themselves to the text over the years.

The programme masquerades as a "Prompt Copy", which explains the supposedly handwritten elucidations presented alongside the printed extracts. The contrast between the printed word of Shakespeare and the pencilled additions is complete; print and scrawl, text and meaning.

The programme reproduces part of Wolsey's speech in the first act in which he is defending his policy of high taxation in the pursuit of the war against France. The Queen is doubtful and expresses her fears of unemployment and civil disorder, to which Wolsey replies:

> ... If we shall stand still,
> In fear our motion will be mocked or carped at,
> We should take root here where we sit,
> Or sit state-statues only.

It comes as small surprise to discover alongside this, the ironic handwritten slogan, "the Resolute Approach - hard measures necessary 'THERE IS NO ALTERNATIVE'." (16)

    I hope I have shown through these examples something of the extent to which images of the sixteenth and seventeenth centuries are reproduced in a variety of institutions in order to construct a distinctive history of the present. The service which this history offers to the ideology of the state in general is an impressive one. The past is presented as a seamless discourse of eternal verities which are thoroughly nationalistic in their character and provide an ideal which may be easily apprehended, simply through the individual consenting to a whole series of practices exercised by the state in the name of "the national interest". Sometimes, as in the present context, the state may mediate its crisis through a more profound conjunction of past, present, and future; a new layer of appeal conveyed by such determinations as "the resolute approach" is only as successful as the layers beneath, cemented into place as much by reformist Labour politicians as by the monetarists of the present regime. The unique value of a sixteenth- and seventeenth-century history to the current appeal is yielded partly through a fictionalized temporal relativity; and also the extraordinary range of meanings available from the components, which are understood as the whole. The epoch pre-dates capitalism, yet can invite a knowledge of capitalism's mechanic in an heroic way; trade and expansion, enterprise and reward, all signify in the present context, yet are "innocent" in the Elizabethan age of, say, their nineteenth-century connotations. It pre-dates socialism and is largely built upon a list of proper nouns, confronting notions of collectivity and class struggle. And the particular "history" speaks to us a truth of events which took place over three hundred years ago. This "space", which is no space at all, encourages consensus and submission to an historical truth and a modern discursive power. The "Discovery of the New World" in the late 1500s is less equivocal than the "Penetration of the Dark Continent" in the late 1800s because liberal humanism has, to some extent at least, cast the later epoch in the role of deviant.

    To some extent the interest paid by the left to the sixteenth and seventeenth centuries reflects the concerns of liberal humanism. It seems that left-wing historians and critics have felt safer dealing with modes of production in the capitalist epoch. If we accept for a moment the usual distinction between "history" and "criticism" (as separate "disciplines"), the former has seen little done in terms of developing theory beyond the seminal work of Christopher Hill. The right, on the other hand, has been more than busy here for decades, and I need only mention Hugh Trevor-Roper in this context. Indeed, the Marxist historian Nora Carlin has remarked that "it is hardly surprising that defending Hill should come to be almost a significant activity in itself". (17) With the exception of the work started at the Essex Conference in 1980, and in some other arenas, few assaults have been mounted against the kind of criticism produced in the 1930s, which continues to hold great sway within the educational institutions. In the face of this neglect the task facing both historians and critics on the left is immense, yet imperative, given the power of these histories in a popular context.

As far as this paper is concerned I can only suggest a few areas of activity which might combine in order to resist this particularly pervasive history of the present. Considering the range of institutions through which it is broadcast, our engagement should be multi-layered. For example, it might well be developed in the area of education within the organized left, and this project is well under way in some quarters. (18) Yet since I have suggested that criticism plays a leading role in shaping this history, and the established canon provides a buttress to its popular appeal, I want to suggest some areas of discussion in terms of our concerns as students and teachers.

The aim is to disrupt the continuum of history and to produce a knowledge of the sixteenth and seventeenth centuries as a period of crisis and of rapid change. Another history is required which engages the present crisis by confronting the construction of a whole range of values as eternal and exclusive, natural and national. The history we produce should be partial to our concerns as socialists in order to confront the "impartiality" and "completion" of the seamless knowledge produced by the opposition.

The areas which might combine to achieve this effect might include the examination of what "writing" means in the sixteenth and seventeenth centuries. It is crucially important to undermine the privilege given to drama, and to Shakespeare in particular, bourgeois criticism's wholly inappropriate sense of value and biography as well as notions of writing as a private realm. This confronts the textuality imposed upon the plays as well as allowing for the alignment of various forms of writing. This also leads to an examination of seventeenth-century theatre itself which is often framed by the assumption that in many respects it was as illusionary as the theatre of later periods and that our "experience" at Stratford or The Barbican is an essentially historical one.

Furthermore the relations between the theatrical and critical institutions should be examined in order to show how the knowledges produced in criticism have developed in the wider context throughout history and how sixteenth- and seventeenth-century writing has been separated into particular realms of, say, fact and fiction, truth and experience. Criticism itself is the major concern - what is its object and effect in terms of education? How has it used particular texts and not others, and what governs the selection?

Finally, it seems absolutely crucial that this politicization of writing and the production of an alternative history for our present should avoid being sealed off, so to speak, from our everyday practices. The great problem with liberal humanism is that it readily assimilates radicalism and that Marxism thus becomes simply another "approach", and is finally given a status as sublime and removed as bourgeois criticism itself. Unless the alternative is agitational and wholly linked to everyday struggle in the wider context, it risks becoming guilty of aiding and abetting the present downturn in the struggle for socialism.

FOOTNOTES

1. I am grateful to Catherine Belsey and David Goldwater for commenting on an earlier draft of this paper.
2. Margaret Rule, *The Mary Rose: the Excavation and Raising of Henry VIII's Flagship* (London, 1983), acknowledgements.
3. *Ibid.*, preface.
4. Warren Tute, *The True Glory* (London, 1983), foreword.
5. Clive Sinclair, multi-millionaire and developer of the first pocket television and chairperson of MENSA, is a keen advocate of Elizabethan values and enterprise.
6. *The Economist*, 25th December 1982, p.15.
7. *Cromwell*, directed by Ken Hughes, 1970.
8. Reproduced in *Gair Rhydd*, No.156 (Cardiff, 1983).
9. Geoffrey Earle, *William Shakespeare* (London, 1981), p.30.
10. L. Du Garde Peach, *The Story of the First Queen Elizabeth* (London, 1958), p.50.
11. *Ibid.*, p.42.
12. *Ibid.*, p.44.
13. R. Mears, *Britain and Europe* (London, 1981), p.82.
14. Derek Longhurst, "'Not for all time, but for an Age': An Approach to Shakespeare Studies", in Peter Widdowson, ed., *Re-Reading English* (London, 1982), p.155. Although new schools of Shakespearean criticism have come and gone since the war, I would argue that the framework of ideas produced by Tillyard and the *Scrutiny* group has not only influenced these later groups, but also survived intact in a variety of educational institutions. Their books still enjoy republication and regularly appear on school and university reading lists.
15. C. Woolf and J. Moorcroft Wilson, eds., *Authors Take Sides on the Falklands* (London, 1982), p.67.
16. Programme for R.S.C. Summer season, 1983.
17. Nora Carlin, "Marxism and the English Civil War", in *International Socialism* 2.10 (London, 1980), p.107.
18. For example, S.W.P./Socialists Unlimited, *The First English Revolution* (London, 1983).

THE POLITICS OF MEANING

Catherine Belsey

What the 1983 general election demonstrated conclusively was the triumph of ideology over experience. By this I don't mean to imply that there is, as empiricism has always protested, a category of pure and innocent experience, the source of true knowledge, which can on occasions be induced to give way to its opposite, ideology-as-dogma. On the contrary, what the election results show is that experience is precisely the location of ideology, the place where it comes into being and is lived. Ideology made the slaughter of 1,000 British and Argentinian troops heroic, unemployment a sacrifice, and poverty inevitable - at least for 43% of those who voted. For another 26% ideology made genteel nostalgia for the lost 1960s world of affluence and consensus the source of a solution to the problems of capitalism in crisis. Which leaves the Labour Party - not just foundering on the rocks of its familiar dissensions, the irresolute approach, but ready to sink, torpedoed by television, which offers close-ups of personalities and so ensures that policies are an expression of subjectivities, and are to be judged on the stability and authority, the sleekness and confidence of the people who put them forward.

Paradoxically, then, the 1983 election was a vindication of theory. The old left can no longer plausibly maintain a commitment to experience as the key to the construction of a class-for-itself, the mainspring of struggle. It's one of the ironies of history that the theory which developed during the last twenty years is precisely what enables us to explain why the ruling ideology is ruling at the moment more effectively than at any period most of us can remember. It might also, though, offer us a clue to what we might do about that state of affairs. "Do" in educational institutions, I hasten to add - in English and Cultural Studies and Communications and Modern Languages. "Do" at that very modest level. (Gratifying though it would be to transform the Trade Unions into instruments of class struggle, and lick the Labour Party into mass revolutionary shape, it's not immediately evident how we should do those things.) Whereas, as Althusser told us in the ISAs essay, paradoxically enhancing our confidence for a few years, until Paul Hirst (inadvertently) and E. P. Thompson (obsessively) rendered it unnecessary ever to read Althusser again, the educational institution is the central ideological apparatus, and if ideology matters there is work to be done at that level.

The project I want to try to define - or offer for refinement - is this. What we can do is teach, demonstrate and exemplify the politics of meaning. By that I mean that whenever we consider meaning in a classroom - and most teachers and students of those subjects I mentioned are considering meaning most of the time - we lose no opportunity to put the case that meaning is plural, not fixed, not rooted in intention, experience, the world, or the mind, not guaranteed by reason, science or law, but the material of ideology, produced in the interests of power, and open to contest in the interests of politics.

In 1963, four years before the publication of Derrida's *Of Grammatology*, Foucault in the Preface to *The Birth of the Clinic* gave an account of the logocentrism of commentary. The traditional notion of meaning, the Preface proposed, assumes an excess of the signified over the signifier, a presence, an intention, a full meaning that is pure concept behind or beyond the signifying process. Within a convention that takes as given the existence of the knowing subject and the objects of knowledge, knowledge of a text is the identification of its essence, its true meaning. "Commentary questions discourse as to what it says and intended to say; it tries to uncover that deeper meaning of speech that enables it to achieve an identity with itself." To produce commentary is to assume a residue of meaning which is not evident, which needs to be made visible, "an unformulated remainder of thought that language has left in the shade", an excess of the signified. (1) This "postulate of depth", as Macherey called it, "the principal inspiration of all traditional criticism", (2) leads to an exegesis which listens, Foucault's Preface goes on, to the Word of God, (3) whispering through and beyond its concealment in an earthly speech which is fallen from the grace of pure intelligibility. The postulate of depth is no less than the desire for a transcendental signified, pure truth, thought in the external present and the infinite understanding of the divine logos. (4)

The project of commentary is to fix meaning. It is a quest for the full, single, but unuttered signified. To know is to recognise the objects of knowledge, a single set of meanings. It is also to collapse together meaning, concept and referent, so that knowledge is a conceptual property of the subject, legitimated by the object, authorised by the facts. To know is to be in possession of the single set of meanings guaranteed by truth itself; it is to be a unified, free subject, fit to choose, consume and vote, the target and the justification of capitalism.

Knowledge of that kind - in the singular - is neither theoretically possible nor politically desirable. The alternative, Foucault argues in the 1963 Preface, is the redefinition of meaning as difference. "The meaning of a statement would not be defined by the treasure of intentions that it might contain, revealing and concealing it at the same time, but by the difference that articulates it upon the other real or possible statements, which are contemporary to it or to which it is opposed in the linear series of time." (5) What is implicit in the concept of meaning-as-difference is that meaning is plural - deferred, Derrida would say - by the *range* of other real or possible statements to which it is opposed. That range is defined and delimited at any specific moment by the knowledges - knowledges-as-discourses - which are available, so that an utterance from another culture, another period, another knowledge, can be variously re-read in the light of our own, and re-read again in the future.

Any single meaning which is attributed to an utterance is thus partial, and the excess is a property not of the signified but of the signifier. If the word "class" defines variously a relation of production, a category of the Registrar General and a set of cultural habits and preferences, according to the particular knowledge I bring to bear on the term, then the excess over each of these meanings belongs to the term itself, to the signifier.

The political implications of the excess of the signifier are predictably - and evidently - plural. Endlessly to deconstruct the metaphysics of presence, to celebrate the unfixing of meaning as an end in itself, is to settle for a relativism which is political paralysis.

(It is also, contradictorily, to opt for a specific set of meanings - Derrida's - as an authority for the refusal to settle for any particular set of meanings.) The alternative is to lay claim to specified meanings in the name of politics, not truth, to argue for "class", say, as a relation of production, not a category of the Registrar General, because the first definition identifies class as a basis of struggle, the second as a ground of inevitable and perfectly natural hierarchy. The Registrar General's meaning is exposed as inadequate, as partial, not in terms of an appeal to the facts, but because it operates so blatantly on behalf of a particular form of power. We need to question discourse in order to identify not its deeper meaning, its concealed residue, but what is at stake in this or that interpretation. If knowledge-as-discourse is power, it is the excess of the signifier which is the location of discursive struggle.

It is in ideology, Marx argued, that people become conscious of their differences and begin to fight them out. (6) Meaning is the material of ideology, and meaning is difference. The control of meaning is power, and power produces practices - economic and military, as well as ideological. As radical teachers and students we may not have much direct influence on some of these practices - except in our spare time - but there is work to be done in the classroom. The right knows this. As John Casey is quoted as saying on behalf of the New Conservatism, "... intellectuals are probably the wrong people to have much political influence. But what they can do, and what is being done is to bring about a change in the political vocabulary, in what can be said and thought." (7) The task of radical teachers, no longer the isolated heroic figures Althusser identified in 1969, is to transform the central ideological apparatus by the introduction of counter-knowledges, counter-meanings which demonstrate the plurality and therefore the politics of what can be said and thought, and what can in consequence be done.

Case Study 1: "English"

The echo of Arnold in John Casey's final cadence, "what can be said and thought", is no accident. John Casey is a member of the English Faculty at Cambridge and therefore witnessed a contest for the meaning of English which issued in a practice, the sacking of Colin MacCabe in 1981. Not a momentous event, it might be argued, in the context of national and international economic recession and the build-up of nuclear arms, but worth a good deal of press coverage at the time, and of some interest to a Sociology of Literature conference. MacCabe got a chair at Strathclyde, and the contest for the meaning of English goes on - overtly during the summer of 1982 in a protracted correspondence in the *London Review of Books*, and early in the spring of 1983 in a symposium and subsequent correspondence in the *Times Higher Education Supplement*; more silently, and I think more importantly, in English departments all over Britain.

There are, of course, a number of ways of understanding this contest for meaning, which is also a contest between practices (not because meaning is authorised by the referent - what English departments actually do - but because meaning generates a referent, produces a practice, determines what they might in future do). I want to confine myself to only one of them here. The contest for "English" is a struggle for absolute meaning as against plurality. What threatens the traditional meaning of "English" is precisely the idea that the meaning of "English" and the meanings of the literary texts which constitute the English syllabus are not fixed, given or guaranteed by anything outside themselves, or inside them, for that matter.

Meaning-as-difference throws into relief the exclusion which is the consequence of absolute definition. Defining itself as the knowledge of literary texts, as commentary, English insists on the belief that meaning is singular, however much it may be open to debate. There *is*, it maintains, a true meaning, by which all accounts of the meaning may be measured, even though the best of them may come short of the absolute, pure truth, the symbolisation of the unformulated remainder which resides in the excess of the signified. Plurality must be excluded because the overthrow of the unattainable absolute would precipitate a crisis in the institution of English. How do you mark (or grade) a reading which invokes the text to demonstrate that Esther Summerson is raped by Mr Jarndyce, or that Giovanni, the incestuous murderer of *'Tis Pity She's a Whore*, is a Christ-figure? If meaning is single, however open to debate, these readings are simply perverse. But if not ...? And if we can't mark exams and grade assessed work, the central location of institutional power crumbles. The institution loses control over its students and the discipline itself. How do we construct a syllabus, or review each other's books? And how do we ensure the reproduction of the institution? How do we decide who is to be appointed, who is to be promoted, who is to be empowered to make decisions on behalf of the institution? Power no longer has its obvious and inevitable place.

But at the same time the institution's definition of itself depends precisely on what is excluded. In practice absolute meaning depends on plurality. The endless supply of books, articles, notes, queries and first-class scripts offering a slightly different reading of the same text(s), evidence of the vitality of English, also testify to the plurality of meaning. Each is offered as an account of the real meaning at last: it doesn't mean *that*, it means *this*. Absolute meaning, invoked in order to transcend difference, is situated within difference (there *is* a *this* and a *that*, but *that* is the wrong one); plurality is exactly the condition of the possibility of absolute meaning (which is the exclusion of other *meanings*), and also its necessity (it means *this*).

Meaning as the institution understands it claims to be natural, obvious and inevitable (though sometimes a bit of background knowledge helps). But the extent to which it necessitates the exclusion of other meanings (Marxist, feminist or psychoanalytic readings, for instance) indicates that meanings are not natural but produced. Something of the strain of holding together the naturalness of the reading process on the one hand and the need for institutions to educate people in the reading process on the other is evident in the current debate. If I cite two contributions to the symposium on the state of English in the *Times Higher Education Supplement* on 11 February 1983, it's not because I attribute to them any particular authority, but because they are reasonably recent and remarkably condensed statements on behalf of two positions, one residual, the other emergent, which display certain assumptions about the meaning of English, and the strains those assumptions impose.

David Holbrook's piece is of value in this context on account of the precision with which it reproduces the vocabulary and the contradictions of the *Scrutiny* movement, with its simultaneous stress on response and training. The Leavisian discourse is all there in miniature in the repetition of "experience", "possession", the "whole response" - natural, like wholewheat and wholefood - and, of course, "life", as mistily present here as it is in any of Leavis's own texts. Meaning is unabashedly singular and absolute: "poetic meaning" is what students ought to "respond" to if they're capable of "good reading". The Downing

College entrance papers asked for "a response to a few simple poems", but the golden world is lost now, as indeed it was when *Scrutiny* was founded, and in consequence few could give "a straight account of *the* meaning" of the set poem. When we do respond, "we live through *an* experience: the art enacts its meaning" (my emphasis).

The reiteration of response, experience, wholeness and life all imply the naturalness of this meaning which art enacts. But the essay also proposes precisely the opposite: students can't do it because they haven't been brought up properly, read the right books, been given the right education. They aren't "trained readers". The emphasis here is precisely that of Leavis's *Education and the University*, where the trained response is the project: "Everything must start from the training of sensibility ..."; "By training of reading capacity I mean the training of perception, judgment and analytic skill ...". (8) This concept of response as a product of training begins to invoke not nature but behaviourism: the trained response to a stimulus which enables rats to find their way through mazes and monkeys to learn to press a lever to get a Smartie.

In other words, it is evident that the response has to be *produced*. Not, as a post-structuralist would argue, by the bringing to bear of certain knowledges, certain discourses (though the emphasis on familiarity with the Bible and Dickens comes close to conceding something of this kind), but by discipline, training. And this must be so if meaning is single and absolute. Holbrook, anxious to demonstrate that he can read foreign philosophers as well as the rest of us, invokes Heidegger's belief that humanity needs "to find a meaning in its existence". This is the way to "fulfilment of the individual person, in his or her uniqueness". But in the context of the piece as a whole "*a* meaning" here is synonymous with "*the* meaning", and not only of literary texts but of "experience", in "existence", "in 'life'". Fulfilment of individuals in their uniqueness is thus the product of submission to a discipline which enables them all to find the same absolute meaning.

Hence the very evident authoritarianism of the piece as a whole. Theory is "philosophically wrong. F. R. Leavis was right ..." "I have just given a fail mark to a candidate who ... could not give a straight account of the meaning". And hence, too, its bitterness. The world of absolute meaning is always already lost for the reasons I have suggested: plurality is the condition of its possibility. Like absolute rule, it is perceived as most desperately needed when it is most evidently threatened. "The assertion of absolute sovereignty in meaning as in the state is always an economy of distrust, desire and fear." (9)

What is at stake here is not, of course, only the meaning of "English". It is also the lynch-pin of capitalism, the knowing, autonomous subject. Subjects are constituted and take up their places in discourses or knowledges which provide them with a set of meanings, and these meanings are not only perceived but lived. The discourse, which pre-exists the subject and is the location of these meanings, dominates the subject to the point where the subject's subordination to it is occluded. The subject, indeed, seems to "possess" it. The relationship between the subject and a specific discourse is realised in the form of autonomy. But that very autonomy depends in turn on the truth of the knowledge inscribed in the discourse. Absolute meaning, the possibility of correct reading, is the guarantee of the free and knowing - free because knowing - subject of humanism and capitalism. (10)

In other words, the individual becomes the subject of his or her discourse by speaking it meaningfully, truly, living its meanings, knowing them from experience, in such a way that the subject's experience becomes the imaginary origin of that set of meanings. Hence the constant appeal to response: "Words in poetry invite us, not to think about and judge but ... to realise a complex experience that is given in the words." (11) The subject is produced in the attribution of meaning; the unified subject of liberal humanism is produced in the attribution of a single meaning; the unified, knowing, free subject is produced in the imaginary recognition of *the* meaning, the only possible, the *absolute* meaning. Liberal humanist freedom is the knowledge of the absolute, the ability to hear the Word of God.

And in case at any time the subject's condition should seem precarious, it can be intersubjectively reinforced. The reader responds to the author, achieves an "inwardness" with the text, "feels into" the experience. (12) And the reader is also entitled to enter into a complicity with other readers who take up their places in the same discourse and "recognise" the same objects and experiences. These subjects become mirrors for each other. Leavis calls it "corroboration"; the institution in general might call it "consensus"; Michel Pêcheux, working in a direct line of descent from Althusser, calls it "collusion". (13)

John Broadbent's contribution to the same *Times Higher Education Supplement* symposium is ostensibly not Leavisian, but it shares with *Scrutiny* a certain secular religiosity (which we can trace back to Arnold), a hostility to theory and a commitment to subjectivity in its emphasis on experience, the personal, depth of feeling. What is relatively new in Broadbent is the overt role of the community: the stress on "interpersonal knowledge" and "group cohesion". Here again the subject is both given, equipped with "subjective resources" and produced, trained by the community. "Subjectivity will be trained, by meditation, writing, encounter. We shall work in interpretative communities ... That is where coherence and consistency will come from."

Broadbent's piece is much briefer than Holbrook's, and I think slightly elusive as it stands. (14) In order to supplement it I want to allude to David Bleich's book, *Subjective Criticism* (1976). I think it is not improper to do so: Bleich goes down well, I gather, in DUET circles, with which Broadbent is involved; and David Punter, who also plays a major part in DUET, associated Bleich at this conference last year with the current "Copernican revolution". (15) I don't think his books have otherwise made a great deal of impact here yet, but subjective criticism is popular in America at the moment, and such are the ways of cultural imperialism that the concept may be scheduled to grow in Britain too.

The subject of *Subjective Criticism* is, of course, given. The book takes as its theory of language roughly the model defined by Locke, but reformulated for the twentieth century. When reading a text the subject undergoes a process of "mentation", which is then "symbolised" in a "response statement", and "re-symbolised" when the subject objectifies its own response statement and studies it in order to achieve self-knowledge. The subject thus becomes its own object and the horizon of its own knowledge. (The theory, of course, traces a direct line of descent from Romanticism.) What the subject learns are the fragments of meaning and truth which (from the post-structuralist position, not Bleich's) are the discursive condition of its own existence.

Though neither the book nor Broadbent's essay says so, I imagine that the experience might be very frightening. Perhaps this is the referent of the "deep feelings of loss" Broadbent cites. Comfortingly, however, "the community" is available to reinstate the subject, reconstitute it if necessary as autonomous, unified and, above all, consensual. The model Bleich invokes is Kuhn's theory of scientific revolutions. According to Kuhn, a new paradigm emerges when scientists manage to convince their colleagues of the authority of a new frame of reference and persuade them to seek answers to the questions the new framework poses. What doesn't conform to the paradigm at any given time isn't science. Bleich adopts Kuhn's relativist belief that knowledge is produced by communities and on this basis argues that knowledge which is not validated by the subject's community isn't knowledge. "To know anything at all is to have assigned part of one's self to a group of others who know the same thing ... The degree to which knowledge is not part of a community is the degree to which it isn't knowledge at all." (16)

A community, which may not be more than two people, is thus by definition consensual, a place where subjects mirror one another and confirm each other's knowledge by recognition of the same objects and experience. To disagree is to incur an obligation "to form a new community defined by other common knowledge". (17) What is assumed in this model is that a community is a spontaneous and voluntary grouping of equal individuals; what is ruled out is the possibility of persuading communities to change what they know. Knowledge is produced by "a collective subjectivity". (18) Individuals agree to this or leave. Thus knowledge remains absolute within the community, though relative from any position outside it, and by this means the knowing subject of *Subjective Criticism* preserves the singularity of meaning while acknowledging plurality ("it's true for *me*"), and so retains its own unity and autonomy, on condition that it remains within the group which validates its knowledge. The group, in turn, is static, thus protecting that knowledge from change. Of course it can learn more about its collective subjectivity, but the paradigm, the problematic, the frame of reference is inviolable, because not to accept it is to exclude oneself from the community. Consensus perpetuates the knowledge, which preserves the subjects as mirrors for each other, which perpetuates the consensus.

This model is, I believe, instructive for us, not because it is in the least Copernican, but precisely because it is so totally Ptolemaic. It seems to me to represent the telos and the terminus of the institution of English as currently constituted, the point to which it tends and beyond which it cannot go. The subjective model accepts the plurality which is the condition of absolute meaning; it accepts that knowledge is produced; but it deflects the radical possibilities of both propositions by repudiating the role of meaning and knowledge in the construction of the subject. It thus retains the reason why capitalism is natural and inevitable (people prefer it) and simultaneously revalorises the self-image of western democracy by defining the community as consensual.

To secure consensus in the largest possible community is, of course, the role of English as the institution defines it. "Our" literary heritage, "our" culture and "our" language are all inscribed in that single word and are the source of "our" identity. Not only does this occlude differences and conflicts of class, gender and discourse, it also guarantees differences between us and them, when *they* are the Argies, the French, the Soviet Union, etc., since they neither speak nor "do" English and do not therefore participate in our knowledge or share our values. To disagree with one's community is to exclude oneself, not only to get bad marks and bad reviews, but also to internalise the censorship which represses alternative knowledges, alternative subject-positions. This self-censorship is precisely the project of the ruling ideology.

Case Study 2: "Peace"

Neither Bleich nor Broadbent discusses what happens when one community feels threatened by another. What happens in practice when English feels its definition and thus its self to be threatened is an attempt to banish the source of the threat by ridicule, abuse and, of course, sacking in the case of MacCabe. (19) What happens when the consensual community English is there to reproduce feels similarly threatened? A parallel set of aggressive utterances and practices, so disproportionate in the scale of their possible effects that it would be absurd to mention them in the same breath, were it not for the ideological chain which links absolute meaning, absolute economic freedom and the capacity for absolute destruction. "We have to be prepared to defend our way of life." The size and commitment of the peace movement testifies to the inadequacy of that "we", and of the consensual model in general.

The plurality of the word "peace" was first brought home to me by the fact that Greenham Common peace women were being arrested for behaviour likely to cause a breach of it. My first thought was that the law had no sense of irony; my second was that the word means different things from different political perspectives. Everyone prizes it, but from the point of view of the law, "peace" means what we have already in this society: a structural conflict of interests which issues in an acceptable level of violence, unauthorised when practised by criminals and terrorists, authorised when consistent with the duty of the police and the army. To the left it means the absence of conflict, something we have to work towards, which is not likely to be realised within the capitalist mode of production.

At the same time there is a third position, a form of idealism within which peace is pure concept, a state of mind, the peace of God which passes understanding and has no practical application in this world. *The Daily Telegraph* began its Christmas Eve editorial in 1982 with a promising quotation from T. S. Eliot's *Murder in the Cathedral*: "Now think for a moment about the meaning of this word 'peace'". The editorial goes on to draw attention to the apparent discrepancy between the Falklands victory service and the message of the angels, "embedded in the folk-memory of the English-speaking peoples, 'in earth, peace, good will towards men'". But of course, it goes on, the discrepancy is only apparent. The world is a violent place. Christmas Day is followed by the feast of Stephen, first Christian martyr, and then by the commemoration of the Massacre of the Innocents. Cheerfully transcending the fact that these Christian victims precisely didn't bomb their enemies, the editorial argues, after a couple of side-swipes at Tam Dalyell and the anti-militarist Bishop of Bristol, that in the light of affairs in Poland, not to mention what happened to the protagonist of *Murder in the Cathedral*, and Christ, of course, the angels were perfectly right, but by "peace" they weren't so naive as to mean not killing people. In a world given over to "evil and guile" there are men (sic) who must be opposed. Precisely what the angels did mean is in the *Daily Telegraph* formulation faintly elusive, but it's something to do with a state of knowing subjectivity which has an ineffable object: "For the Christian, to kneel before the Christ child is to know the unknowable" - and to rehearse a stanza of Crashaw on "Eternity shut in a span".

The editorial may cast some light on the Archbishop of York's position, which is that Christians shouldn't worry unduly about the bomb because the apocalypse is, after all, the gateway to the kingdom of heaven. But it's still more illuminating if we attend to the real heroes of the *Daily Telegraph* text. They are Becket, St. Stephen, the Innocents, Christ, the "glorious dead" of the Falklands conflict, and the Poles, "prepared for what, for some of them, was to be a martyrdom by receiving their Christmas communion. And in a sense it is they who have been the victors." At the same time as it is a plea for a "realistic" definition of peace, the editorial is also a celebration of death. Consistent with the metaphysical construction of difference as polarity, the privileging of subjectivity leaves the body to the glory of violent death, wrenching eternity from the span that shuts it in. Medieval otherworldliness, privileging the soul, led to the mutilation of the flesh. Peace as a state of mind does more than leave open the possibility of war: it valorises physical suffering. Conflict is heroic not only because people win but also because people die. The supreme instance of the peace of God is violent death.

On 11 February 1983 the Prime Minister declared that the word peace "has been hi-jacked by those who seek one-sided disarmament". In the *Guardian* Roger Scruton, always one to follow where Thatcher leads, accused the Campaign for Nuclear Disarmament of "shamelessly appropriating the name of 'peace', as though its opponents have some other ultimate intention." The right's recognition of the contest for meaning is one of the reasons why the left cannot afford to ignore it. For the right, however, meaning remains absolute: their meanings are the correct ones. The Conservative Party's definition of "peace" may be extrapolated from the current White Paper on defence expenditure. (20) From the beginning peace is linked with freedom (another remarkably plural word), and the Soviet Union is shown to be the inveterate enemy of both - and therefore of the West. (Ironically, one of the crimes attributed to the Soviet Union is that it takes measures to silence groups which raise questions about nuclear disarmament.)

Among the many problems the White Paper presents, I want to confine myself here to two: the slide between defence and deterrence, and the construction of a position for the reader which is one of intense hostility to the Soviet Union. The conjunction of the two leads to a definition of peace which calls in question the difference which gives meaning to the terms "peace" and "war".

Deterrence or defence? Defence implies fighting to ward off attack; deterrence implies avoiding having to fight. In paragraph 101, 'we must plan our defences on the world as its exists ... The key to our continued peace and freedom remains ... the collective determination of the Allies to prevent war in Europe, by a policy of deterrence." Later, "Since 1949 the North Atlantic Alliance has maintained the peace and freedom of its member nations by a policy of deterrence. This is an essentially defensive strategy ...". (21) The two terms seems to be interchangeable rather than differential.

"We cannot afford policies based on emotion rather than logic" (paragraph 101). Let us look at this logic. The emphasis throughout the White Paper is in practice on deterrence, and the argument, constantly reiterated, is that "they" (the Soviet Union) wouldn't dare attack "us" (Britain and/or NATO) knowing the danger they would incur. In other words, the fact that we possess nuclear weapons means that the Soviet Union will be deterred from attacking us. By the same logic it must follow that the fact that the Soviet Union possesses a vast nuclear capability deters us from using nuclear weapons against them, knowing the danger we should incur. But this is not the case. NATO includes in its policy of "flexible response" the possibility of the first use of nuclear weapons. (The Soviet Union doesn't, but says that if we use them first it will annihilate us.) Margaret Thatcher has stated, under provocation from Enoch Powell whose remorseless logic on this issue reached the headlines in May 1983, that she would press the Polaris button. Asked directly whether she would be prepared to fire nuclear weapons, she replied, "Of course."

In other words, the unacceptable damage which we know the Soviet Union is prepared to inflict does not constitute a deterrent to the NATO Allies. Deterrence is apparently not symmetrical. Enoch Powell's argument that the British use of nuclear weapons would incur "national suicide" had no force for the Prime Minister, who shifted the argument back to the Russian peril by insisting that she'd rather be dead than red. (22)

What does this imply? It implies that what is supposed to deter the Soviet Union does not deter the West. Why, then, should we suppose that it deters the Soviet Union? The only possible grounds would be that the Soviet Union values human life more highly than the West, is more moral, and is more seriously committed to peace than the West. And if it is, why do we need to point all these nuclear weapons at it to deter the ruthless aggression which would otherwise be inevitable?

But of course it's not. It's "the focus of evil in the modern world", as Reagan has made clear. (23) Or in the more moderate but equally propagandist formulations of the White Paper, it is entirely hostile to the peace and freedom the West prizes so highly (paragraph 102). In order to justify the immense expenditure (or "taxpayers' money") on nuclear weapons, the government has to intensify taxpayers' fear of and aggression towards the Soviet Union. This is a precarious policy, however, in a political system where the government needs to be popular to retain power. The more evil the Soviet Union is believed to be, the more any government may be under pressure to implement the resolute approach if the Soviet Union takes any step which could be construed as provocative.

Evidently the financial aspect of the preservation of peace and freedom depends on the development of strong feelings of hostility. This will have the additional advantage of ensuring that the Soviet Union will see that we mean what we say, and will consequently be deterred. But the deterrence argument has just collapsed under the weight of its own contradictions. We are left with defence. Defence involves fighting. (The strong feelings of hostility will help there.)

What remains of government policy? "The key to our continued peace and freedom" is defence. The key to our continued peace and freedom involves war. In wartime there is not much freedom. The key to our continued *peace*, then, is war. Roger Scruton concluded his *Guardian* analysis of CND and the Soviet Union with the following sentence: "If the so-called 'peace' movement has a duty it is this: to work, at whatever risk, for the overthrow of the only system which has so far succeeded in suppressing movements like itself". Is it seriously supposed that there is any way other than a nuclear war of *overthrowing* the Soviet Union? The only peace in a nuclear war is the peace of the grave - if there are any graves. What peace means in its Conservative definition is the possible annihilation of the planet.

What is to be done?

In the case of "peace", I'm not sure. Absolute meaning is metaphysical. Peace as the polar opposite of war always contains the inscription of its other. Pacifism can legitimate violence by refusing to resist it. If meaning depends on difference rather than polarity, peace is both different from war and the deferment of war, but it is itself also a difference and a deferment. "There can never be an isolated, unique, proper, selfsame thing that would be the object of an absolutely adequate proper name." (24)

We are not wise to expect absolute peace, but we are entitled to expect something more than we are offered: a deterrent which is not a deterrent, defence which threatens annihilation, and peace which is not a probability in this world but is something to look forward to in the next. We need a definition of peace produced in the margins of its difference from war - if only to counter the argument that nuclear disarmament would leave Britain defenceless.

And it's here, perhaps, that my two case studies, so disparate in scale, come together in their implications for practice. As a teacher of English, I'm not sure how much I can contribute to planning a strategy for peace. But perhaps I can productively attend to the politics of meaning, by trying to put across an alternative to the commonsense belief that meaning is a matter of intention or reference. The signified is not produced or authorised by thought or by the world, but by the difference between signifiers within a discourse-as-knowledge. Absolute meaning emanates from and addresses itself to the free subject, who is paradoxically not free but subjected to the discourse in which he or she is constituted as recognising and giving meaning. The plural subject of plural meaning makes choices - of discourse and of meaning - and these choices are political choices. In choosing between the meanings of peace we choose a political commitment, and to identify *that* knowledge is simultaneously to identify a meaning and a project for English.

Whatever the departments and the examination boards may formally call it, everyone always abbreviates it to "English", which designates not primarily a literature but a language. We don't have to do away with English; we don't even have to re-name it. We need only acknowledge one of the meanings of the word to include English departments among the places where we can study the language which is the location of the set of meanings by which we live, and the set of contests for meaning by which we might struggle to live differently.

FOOTNOTES

1.   Michel Foucault, *The Birth of the Clinic*, tr. A. M. Sheridan (London, 1976), p.xvi.

2.   Pierre Macherey, *A Theory of Literary Production*, tr. Geoffrey Wall (London, 1978), p.81.

3.   Foucault, *Clinic*, p.xvii.

4.   See Jacques Derrida, *Of Grammatology*, tr. Gayatri Chakravorty Spivak (Baltimore and London, 1976), pp.11, 49, 73.

5.   Foucault, *Clinic*, p.xvii.

6.   Karl Marx, Preface to *A Critique of Political Economy*, *Selected Writings*, ed. David McLellan (Oxford, 1977), p.390.

7.   *Guardian*, 1 March 1983.

8.   F. R. Leavis, *Education and the University* (Cambridge, 1979), pp. 120, 69.

9.   Michael Ryan, *Marxism and Deconstruction* (Baltimore and London, 1982), p.6.

10. Michel Pêcheux, *Language, Semantics and Ideology*, tr. Harbans Nagpal (London, 1982), pp.111 ff.

11. F. R. Leavis, *The Common Pursuit* (Harmondsworth, 1962), pp.212-13.

12. Leavis, *Common Pursuit*, p.212.

13. Leavis, *Education*, p.70; Pêcheux, *Language*, p.118.

14. I was happy to find this impression intersubjectively reinforced by Ellen Challis in a letter to *THES*, 18 February 1983.

15. Francis Barker *et al*, eds., *The Politics of Theory* (Colchester, 1983), p.83.

16. David Bleich, *Subjective Criticism* (Baltimore and London, 1978), p.296.

17. *Ibid.*

18. Bleich, *Subjective Criticism*, p.264.

19. For examples see especially Tom Paulin, "Faculty at War", *London Review of Books*, vol.4, no.11, 17-30 June 1982, and subsequent correspondence.

20. *Statement on the Defence Estimates* (London: HMSO, 1983), 1.

21. *Defence Estimates*, 1, p.4.

22. *Guardian*, 1 June 1983.

23. *Guardian*, 9 March 1983. Cf. Paul Johnson, *Times*, 29 January 1982; Roger Scruton, *Guardian*, 28 March 1983.

24. Ryan, *Marxism*, p.14.

ON NUCLEAR TERMS IN THE UK

Gordon Brotherston

Of the many factors that make up the current crisis, hard on Orwell's date-line, the nuclear one exists in a class of its own, and is intellectually unique, for the following reason. It conjoins, as no other factor does, different orders and levels of reality each with its own discourse, problematic and time-scale. These range from the here and now of party politics to vistas of planetary apocalypse, from the manifestos of June 1983 and the quirks of what Stuart Hall (1983) has helped to identify as Thatcherism in the UK to homilies on the fate not just of the species but of the earth itself (to borrow Jonathan Schell's 1982 title). Discussion at any one of these levels may be locally fruitful but will always miss the larger urgent question: how are we to save ourselves? Dealing with the circumstance of politics in this country at this time leaves little space for what Einstein, one of its chief architects, called the nuclear revolution of 1945, adding: 'The power unleashed from the atom has changed everything, except our ways of thought ... We need an essentially new way of thinking if mankind is to survive.' Conversely, just to track back into the origins and quanta of this revolution tends not to help us to work out what we can or should do politically, now, an obvious limitation of Schell's otherwise excellent study.

A main objective of this enquiry into the present crisis will in fact be to identify and hold together these different levels of its nuclear discourse. The procedure is basically historical and literary critical and involves locating and dissecting two texts, one from the military beginnings of the nuclear age, the other from the run-up to the election of June 1983.

The Atomic Energy Report of 1945

Without too much exaggeration the nuclear problem can be said to have been foreseen and prestated in its entire scope even before the first explosion at Los Alamos. The source in question is a booklet entitled *Atomic Energy. A general account of the development of methods of using atomic energy for military purposes under the auspices of the United States Government*; authored by the Princeton physicist H. D. Smyth, it was first published by the US Government Printing Office in August 1945 and reproduced shortly afterwards in Britain by HMSO. For our purposes the most pungent paragraphs are those that form the final

---

In preparing this essay I have been indebted to Jules Lubbock, for finding and lending me his copy of *Atomic Energy*; Val Lucas, for digging out useful sources from *New Scientist* and for other research; Herbie Butterfield, for comments on the *Times*; Tony Loynes, for comments on the local press; to Gisela Langsdorff for comments on the draft; and to my companions in Colchester CND, Tony Young and Francis Barker, for frequent and good conversation. I should also like to point out that throughout I have found especially useful the recent publication of the Cambridge University Disarmament Seminar *Defended to Death* (edited by G. Prins).

General Summary (pp.134-6), where Smyth offers an apologia for what had been done.

A variety of beliefs are invoked in this apologia. The three appealed to initially may be listed as the necessity of scientific progress; the value of hard work; and the need to be better equipped than one's enemy in war. There follow some thoughts on the value of nuclear power along the 'paths of peace', as man's newest tool and technology; and on the need for the people of the United States to debate the nuclear issue, insofar as national security allows information to be made available to them. Though most reasonable in terms and tone, the language used at every turn shows the strain of the task in hand; the impersonal verbs of the laboratory experiment alternate with a populist 'we', neutral data with moral exhortation, in the effort to inform and convince the reader that all is still well.

Integral to ideology of the west since the Enlightenment, the first of the justifications given by Smyth is at once the easiest and the hardest to focus on. The text of the first paragraph puts it this way:

> ... the end of June 1945 finds us expecting from day to day to hear of the explosion of the first atomic bomb devised by man. All the problems are believed to have been solved at least well enough to make a bomb practicable. A sustained neutron chain reaction resulting from nuclear fission has been demonstrated; the conditions necessary to cause such a reaction to occur explosively have been established and can be achieved; production plants of several different types are in operation, building up a stock pile of the explosive material. Although we do not know when the first explosion will occur nor how effective it will be, announcement of its occurrence will precede the publication of this report. Even if the first attempt is relatively ineffective, there is little doubt that later efforts will be highly effective; the devastation from a single bomb is expected to be comparable to that of a major air raid by usual methods.

As if predicting the inevitable, the passive perfects (have been solved, has been demonstrated, have been established) lead to the future 'occurrence', according to the best traditions of scientific law. With a certain literary finesse, Smyth even dispenses with the need for the occurrence to have occurred before reporting on it, the laws of science themselves being the guarantee and enabler. The surreptitious excitement generated by this thought, at so major a juncture, succeeds in entirely obscuring the distinction between discovering a physical law in principle or theory and its possible application materially, i.e. someone has to put the bomb together and explode it, even in a test. The mystification is increased by the author's feint of ignorance ('although we do not know when ...') followed by the certainty of success by the time the reader is reading the lines he is then writing. There is here a fundamental determinism of enlightened and Positivist origins which can be found likewise in reports by other members of the Bomb Project and which has been endlessly echoed since in the rhetoric of 'you can't disinvent', and of scientific progress generally, on the subject of the bomb (see for example the *Times* leader below, and the argument in Defences Estimates 1981 Command 8212; HMSO, reprinted in *Armed Forces* 12, pp.3-4).

Compared with his first, Smyth's next paragraph, about what hard work it was to produce the bomb, is far richer in grammar and epithet. The 'we' that was at first circumspectly restricted to the small, privileged and expectant group of the nuclear scientists themselves is now broadened to include their fellow workers, the 'normal' humans of the supply and support teams; then, wider still to embrace the whole country or nation. As historical testimony the paragraph is worth quoting in full, especially insofar as it finds a way of putting the scientific law noted above into local practice:

> A weapon has been developed that is potentially destructive beyond the wildest nightmares of the imagination; a weapon so ideally suited to sudden unannounced attack that a country's major cities might be destroyed overnight by an ostensibly friendly power. This weapon has been created not by the devilish inspiration of some warped genius but by the arduous labor of thousands of normal men and women working for the safety of their country. Many of the principles that have been used were well known to the international scientific world in 1940. To develop the necessary industrial processes from these principles has been costly in time, effort, and money, but the processes which we selected for serious effort have worked and several that we have not chosen could probably be made to work. We have an initial advantage in time because, so far as we know, other countries have not been able to carry out parallel developments during the war period. We also have a general advantage in scientific and particularly in industrial strength, but such an advantage can easily be thrown away.

Of course only in a culture as exemplary of Weber's protestant ethic as the war-time US could the full force be felt of terms like 'arduous labor', 'costly in time, effort, and money', 'serious effort', etc. Even so, what impertinence to relate them at all, as justification that is self-evident, to the atomic bomb. In any wider view of 'human achievement', this last is clearly incommensurable as a phenomenon.

That this 'hard-work' ploy is however more than contingent is suggested by the remarkable disavowal in the second sentence, which is adjectivally more loaded than any other sentence in the whole report ('This weapon has been created not by the devilish inspiration of some warped genius ...'). In other words the larger identity of the we who made the bomb can be most readily deduced from their capacity to recognise inspiration that is devilish when they see it. Their own hard work is worthy because it refuses Faust's short cut, because it is consonant with the duty of fallen man in the moral scheme of Calvin and the Old Testament. A similar religious atavism was provoked by the bomb among some of Smyth's more illustrious collaborators, the case of Oppenheimer having been acutely diagnosed for example by Paul Chilton in his article 'Nukespeak: nuclear language, culture and propaganda' (1982). Yet of course, as so often in Judeo-Christian rhetoric, the irony is total and the value-switch via language complete (Oppenheimer and co. were nothing if not Faustian). In Smyth's particular argument, this pretence at labouring worthily for salvation before Jehovah, when in fact plotting the destruction of the earth, complements and much enhances the merely scientific determinism of the previous paragraph. Historically, the sequence of terms, scientific and religious, was of course the inverse; in any case, the bomb here reveals them to be most intimately allied in a fatalistic cult of progress, one moreover that is capable of wide populist extension among the we of the text. In particular, the play on 'our' fallen condition as grounds for accepting the bomb survives powerfully in theology today, not just in the American quagmire of Born Again, but in such measured European tones as those of Dr. Graham

Leonard, Bishop of London, who recently said of nuclear arms: 'I believe that their possession *and use* [my italics] can be morally acceptable, as a way of exercising our moral responsibility in a fallen world' (lecture at the Church of St. Lawrence Jewry, quoted in the *Guardian*, 4 November 1982, front page).

Having scaled relative heights of moral discourse in his first two paragraphs, Smyth turns in his third to a far simpler and pragmatic mode: if we hadn't made the bomb, our enemies would have done. This was written in that fateful space between May and August 1945, that is after the surrender of Germany, against whom the nuclear effort was initially directed (although she had long been known not to be a nuclear threat), but before Hiroshima. And as a result his hypothetical argument acquires a strange ring. For it is openly admitted that Japan was at that moment not suspected of having the bomb, at the same time as the intent to bomb that country is not precluded.

This silence can be seen as symptomatic, already before the event, of the loss of even the notional distinction between military and civilian targets which had been so monstrously demonstrated earlier in 1945 over Dresden and Chemnitz. It also points, equally before the event, to a fallacy in the 'deterrence' argument, which is here being inaugurated by Smyth, and of which a logical extension would be: if Japan had had the bomb she would not have been bombed by the US. For, historically rather than hypothetically, having the 'advantage' of a weapon 'potentially destructive beyond the wildest nightmares of the imagination' did not deter the US from actually using it as logically it should have done in strict deterrence theory. Trapped in their solipsistic guilt, the nuclear pioneers of the US can presumably only have hoped at heart for the rest of humanity to prove less devilish than they. Since then of course, the falsity of US deterrence has been corroborated by NATO's policies of first use (using nuclear weapons not as some ultimate threat but as a fairly immediate response to conventional weapons in the European 'theatre'), and of counterforce, which hugely raises the pressure to strike first in 'a sudden unannounced attack' (cf. J. M. Lee *et al.*, 1983). And now, scientists at The World After Nuclear War conference held in Washington in November 1983 have demonstrated that such a first strike *alone* would so harm the atmosphere as to make the world humanly uninhabitable (cf. *New Statesman*, 13 January 1984, pp.13-4; also the insane apologia for counterforce by Gray and Payne of the Hudson Institute, 1980).

By this stage it might be thought unfair to be exposing Smyth to such prolonged analysis, and that his report was after all only a minor moment in what was and is a huge debate. Yet it must be held a key document in that debate, by virtue of the exact moment it was written, of its official status, of what it seeks to defend, and of the particular combination of reasons with which it chooses to do that; and as far as I am aware it has not received critical attention. Also, it provides an historically exact term of reference for us now in the 1980s, this being particularly true of the further paragraphs in the General Summary, on the 'peaceful' use of nuclear power (Prognostication; Planning for the future) and on public information (The questions before the people). In this further 'debate' it is clear that the crucial decision has already been made, quite undemocratically by only few of the 'we' and on necessarily limited scientific information. For there is never any question but that mankind should proceed along the nuclear path, despite the open prediction that it could lead to humans having 'the means to commit suicide at will'. Today we know that it doesn't have to be will just accident, an electronic malfunction.

Referring to the Tolman committee of 1944, of which he was a member, Smyth points up the need for some sort of 'continuing organization', to enable the nuclear weapons industry to survive and grow ('It has been apparent for some time that some sort of government control and support in the field of nuclear energy must continue after the war'; cf. Jungk, 1979; Garrison, 1980; Pringle and Spigelman, 1981). Today in the UK, the shadowy nature of just such an organisation and of its blurred distinctions between military and civil has of course been the reason for the nervous responses of the CEGB to scientists like Dr. R. V. Hesketh, who lost his job simply for asking where enriched plutonium from Windscale had been going in recent decades and for giving voice to the opinion: 'I do not think it could be rationally maintained that we, the United Kingdom, have distinguished civil use from military use' (*Times*, 30 October 1981; cf. Prins, 1983:256). It is also at the centre of the paranoid web of official secrecy on nuclear matters referred to recently by Tony Benn at the Sizewell enquiry when, drawing on his experience as minister, he said that every British nuclear power station had become a nuclear bomb factory for the United States (*Guardian*, 9 December 1983). And this leaves quite on one side the whole question of environmental pollution and waste disposal, which the National Union of Seamen and Greenpeace have selflessly succeeded in alerting the public's attention to and which likewise has led to the sacking of scientists, Dr. Barry Matthews being a case in point, he having warned people about radioactivity on Cumbria's beaches (*Guardian*, 14 November 1983; cf. also Rob Edwards in the *New Statesman*, 22 July 1983). Extreme as these examples may appear, they do no more than reflect the situation envisaged in principle in Smyth's report. So that the stout instruction with which he concludes his Summary must seem laughable, or sinister: 'It is a semi technical report which it is hoped men of science in this country can use to help their fellow citizens in reaching wise decisions. The people of the country must be informed if they are to discharge their responsibilities wisely'.

The J. Walter Thompson Affair 1983

What exactly 'public information' on nuclear matters has come to mean for us, here in the UK forty years after Smyth, can be well deduced from an incident of late January 1983, that had everything to do with the coming election. Over the weekend of 29th-30th ministers confirmed that the government was actively considering collaboration with the US advertising agency J. Walter Thompson, in order to get its nuclear policies across better to ordinary people: this came in response to the headway then being made by the Campaign for Nuclear Disarmament, particularly on the question of Cruise and Pershing missiles. According to this arrangement British tax-payers would be being asked to reward a US commercial advertiser with a million pounds for informing them how they stood in need of accepting US-controlled missiles on their soil (cf. Pringle and Arkin, 1983). As it happens, the government backed off quickly, sensing trouble. Nonetheless, that such a course could be contemplated at all is significant as part of the present crisis, on several counts.

First of all the J. Walter Thompson affair highlighted a Tory fascination with and reliance on media advertising, which historically distinguished the 1979 British election from all others before it. Moreover the shift in their favour in that election, sustained and shown to be not a fluke in the yet more US-style commercial election of 1983, was in precisely those groups, like young people, which the government frankly said it most wanted to influence on the nuclear question (cf.

Peter Kellner in the *New Statesman*, 17 June 1983). And this involvement of the world's top opinion-mongers in the Tory 'Kulturindustrie' has gone hand in hand with a recourse to new tactics in the press, at all levels. In May, to save the country from communism (i.e. the Labour Party) readers of local small-circulation newspapers were being asked to subscribe to Tory party funds, when clearly it was not the money (there was already more than enough around) but the participatory act, especially on the part of the old and lonely that was being sought. This followed upon a series of typical smears, also in local papers; one such in the *Colchester Evening Gazette* ('CND and the Russian link', 9 July 1981; Fig.1) was taken up by the journalists' union, *Tribune* (17 July), Duncan Campbell in the *New Statesman* (7 August, pp.12-13) and the Campaign for Press Freedom (cf. Brotherston, 1981). At the same period this threshold lowering became likewise evident in pro-nuclear posters, leaflets, badges, etc. infiltrated into schools by such odious outgrowths of the British Atlantic Committee as the Coalition for Peace through Security (Fig.2).

Second, the proposed offer to Thompson brought out the faint confidence of the government in its own propaganda organs in the Civil Service and the HMSO, and the Central Office of Information (which was however allowed to participate in the talks about the offer). The reason for this is not hard to perceive: a loss of touch on the part of these agencies which had begun to prove counterproductive over the previous decade or so. The very British mixture of pragmatism and public-school protectionism which had produced such a stunning propaganda machine during the 1939-45 war, was at last showing serious signs of weakness, and a particular incapacity to handle the nuclear issue. This may be illustrated by reference to two HMSO pamphlets, *Nuclear Weapons* (3rd edition, 1974) and *Protect and Survive* (1980).

While giving a range of data on their effects, the first pamphlet attempts to reassure the reader that nuclear weapons are somehow just another bit of modern technology. This is done by a chapter and paragraph division which cuts short any argument as such, and by an unashamedly pragmatic choice of the effects to be studied. Hence we learn what nukes do to cows but not any form of wildlife, to motor vehicles but not the stratosphere; we are told how to clean and thresh cereals to lessen the 'ingestion hazard' but not what to do with the dust and chaff; and so on, to the degree that the authors cannot but appear not just pragmatic but evasive and muddle-through. More seriously, since 1974 many of the data so authoritatively passed on by these Home Office 'scientists' have been exposed as fallacious, by such bodies as Scientists Against Nuclear Arms (cf. Greene *et al.*, 1982), the British Medical Association (cf. Stallworthy, 1983), and International Physicians for the Prevention of Nuclear War (cf. *New Scientist*, 8 October 1981, p.84); and the suggestion has been made that casualty figures have been underestimated and environmental effects all but ignored in order to make less incredible the civil defence rhetoric with which the government seeks to support NATO's nuclear policies (cf. Phillips and Ross, 1983). As far as propaganda goes, then, it is clear that the HMSO can no longer rely so easily on its old national image of scientific infallibility. Indeed, so severely did the Home Office sense this possibility that they denounced the BMA report, *The Medical Effects of Nuclear War*, for having an allegedly CND bias, an act described as 'infamous' and 'the last straw' by Sir John Stallworthy, emeritus professor of obstetrics and gynaecology at Oxford (*Guardian*, 7 July 1983).

As for the other pamphlet, *Protect and Survive*, which tells you 'how to make your home and your family as safe as possible under nuclear

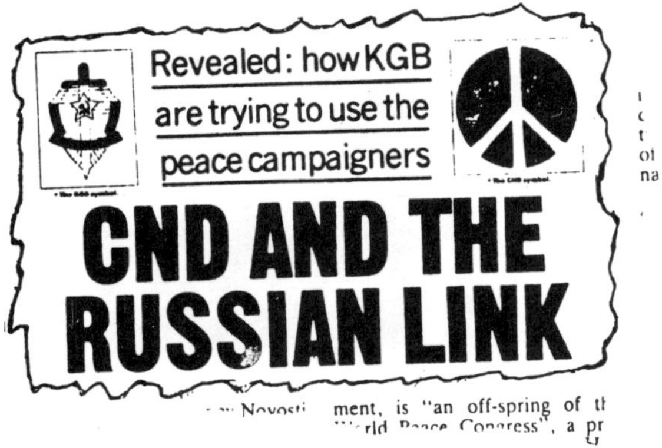
Revealed: how KGB
are trying to use the
peace campaigners
CND AND THE
RUSSIAN LINK
ment, is "an off-spring of

Fig. 1 The smear headline in the *Colchester Evening Gazette*.

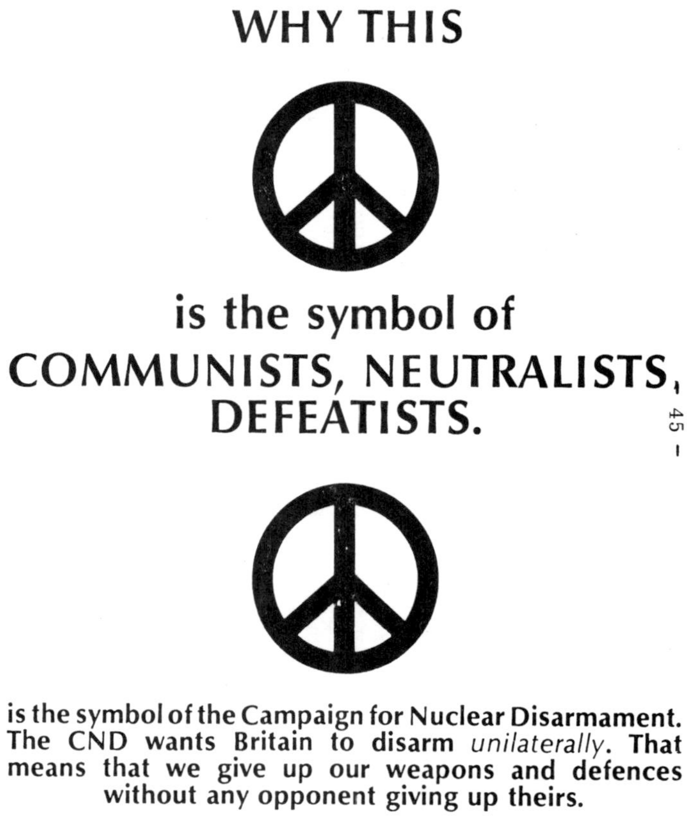
WHY THIS
is the symbol of
COMMUNISTS, NEUTRALISTS,
DEFEATISTS.
is the symbol of the Campaign for Nuclear Disarmament. The CND wants Britain to disarm *unilaterally*. That means that we give up our weapons and defences without any opponent giving up theirs.

Fig. 2 Abuse from the Coalition for Peace through Security.

attack', it has been so widely ridiculed as to count as the most valuable item of propaganda to date *against* the cause it seeks to promote, civil defence (Fig.3). The protective, reassuring voice of government persuasion, developed over decades by the Civil Service and the classical BBC, is here simply stretched beyond its competence. With its pathetically misleading echoes of 1939-45 patriotism, this pamphlet expects a phlegmatic public obedience of the kind terminally portrayed in Raymond Briggs's *When the Wind Blows* (Fig.4); and not without a certain black humour of its own. The doughty male of yesteryear is now urged to protect his family by burying himself along with it in a makeshift domestic grave, being reminded 'The longer you spend in your refuge the better'. This kind of approach can succeed only in undermining traditional gender roles, with all their conservative force, and ultimately threatens to expose the protectionist game on which the very idea of the state and defence are founded. At any event the ineptitude of *Protect and Survive* has undoubtedly been a factor in the resistance to official civil defence, bureaucratically and through outright non-cooperation, by over 150 local authorities in Britain (cf. *Guardian*, 3 December 1983).

Elaborating this, we may diagnose the Tory favouring of J. Walter Thompson and the ad-man over the trusty civil servant as symptomatic of a larger change and decay in what once was known as the British establishment. Telling and impeccably placed signs of this anatomical change, all of them related to the nuclear issue, have appeared in the *Times* leaders, especially since that paper has been sharing stables with the *Sun*; and perhaps the most telling of all is precisely the one occasioned by Thompson's million: 'Where there is life' (*Times*, 31 January 1983; Fig.5). For even as ministers were beginning to get cold feet over the Thompson plan late on Sunday 30 January, the *Times* leader writer for Monday 31 was intrepidly finding ways of justifying, nay, commending it to his readers. The result is a masterpiece of the genre, of bad English and bad faith, a privileged symptom of the nuclear malaise in nine paragraphs.

The merest precis would run: Britain needs defence; people have been distracted from seeing this need; people need education, ergo JWT. In fact, to sustain this spare logic the piece draws heavily on a whole range of unspoken assumptions, misdirects, mystifies, lies, and at moments lapses into a gibberish wonderfully eloquent of the present crisis. For these reasons, given its traditional revered status as a *Times* leader, this bit of British nuclear orthodoxy from early 1983 is worth looking at further.

The lead-in to the 'Britain needs defence' argument is provided by a speech made in Cambridge on Saturday 29, by the then Foreign Secretary Francis Pym. It serves perfectly to enforce the two major tenets to which the foreign policy of every British government since 1945 has adhered: one, Atlanticist grandeur and the great-power special relationship with the US (Britain as Greece to America's Rome, etc.); two, the total failure to distinguish in kind between nuclear and other weapons. 'Our way of life' is said to be threatened by a 'system' that is alien yet somehow its match and equivalent geo-politically: the UK nowhere emerges as a sovereign unit with boundaries, needs, strengths, opportunities and so on of its own. 'Unilateralists' are therefore denounced as 'one-sided', as if Britain alone amounted to a side. Further, they are deliberately and persistently denied their nuclear definition, as 'one-sided disarmers' who would leave Britain altogether naked militarily; nowhere is it said that the weapons in question are specifically *nuclear* ones, a favourite trope of omission in Thatcher's and Tory

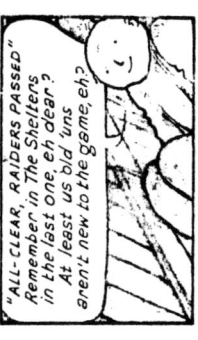

Fig. 4 From Briggs *When the Wind Blows*.

What to do on hearing the Fall-out Warning:

(Remember you may hear a fall-out warning without hearing an explosion.)

In the open

If you are out of doors, take the nearest and best available cover as quickly as possible, wiping all the dust you can from your skin and clothing at the entrance to the building in which you shelter.

At home

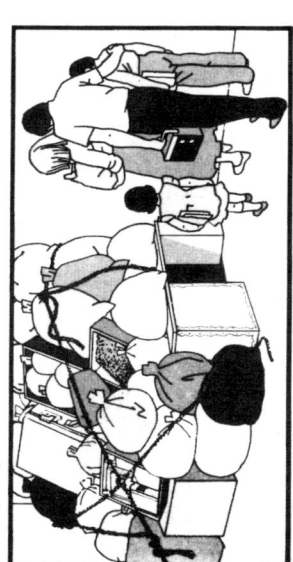

All at home must go to the fall-out room and stay inside the inner refuge, keeping the radio tuned for Government advice and instructions.

Stay in your refuge

The dangers will be so intense that you may all need to stay inside your inner refuge in the fall-out room for at least forty-eight hours. If you need to go to the lavatory, or to replenish food or water supplies, do not stay outside your refuge for a second longer than is necessary.

After forty-eight hours the danger from fall-out will lessen — but you could still be risking your life by exposure to it. The longer you spend in your refuge the better. Listen to your radio.

Fig. 3 A page from *Protect and Survive*.

P.O. Box 7, 200 Gray's Inn Road, London WC1X 8EZ. Telephone: 01-837 1234

WHERE THERE IS LIFE

In all the argument about nuclear weapons which swings through morality, technology, economics, propaganda and back again, we are in danger of losing sight of what their purpose is. It is defence. It is as the Foreign Secretary said on Saturday, because "We have a way of life which the vast majority of the population of this country agree is worth preserving". Mr Pym went on to point out that the challenge to our way of life was not only a military one, leading as that has for the whole nuclear dimension, but an ideological one based on an attempt to show that our democracy is a fraud and challenged by a system which though in trouble with itself, is dedicated to the priority of a system secured by coercive rather than cooperative power.

Faced with that power, and Mr Pym gave all the necessary figures of its quite unjustifiable growth, the answer for those who must believe in democracy is to persist patiently with countermeasures of defence. But for those who have become too obsessively caught up in the rights or wrongs of the arithmetic of the current nuclear negotiations, he had some comforting words.

"the fact that the deployment of cruise and Pershing missiles will occur over a 5 year period ensures that the programme could be stopped or changed or even reversed at any time if success in the negotiations warranted. So there is plenty of scope for progress, if the Russians are serious".

However, behind these speeches, as behind all the other noise about nuclear weapons, it is important, as Mr Pym stressed at the start, to return to first principles. That is because most of the critics of nuclear weapons, as Paul Johnson pointed out in his demolition of the Church's unilateralist case on Saturday, curiously casual about the principle of defence, and seem to prefer to indulge only in the absolutist projection which they can extract from the nuclear dimension.

The instinct for self-defence is natural and undeniable. It also spreads more naturally to embrace one's own and, wider still, one's community, so that the instinctive and individual response of seeking defence to meet danger is altogether more responsible than the pacifist one, let alone the unilateralist approach. If one excludes from the one-sided disarmament camp those whose purpose is surreptitiously to build up the other side – of which it has to be admitted there are considerable numbers – that still leaves the one-sided disarmers who seem motivated by a desire either to perish gloriously or at least not in any way to consider the consequences, let alone alternatives.

We hear nothing, for instance, about the perfectly respectable but onerous disciplines of neutrality, in all the arguments put forward, even from the Labour Party or the CND, both of whom want American bases out, and who would thereafter wish for Britain's departure from Nato. Indeed it is just one more of the many paradoxes in these arguments that so many of those voices - sadly from within the Churches as much as from without - are the same people who say we must strike out such and such a scourge, and who promote armaments and liberation movements to do that elsewhere, while simultaneously pressing disarmament on themselves and their fellow citizens.

The trouble with nuclear weapons has been that they have taken the responsibility for thinking and acting about defence too far from the average citizen. The debates are conducted by experts. The people are left with nothing, or with propaganda which seeks to alarm them about the unseen horrors of tomorrow while obliterating memory of the all too visible horrors of yesterday in Europe, and those many horrors which affect the rest of the world still today.

The spirit of communal defence and responsibility so visible, say, in Sweden or Switzerland - both non nuclear countries - is activated by an instinctive and persistent commitment which has no illusions about the fact that modern warfare has invented nuclear weapons, that they are on the increase, and that they will be neither dis-invented or dis-continued.

Why are no serious measures for civil defence proposed by the nuclear critics here, therefore? Why, indeed, is the government itself less concerned than it should be with the whole philosophy of civil defence? Without engaging the common man in the every day responsibilities and ideas of his country's defence, the nuclear debate will stay confined to experts, obsessives and propagandists. This can only be unwelcome, and unhealthy. Perhaps that is why CND seeks to criticize the perfectly respectable attempt of the government to use money for a campaign of proper public education.

Without such a campaign we are left with criticisms of a policy which of course has its dark side, its doubtful corners, and its paradoxes. But the criticisms have no clear alternative, only a form of escapism, equivocation, for a persistent denial of hope in the face of what is claimed to be a critical "truth", which is never, and could never be enough to extinguish man's essential hope of his future.

Fig. 5 _The Times_ leader, 13 January 1983.

rhetoric in the pre-election weeks. 'Defence' may indeed be the stated purpose of nuclear weapons. But unfortunately it is one to which they are ideally unsuited, since on the scale they have come to exist on even in the UK they must destroy the attacker no less than the attacked and with both an environment and ecology that have evolved over millions of years. The will to suppress this fact leads to these unilateralists being presented as yet greater extremists than the pacifists, a nonsense in even the crudest political science:

> The instinct for self-defence is natural and undeniable. It also spreads more naturally to embrace one's own and, wider still, one's community, so that the instinctive and individual response of seeking defence to meet danger is altogether more responsible than the pacifist one, let alone the unilateralist approach.

Just as the *Times* would get away with all this by indulging the two illusions dearest to post-1945 Britain, Atlanticist grandeur and nuclear-military might, so it is only by at last shunning them both that the post-election Labour Party has been able to begin to work out a 'defence' for Britain that bears any connection to the original meaning of the word.

Uninspiring no doubt, the *Times* argument so far at least has the virtue of following well-worn establishment paths. Not so by stage two: 'people have been misled'. For the people have been misled and deceived not just by CND propagandists and fanatics, of whom little else could have been expected in any case, but by powers much nearer to home: experts obsessed with figures, and Christians who have got their pastoral priorities wrong. In context this cannot but represent a rounding on what Smyth's piece showed to be the twin enablers of the nuclear adventure in the first place - Positivism and Judeo-Christianity - in their local UK forms, professional scientists and the great Anglican Church itself. That scientific experts were beginning to irk the establishment, with their worries about nuclear waste and quibbling over Home Office figures and so on, had become clear long before the publication of the BMA report in May 1983 or the first official admission of radioactive leaks later in the year. And it is notable that the *Times* piece again and again derides the expert's concern with facts as somehow obsessive and reprehensible, an irrational position in terms of its own traditional rhetoric. For their part, the Anglicans had just produced their report, *The Church and the Bomb*, and were to debate it in February. At that time, refuting in particular the fatalist 'fallen-world' line of Thatcher's appointee Dr. Graham Leonard (quoted above), they voted overwhelmingly against NATO's key European policy of nuclear first-use - a remarkable decision in the history of an institution whose prime reason for existence was after all supporting the establishment. (Also, on the larger stage of Christendom, it points to a shift away from that imperialist theology, born of the Semitic pastoral and flock economy, in which man rules as species and gender; cf. also Easlea, 1983.)

In the *Times* leader this waywardness on the part of the Anglicans provokes the extraordinary ploy of hailing a paladin of truth and right-thinking in their stead, who is none other than the hapless Paul Johnson, plucky Paul who took the whole edifice single-handed 'in his demolition of the Church's unilateralist case on Saturday'. 'Demolition' - can this be right? Are our worthy bishops and pastors as nothing beside this luminary of modern British thought? The desperateness of the ploy can be fully understood only by recognising the blanket coverage the Church had hitherto provided. Witness for example this hunk of unregenerate theology from the leader of 24 June 1981, 'Making room for Trident':

> There is therefore no point in possessing a nuclear weapon and maintaining a posture of deterrence unless one is also prepared to contemplate the awful possibility that the weapon might have to be used. War and the Christian conscience have never been wholly reconciled even before the nuclear age. Christian morality, when it is not simply pacifist, rests on the theory of the "just war". It is a theory more difficult to square with the scale of indiscriminate destruction in wholesale nuclear war. But it is not wholly invalidated either.

From any point of view, the *Times* attack on the scientific professions and the Church equals a radical departure in its own and Establishment practice. As no other, the imposed need to promote nuclear madness cracks its would-be liberal discourse and exposes as utterly bankrupt all inherited notions of balanced independent powers within the state. We are faced here with a populism and crypto-fascism that are the hallmarks of Thatcher's Britain. To this degree, the nuclear revolution can be said to have elicited more direct evidence than ever before in the UK of an identifiable ideological state apparatus. By the same token we find corresponding evidence of a repressive state apparatus, in the revised civil defence regulations, with their threat to and coercion of possible 'disgruntled' elements: in the ever bolder and crasser behaviour of the Special Branch towards 'peace' suspects; in the national build-up of the secret and legally unbridled nuclear police; and in effective government complicity with gangs like that which murdered Earl Mountbatten, not long after he had uttered his heroic anti-nuclear cry (Enoch Powell believes it was the CIA, *Guardian*, 9 January 1984; cf. also Campbell, 1982, and his two articles in the *New Statesman*, 28 October 1983).

After this decided plunge in the tone of the *Times* argument, the third stage, 'people need educating by JWT', comes as perhaps less of a surprise. Indeed it follows quite naturally: if we're to keep this show going, we need the strongest persuaders of 'average citizens' we can afford. So that it remains only to examine further the language and rhetoric of the leader as an example of just the sort of propaganda it seeks to recommend, a literary-academic task maybe, but one not too often practised on this privileged genre.

For a start no problem is caused by such classical flaws as self-contradiction, as long as the two conflicting statements are separated by enough intervening prose. Example: a major point in Pym's favour at the start is that he promises to discontinue Cruise if the Russians show signs of sense; yet by the end we are assured, ungrammatically and as if the second verb were the same as the first, that nuclear weapons 'will be neither dis-invented or [*sic*] dis-continued'. Which statement are we to believe? Looking closer we see that Pym's promise is in fact presented as something like an insult to those witless enough to be at all alarmed by Cruise ('But for those who have become too obsessively caught up in the rights or wrongs of the arithmetic of the current nuclear negotiations, he had some comforting words'). Correspondingly, the assertion that nuclear weapons will *not* be discontinued forms part of an extremely emphatic assertion about 'the fact that modern warfare has invented nuclear weapons, that they are on the increase, and that they will be neither dis-invented or dis-continued'. It is as if the writer, lemming-like, *wants* it so (cf. Humphrey, 1981). There is the same appeal to god-like abstract subjects of verbs that there was in

Smyth (Oppenheimer and co. not 'modern warfare' invented the bomb), plus an almost schoolmasterly tetchiness at the idea that anything contrary could ever have been or be the case. Can we detect here a dimly perceived discomfort at what the nuclear nightmare has done, even within the confines of the leader, to the establishment authority and respect such literary offerings once enjoyed?

A similar example of subject misattribution occurs when nuclear weapons, having been 'invented' by modern warfare, are said themselves to confuse people: 'The trouble with nuclear weapons has been that they have taken the responsibility for thinking and acting about defence too far from the average citizen'. This mystification helps to justify the need for JWT, and 'the perfectly respectable attempt of the government to use money for a campaign of proper public education'. For it makes the problem seem less ideological after all - though 'responsible' the weapons can hardly think - and more one of habilitating and making attractive an abstract and admittedly not very cuddly object, par excellence the task of the commercial advertiser. Nonetheless the old arrogance can't help asserting itself, in the faintly contemptuous 'p's (perfectly proper public) though again self-contradictorily, in the name of old establishment educational values which the argument overall has left in shreds. The prize exhibit must however remain the concluding paragraph, where the syntax visibly explodes. Instead of even an attempt at argument we are offered echoes of the folk adage about life and hope half quoted in the title. The result is a gibberish of the age which defies all parsing:

> Without such a campaign we are left with criticisms of a policy which of course has its dark side, its doubtful corners, and its paradoxes. But the criticisms have no clear alternative, only a form of escapism, equivocation, for a persistent denial of hope in the face of what is claimed to be a critical "truth", which is never, and could never be enough to extinguish man's essential hope of his future.

(Is or isn't 'clear alternative' supposed to connect with 'for a persistent denial of hope'? Is this hope the same as the essential hope later in the same sentence? What is a criticism's critical truth? And so on.) One moral to all this might be: if you're not good enough to work for JWT stick with the *Times*. Another: if we let it, the nuclear nightmare will finish our language before us.

In Sum

In both what it says and fails to say, the *Times* leader of 31 January 1983 reveals how intricately the nuclear nightmare is part of the present crisis. It exposes the latent strength of a state apparatus within the party politics and the old idea of the establishment in Britain. At the same time in the larger time-scale of western scientific and religious discourse, it shows the bankruptcy of the argument which in the US originally sanctioned the nuclear adventure, as we saw in Smyth's report. Beyond that again it suggests an urgent need for the reappraisal of concepts at least as old as the social phenomenon of the State, like defence, war, weapon. Taken together, these separate considerations highlight in turn a suicidal arrogance of man as species, gender and technocrat, one reinforced by the old rhetoric of Christianity, scientism and Marxism alike, within this earth household.

Faced with such a range of temporal factors, what to do? In the UK the short answer would point to support of those groupings which contrive still to resist the advance of the nuclear nightmare, like the councils of nuclear free zones, doctors, clergy, unions, CND, Greenpeace, Greenham women. The longer answer, which we may not be granted the time to discover, would involve rethinking the so-called ascent of man.

REFERENCES

(Excluding HMSO pamphlets and newspaper items)

Aubrey, Crispin (ed.), 1982, *Nukespeak. The media and the bomb*, London: Comedia.

Briggs, Raymond, 1982, *When the Wind Blows*, London: Hamish Hamilton.

Brotherston, Gordon, 1981, 'Press plot against CND', *Free Press* 9.

Campbell, Duncan, 1982, *War Plan UK. The Truth about Civil Defence in Britain*, London: Burnett Books (2nd edition, 1983).

Chilton, Paul, 1982, 'Nukespeak: nuclear language, culture and propaganda', in Aubrey, 1982:94-111.

Church of England Board for Social Responsibility, 1982, *The Church and the Bomb. Nuclear Weapons and Christian Conscience*, London: Hodder & Stoughton.

Easlea, Brian, 1983, *Fathering the Unthinkable. Masculinity, Scientists and the Nuclear Arms Race*, London: Pluto Press.

Garrison, Jim, 1980, *From Hiroshima to Harrisburg. The Unholy Alliance*, London: SCM Press.

Gray, Colin S. and Keith Payne, 1980, 'Victory is possible', *Foreign Policy* 39:14-27.

Greene, Owen *et al.*, 1982, *London After the Bomb. What a nuclear attack really means*, Oxford and New York: OUP.

Hall, Stuart and Martin Jacques, 1983, *The Politics of Thatcherism*, London: Lawrence & Wishart.

Humphrey, Nicholas, 1981, 'Four Minutes to Midnight', *The Listener* 1981: 493-9.

Jungk, Robert, 1979, *The Nuclear State*, London: John Calder.

Lee, John Marshall *et al.*, 1983, *No First Use. A report by the Union of Concerned Scientists*, Cambridge, Mass.

Phillips, C. and I. Ross, 1983, *The Nuclear Casebook. An illustrated guide*, Edinburgh: Polygon.

Pringle, Peter and William Arkin, 1983, *SIOP: Nuclear War from the Inside*, London: Sphere.

Pringle, Peter and James Spigelman, 1981, *The Nuclear Barons*, New York: Holt Rinehart & Winston.

Prins, Gwyn (ed.), 1983, *Defended to Death. A study of the nuclear arms race*, Harmondsworth: Penguin.

Schell, Jonathan, 1982, *The Fate of the Earth*, London: Picador.

Smyth, H. D., 1945, *Atomic Energy. A General Account of the Development of Methods of Using Atomic Energy for Military Purposes*, Washington: Government Printing Office; London: HMSO.

THE FALL AND RISE OF LABOURISM

Ian H. Birchall

I.

The starting point of this paper was the observation that at last year's Conference, virtually everybody with whom I had informal discussion in the bar or restaurant turned out to be a member of the Labour Party. Yet at a Conference ostensibly devoted to the 'Politics of Theory' there was virtually no reference to the Labour Party. Such a disjunction of theory and practice seems to be peculiar to the present period. One can scarcely imagine an analogous conference in the thirties where the question of political organisation was similarly avoided. 'Joining the party' was a major topic of intellectual debate, and is a *motif* of much of the literature of the period. The aesthetic debates of the thirties have direct political relevance, above all to the question of how to fight fascism. But what is there in common between the theoretical work produced at conferences like this and the day-to-day political practice of the participants? Is it no more than a somewhat problematical reference to 'Marxism'?

The question fits well with the dates proposed for this year's Conference. 1968 was the year when, for the first time in Britain since the 1920s, a significant political current emerged outside of and to the left of the Labour Party. By 1983 much, though not all, of that current had been reabsorbed into the Labour Party.

The capacity of reformist socialism to coopt currents to its left has been a widespread one during this period. In France Mitterand's achievement in rebuilding the Socialist Party was to persuade much of the independent left that had emerged from May 1968 to either enter the PS or to tail behind it. In a rather more dramatic context Mario Soares in Portugal was able to head off and contain a working-class upsurge of proportions that a straight bourgeois party could never have dealt with. (1)

This paper will attempt to look briefly and tentatively at some of the political and ideological issues raised by this process of cooption. It will begin by examining the critique of labourism developed in the conjuncture of 1968; then look at the alternative political strategies available in the seventies; and conclude by discussing some examples of the discourse of the left in the eighties.

II.

At a time when critiques of labourism are somewhat thin on the ground, it may be interesting to look back to a period when the attack on labourism seemed central to Marxist politics. The most extensive and influential critique of labourism was that developed in the pages of *New Left Review* and especially in the writings of Perry Anderson and Tom Nairn. (2) Very briefly, the argument ran as follows. England had had the first industrial revolution, producing a bourgeoisie 'polarised ... towards the aristocracy' and a proletariat for which socialist theory was largely unavailable. As a result 'a supine bourgeoisie produced a subordinate proletariat'. (3)

Consequently the English working class had 'almost no hegemonic ideology' and, in the words of Tom Nairn, 'it embraced one species of moderate reformism after another, became a consciously subordinate part of bourgeois society, and has remained wedded to the narrowest and greyest of bourgeois ideologies in its principal movements'. (4)

A notable feature of this analysis is that it sees the history of theory and the history of the working-class movement as separate and autonomous of each other. As a result, the real problem of the English working class seems to have been the product of bad timing: 'In England, in contrast to countries that industrialised afterwards, Marxism came too late: the *Communist Manifesto* was written just two months before the collapse of Chartism.' 'In consciousness and combativity, the English working class had been overtaken by almost all its continental opposites. Marxism had missed it. Mature socialist theory was developed in precisely the years of the British proletariat's amnesia and withdrawal. In France, in Germany, in Italy, Marxism swept the working class.' (5)

The autonomy of theory from class struggle meant that the analysis could lead to a variety of conclusions. Initially it meant that Anderson was highly optimistic about the radical potential of the Labour Party. A change of leadership, produced by the accident of mortality, could work wonders. In September 1964 he wrote: 'All the most crippling limitations of the British Labour movement have been incarnated in the lamentable succession of its official spokesmen. Now, suddenly, this is over. The Labour Party has at last, after 50 years of failing, produced a dynamic and capable leader.' (6) The reference was, of course, to Harold Wilson.

Four years later, Anderson's position had shifted sharply. In 1968 he published perhaps his most influential article, 'Components of the National Culture'. (7) This makes a devastating attack on the inadequacies of British cultural and intellectual life, and lays the basis for *New Left Review*'s seminal work in engaging on the enterprise of systematically translating and presenting the key texts of Western Marxism, an enterprise which was to have a major impact in a number of fields, among them the sociology of literature.

III.

> The English working class, immunised against theory like no other class, by its entire historical experience, *needed* theory like no other.
> It still does. (8)

Thus wrote Tom Nairn in 1964. The statement itself might meet a considerable degree of assent. The problem arises when we start to enquire as to the source, nature and content of such theory. The question of theory was posed, not in terms of a party conducting ideological struggle inside the working-class movement, but rather as something to be brought to the working class by a benevolent intelligentsia. Thus on Nairn's own account Marxism did not 'penetrate the working-class movement' at the end of the nineteenth century because 'the British intelligentsia had other preoccupations'. (9)

From this Anderson drew the strategic conclusion that 'the full conversion of the Conservative working class, for instance, can only be achieved through a *detour* through the sociological groups that generate the consciousness which mystifies it. In other words, the necessary ideological contest for a permanent majority must also be fought and won where the ideology originates - in the intelligentsia'. Ten years later Anderson was to adopt a more gloomy view. 'All that can be said is that when the masses themselves speak, theoreticians - of the sort the West has produced for fifty years - will necessarily be silent'. (10) The earlier attempt to by-pass the working class has given way to a fatalistic passivity; but both derive from a notion of 'theory' as something autonomous from the day-to-day practice of the class struggle.

In the conjuncture of 1968 the consequences of such a concept of theory were necessarily voluntaristic. The specific form of such voluntarism was on the one hand the advocacy of student 'red bases', on the other the dismissal of the day-to-day struggles of the working class as 'economism'. (11) A reading of Althusser was developed which specifically encouraged such voluntarism. In his introduction to the Penguin *Student Power* Alexander Cockburn cited Althusser in defence of the independent political role of students and against the notion that 'capitalism is riven by one, simple master contradiction which determines all else, and the revolution is a question of unlocking its progressive potential'. (12)

Such voluntarism could not offer any effective critique of reformism. (13) Political practice was centred on the student movement, a social grouping relatively untouched by reformism; in the heady atmosphere of 1968 the traditional organisations of the working class were to be forgotten or wished away rather than struggled against. Such an underestimation of their resilience led a few years later to an overestimation, once it became clear that they had not evaporated after all.

Nonetheless the analysis emanating from *New Left Review* was to prove widely influential over the coming years. Among many examples we might note the work of Terry Eagleton and his critique of the 'corporatist, evolutionary discourse of Labourism' in the work of Raymond Williams. (14)

IV.

The rejection of labourism in 1968 led to a variety of political alternatives. This is no place to attempt to map the complexities of the political left in the seventies. (15) But two main alternatives may be briefly noted.

The first was Maoism. Althusser himself had Maoist sympathies, albeit, in Anderson's words, 'delphically expressed'. (16) The influential French journal *Tel Quel* was explicitly Maoist in the early seventies, and as Peter Wollen pointed out to last year's conference, *Screen* in Britain was influenced by a 'crypto-philo-Maoism'.

Maoism was influential, not so much in the form of a transplanting of the neo-Zhdanovism of the Cultural Revolution but rather as a generalised voluntarism, expressing the need of a Third World ruling class to pull itself up into the industrialised world by its own bootstraps, and typified by Chairman Mao's reported achievement of swimming the Yangtse four times faster than the world record for the distance. Such voluntarism could not account for labourism; it sought rather to by-pass it. A classic Maoist slogan of the early seventies was 'Don't vote - strike'.

Maoism could scarcely survive the Chinese alliance with US imperialism, the death of Mao and the purge of the Gang of Four. But its decline in the mid-seventies was paralleled by the rise of Eurocommunism.

Once again Eurocommunism was deeply influenced by Althusser and Poulantzas, in particular by what Alex Callinicos has called their 'ideologism', the belief that power can be won through ideological struggle rather than by violent smashing of the state machine. (17)

But if Maoism failed to criticise reformism, Eurocommunism could not criticise it either, for it was not radically different from it. Time and again Eurocommunism was to serve as a bridge into social-democratic reformism. In Western Europe, most notably in France and Spain, Eurocommunism collapsed when voters, who were offered the alternative between an authentically reformist party, and an ex-Stalinist party desperately trying to prove that it had become reformist, preferred the former.

In Britain the demise of Eurocommunism was symbolised by the collapse of the Communist University of London, the only area where the Communist Party had some significant intellectual and cultural influence. As the Communist Party became a federation of disparate discussion groups that could not control its own daily paper, more and more Eurocommunists voted with their feet and joined the Labour Party.

This account omits a third current, Trotskyism of various shades, which has been far less influential in the area of theory central to the Essex Conference. Trotskyism has potentially a more radical critique of labourism and of reformism in general, but for a set of historical reasons (18) has often proved susceptible to cooption. Virtually all the British variants of 'orthodox' Trotskyism are now inside the Labour Party.

V.

Yet for those concerned with what the Conference poster calls 'political struggle in the cultural field', the Labour Party does not appear to offer very promising terrain. In 1926 Herbert Morrison had organised some twenty London labour choirs (19) and in the forties J. B. Priestley's broadcasts propagated the labourist message. No such cultural intervention now remains. The 1983 Labour Party Manifesto promises more funds and less VAT for the arts - but there is no reference to the content of the activities to be thus subsidised. (20) As Edward Thompson pointed out many years ago, commenting on Richard Wollheim's Fabian pamphlet on *Socialism and Culture*, 'the imagery is that of the prospectus of a new self-service store. Mr Wollheim will draw Proust and Mr Jones will draw *Seventy Splendid Nudes* and Mr Brown will draw the Book of Revelation and I will draw the *Niebelungenlied* - and what the hell shall we all *do* with what we draw.' (21)

The Labour Party has been unable to make the sort of cultural mobilisations achieved by the Anti-Nazi League, Rock Against Racism and to a lesser extent CND. And this is despite the fact that the hegemony of the established order is vulnerable in this respect. The only singer that the Conservative Party could get to perform at its pre-election youth rally was a woman whose last top ten entry was in 1974. (22) And just after the end of the Falklands War *The Economist* published an editorial called 'At the end of the day' which argued that the war might serve as a 'sort of cultural revolution' showing the younger generation the need to respect military values. It concluded: 'Colonel "H" Jones, killed; General Jeremy Moore, alive. Both men a bit more handsome and heroic than Mr David Bowie.' (23) The success of *Let's Dance* shows that the 'cultural revolution' has failed. But there is no sign that the Labour Party could mount its own 'cultural revolution'.

VI.

The post-Althusserian left has devoted a great deal of time and energy to the problem of ideology. Yet these efforts have not served to protect it against the blandishments of the Labour Party. It is one thing to root out traces of 'metaphysics', 'organicism' or 'realism' in the work of allegedly progressive writers like George Orwell or Bernard Shaw. But it is much rarer to find a similar rigour being applied to the spokespersons of labourism. (24)

Part of the problem is that many of the forms of 'discursive analysis' used on literary texts are based on a theory of the subject that is unsuited for a political critique. For the tradition emanating from Althusser and Barthes seeks to deconstruct the subject that produces the text; to detach the biography of the author from the text; in short, to break the connections between what people write and what they do.

Thus Eagleton has written: 'The phrase "George Eliot" signifies nothing more than the insertion of certain specific ideological determinations - Evangelical Christianity, rural organicism, incipient feminism, petty-bourgeois moralism - into a hegemonic formation which is partly supported, partly embarrassed by their presence'. (25) Now if we replace 'rural organicism' by 'Fabian Zionism' this would be a reasonably accurate description of Tony Benn. But no-one is going to vote for an insertion as deputy leader of the Labour Party.

For this reason my own approach will be more open to criticism as 'impressionistic' and 'pragmatic', but it will attempt to relate discourse to total political practice. For the discourse of labourism deserves critical analysis. As Lukács pointed out, only a concept of totality can overcome the dichotomy between moralistic voluntarism and fatalistic passivity. The oscillation between these two can be seen by examining the discourse of two prominent representatives of the left today. Tony Benn represents the euphoric voluntarism of 1981; Eric Hobsbawm the rightward-moving defeatism of 1983. I shall examine a few brief examples of the discourse of both men, referring in particular to the use (or abuse) of 'History'.

VII.

The political role of Tony Benn is to attract into the Labour Party those sections of the left who have been radicalised in non-party extra-parliamentary activity. As long as he performs this task, he is no threat to the right-wing leadership, although unless he from time to time *seems* to be a threat, he is not able to perform his function. Benn himself has declared this project openly:

> The Labour Party must align itself with the women's movement, the black movement, the environmental movement, the peace movement, the rural radical movement, the religious movements that object to monetarism and militarism, and bring back into the mainstream of the Labour Party those socialists who have been isolated in sectarian loneliness. (26)

Benn himself has said that 'the language we use has to be precise, because people are entitled to know what we are saying'. (27) Yet any examination of Benn's discourse will show that language is used with deliberate vagueness in order to fudge issues and to create bridges between the radical left and labourism. Thus Benn's interpretation of 1968 is designed precisely to drown it in platitudes:

> People want a much greater say. That certainly explains some of the student protests against the authoritarian hierarchies

in some of our universities and their sense of isolation
from the problems of real life. (28)

Of course even Norman Tebbit wants people to have a 'greater say'.

Benn is notorious for his attempts to appropriate history; his speeches are littered with strings of names, designed to serve as posthumous supporters. Thus he sees the roots of democratic socialism as being 'deep in hour history'; (they) 'have been nurtured by the Bible, the teachings of Christ, the Peasants' Revolt, the Levellers, Tom Paine, the Chartists, Robert Owen, the Webbs and Bernard Shaw who were Fabians, and occasionally by Marxists, Liberals and radicals who have all contributed to socialist analysis.' (29) There would seem to be something to please everyone in this teleological view of all human dissent culminating in the Labour Party.

But Benn is not satisfied with a roll-call; he wants to mobilise. Thus:

> The political message left by the Levellers, the Agitators and the Diggers for today can easily be summarised and made relevant.
> They would certainly be urging a redistribution of wealth and power in favour of working people and their families. They would be campaigning against the military industrial complex with its world-wide network of influence. And there is no doubt about the attitude they would adopt towards the need for industrial democracy and the growth of trade unionism. (30)

This attempt to jump right out of history is typical of Benn's voluntarism. The disembodied will can pursue moral abstractions regardless of the historical conjuncture. It is of a piece with the politics which thinks that getting the right leader elected can change the nature of the Labour Party.

VII.

In the case of Eric Hobsbawm, on the contrary, History weighs heavy. (31) In his article 'Falklands Fallout' he twice reminds his readers that he is speaking 'as an historian'. Evidently his political judgments cannot stand on their own merits; *Industry and Empire* and *The Age of Revolution* must be mobilised to back them up. (32)

Although a life-long member of the Communist Party, Hobsbawm has considerable influence in the Labour Party. At last year's Labour Party Conference Tribune Rally Neil Kinnock defended himself against the left of the Tribune group by quoting Hobsbawm. (33)

Hobsbawm's role is to provide a left cover for a move to the right. Thus he can invoke a heroic past of dedicated Communist militants, like the CP members in Auschwitz who paid their dues in cigarettes. (34) But romanticisation of the past reinforces pessimism about the present, and enables him to deploy the full force of empiricism; revolution would be nice but the facts won't permit it.

Thus in his article on the Falklands, tradition and the mood of the people are not something to be struggled against, but rather facts that are given and immutable:

> Michael Foot may be blamed for thinking too much in terms of "Churchillian" memories - 1940, Britain standing alone, antifascist war and all the rest of it, and obviously these echoes were there in Labour's reaction to the Falklands.

But let us not forget that our "Churchillian" memories are
not just of patriotic glory - but of victory against reaction both abroad and at home: of Labour triumph and the
defeat of Churchill. It's difficult to conceive this in
1982 but as an historian I must remind you of it. It is
dangerous to leave patriotism exclusively to the right. (35)

In the same article there is an even more dishonest use of empiricism. Hobsbawm claims that the Argentine invasion of the Falklands produced 'an almost universal sense of outrage'; how does he know?

This I think was a public sentiment which could actually be
felt. Anybody who had any kind of sensitivity to the vibes
knew that this was going on, and anyone on the Left who was
not aware of this grass roots feeling, and that it was not
a creation of the media, at least, not at this stage, but
genuinely a sense of outrage and humiliation, ought seriously
to reconsider their capacity to assess politics. (36)

Here Hobsbawm the painstaking economic historian gives way to Hobsbawm
the pseudonymous jazz critic. How is it possible to deny the vibes?
Intuition has replaced rational discourse; reality is conceived as an
external sphere in which no intervention is possible.

Yet sometimes this empiricist appeal to the irrational leads
Hobsbawm to fall flat on his face. In *The Forward March of Labour
Halted?* Hobsbawm makes a similar appeal to the spirit of the common person: 'The future of Labour and the advance to socialism depends on
mobilising people who remember the date of the Beatles' break-up and not
the date of the Saltley pickets'. (37) Writing in 1981, Hobsbawm, aiming
to prove how contemporary he is, is still back in the sixties with the
Fab Four.

To conclude: the discourse of contemporary labourism is shabby and
dishonest; its aim, through moralism and empiricism, is to coopt the
left behind a rightward-moving apparatus. It deserves criticism just as
rigorous as that which it received in the sixties. To invert an old
1968 slogan: Labourism isn't part of the solution, it's part of the
problem. (38)

FOOTNOTES

1.   Cf. I. Birchall, 'Social democracy and the Portuguese "Revolution"',
International Socialism 2:6 (1979).

2.   The key articles are: P. Anderson, 'Origins of the Present Crisis',
New Left Review 23 (1964); T. Nairn, 'The English Working Class', *NLR* 24
(1964); P. Anderson, 'Critique of Wilsonism', *NLR* 27 (1964); T. Nairn,
'The Nature of the Labour Party', *NLR* 27-28 (1964).

3.   'Origins of the Present Crisis', pp.28-35, 43.

4.   'Origins of the Present Crisis', p.41; 'The English Working Class',
p.44.

5.   'Origins of the Present Crisis', pp.34, 36.

6.   'Critique of Wilsonism', p.22.

7.   *New Left Review* 50 (1968).

8.   'The English Working Class', p.57.

9. 'The Nature of the Labour Party Part I', p.44.

10. P. Anderson, 'Problems of Socialist Strategy', in P. Anderson and R. Blackburn (eds.), *Towards Socialism* (Fontana, 1965), p.270; P. Anderson, *Consideration on Western Marxism* (New Left Books, 1976), p.106.

11. Cf. *New Left Review* 53 (1969), especially J. Wilcox, 'Two Tactics'.

12. A. Cockburn and R. Blackburn (eds.), *Student Power* (Penguin, 1969), pp.15-16.

13. Cf. T. Lovell, *Pictures of Reality* (British Film Institute, 1980), p.38.

14. T. Eagleton, *Criticism and Ideology* (Verso, 1978), p.25.

15. Cf. C. Harman, 'The Crisis of the European Revolutionary Left', *International Socialism* 2:4 (1979).

16. P. Anderson, *Arguments within English Marxism* (New Left Books, 1980), p.109.

17. A. Callinicos, *Is There a Future for Marxism?* (Macmillan, 1982), p.78.

18. A historical explanation would have to begin with the 'French turn' of 1934. For a critique see: I. Birchall, 'Too much, too little, too late; left Social Democracy in the French Popular Front', *International Socialism* 2:13 (1981).

19. Cf. B. Donoghue and G. W. Jones, *Herbert Morrison* (Weidenfeld & Nicholson, 1973), p.72.

20. *The New Hope for Britain* (The Labour Party, 1983), p.32.

21. 'The Long Revolution - Part 2', *New Left Review* 10 (1961), p.36.

22. *The Guardian*, 6 June 1983.

23. *The Economist*, 19 June 1982.

24. When I asked one long-standing participant in the Essex Conference how he reconciled his literary theories with his activity in the Labour Party, he replied that he didn't have to as he was a 'split subject'.

25. Eagleton, *op. cit.*, p.113.

26. Interview in M. Jacques (ed.), *The Forward March of Labour Halted?* (Verso, 1981), p.89.

27. A. Freeman, *The Benn Heresy* (Pluto, 1982).

28. Speech at Llandudno, 1968, cited *ibid.*, p.23.

29. *Ibid.*, p.91.

30. Foreword to F. Brockway, *Britain's First Socialists* (Quartet, 1980), p.xi.

31. For a fuller treatment of Hobsbawm, see N. Carlin and I. Birchall, 'Kinnock's Favourite Marxist', *International Socialism* 2:21 (1983).

32. 'Falklands Fallout', *Marxism Today*, January 1983, pp.17-18.

33. *Labour Weekly*, 8 October 1982.

34. E. J. Hobsbawm, *Revolutionaries* (Quartet, 1977), p.6.

35. 'Falklands Fallout', p.18.

36. *Ibid.*, p.14.

37. *The Forward March of Labour Halted?*, p.181.

38. When I delivered this paper in July 1983, one questioner expressed concern that I had offered no positive alternative. I was a little surprised, at a Conference which in the past has owed so much to Brecht, to be asked for a 'happy ending':

>It is for you to find a way, my friends,
>To help good men arrive at happy ends.
>*You* write the happy ending to the play!
>*(The Good Person of Sezuan)*

My own solution - which I commend to others - is membership of the Socialist Workers Party.

THE FALKLANDS/MALVINAS WAR - 1982:
A PERSPECTIVE FROM THE REPUBLIC OF IRELAND

John Arden

> FLEET STREET DECLARES WAR ON IRELAND: A visitor from another
> planet reading the British press this month could be forgiven
> for thinking that Ireland as well as Argentina is locked in
> deadly military conflict with Britain, such is the anti-Irish
> tone that permeates much of the newsprint spewing daily out
> of Fleet Street ... since Ireland decided along with Italy to
> pursue a neutral policy on the Falklands dispute and oppose
> mandatory EEC anti-Argentinian sanctions ... Even the rabidly
> xenophobic 'Dago Latins' *Sun* is prepared to make a seemingly
> moralistic distinction between the merely 'frightened'
> Italians and the 'treacherous' Irish. One might think that
> it was Ireland that sold the Aer Macchi planes which sunk
> British warships ... The *Sun* repeated its earlier demands
> - 'Don't buy Irish golden butter' and 'Don't holiday there
> this summer' ... It would have been ... interesting to ask
> [the editor] whether the *Sun* intends to go ahead with the
> 'IRA hit squad sent to kill Pope' story, concocted by one of
> their more imaginative journalists and ready for publication
> this week. (1)

I am a British citizen, resident for the past twenty years, off
and on, in County Galway, Ireland; married to - and in constant literary
and theatrical collaboration with - an Irish citizen (Margaretta D'Arcy).
Much of our joint work as playwrights has concerned the historical relationship between Britain and Ireland and the propaganda that has surrounded it. When the Argentinian troops invaded the Falklands/Malvinas
I was, as it happened, in Britain. I returned home to Ireland the day
after the *General Belgrano* was sunk, and remained there until after the
hostilities in the South Atlantic ceased. This physical removal in the
middle of an international crisis was accompanied by, and received poignant emphasis from, the strong psychological shift in my perspective of
world affairs that has always (perhaps irrationally) taken place whenever I have travelled between the two islands and subjected myself to
the news-media of the one rather than the other: but in this case far
more extreme than usual. To those of the left in Britain who are still
suffering from the aftermath of the 'Falklands Factor' trauma of 1982-3
(indeed, to anyone in Britain who feels, as I always do when there,
hemmed in by the parochialism of British public thought), a brief, subjective, account of how it all looked from the far side of the Irish Sea
might be of some use. The war itself, and the election that followed it,
proved a severe defeat for good sense, common decency, and the political
competence of British democracy: a defeat needing to be faced, sustained,
and finally reversed. I see introverted self-pity and recrimination as
the greatest obstacles to such a reversal.

The quotation at the head of this paper, from a Dublin Sunday newspaper, well illustrates the type of thinking that was going on at the time in the minds of Irish writers and readers. Priorities were quite different from those of the British media. For the majority of the reporters and commentators in the UK the questions posed by Galtieri's military stroke were something on these lines: (a) as the Argentinians have no right to the islands, and as the only inhabitants are thoroughly British, it follows they have no right to occupy them: so how do we get them out? (b) negotiation to that effect seems unlikely to do more than confirm the Argentinians in their belief that they have some sort of right: so have *we* then the right to expel them by force? (c) of course we have, but what is the best way of doing it? We don't want to lose too many (British) lives; (d) but loss of British lives may, may it not, produce a revival of British traditional virtues, which we sorely need, don't we? (e) finally, and crucially: have we the stomach?

In Ireland, on the other hand, where British patriotic partisanship was not a determinant, the inquiry went more like this: (a) do the Argentinians in fact have as much right to the islands as the British? (b) how far would such a right give them the right to a unilateral take-over? (c) would not Britain, indeed *has* not Britain, many times in the past carried out such a take-over herself? And how else did the islands get included in the Empire in the first place? For that matter how else did Derry come to be called Londonderry? (d) if Britain uses force to expel the Argentinians, would this not be a case of two blacks failing to make white? (e) loss of British, and Argentinian, lives may be no skin off Irish noses, but who else is going to be involved before it's finished? (f) if the inhabitants are thoroughly British, so too, it is claimed, are the northern Six Counties, and where does that leave the Irish aspiration to a thirty-two county republic? Could not the Falklanders be British somewhere else?

There was one question which certainly cropped up on both lists: the Galtieri Junta consists of violent torturing fascists with an atrocious record against their own people, so why should they be allowed to assert their rule over any additional subjects? Because it cropped up on both lists, and because it is clear that the average British nationalist opinion-maker conventionally regards all hostile foreigners as necessarily 'fascist' (cf Nasser in 1956) unless they are 'communist' (in such a context there is not much to choose between the two breeds), and because the Irish are well aware of this attitude (having had it applied to them more times than they care to remember - cf the British view of De Valera, 1939 ff), I think this particular question cancels itself out.

It is true that my 'Irish' list of questions will seem very similar to that meditated in such quarters as *The Guardian*. If you like, the general 'liberal' line. But not entirely. Even the 'liberal' British remain incontrovertibly British: their observation of their own country can never be truly external. Despite all the appeals to international socialist solidarity, class-identity, and so forth, I regard the same as being true of the 'left-wing' British. There have been some very strange contortions in the marxist journals, for example, over the dilemmas posed by anti-fascist working-class Argentinians. If they, through their oppressed spokespeople, support Galtieri's 'Argentine Malvinas' demands, are they to be disregarded as dupes of the Junta, or backed up as the true voice of anti-imperialism? Such controversies always seem to contain an element of 'foreign comrades never know quite what they are up to until we the British theorists have analysed their position for them': the regular characteristic, in fact, of opposition to colonialism as practised from a colonial country. It could, unkindly, be argued that such opposition is only a more sophisticated form of colonialism itself ...

Let me make it clear that when I talk about 'Irish opinion' or 'the Irish view' I am not suggesting that Ireland is any less divided than Britain or anywhere else by class and ideology, or that attitudes there are in any sense monolithic. But underlying all Irish viewpoints is a totally different experience of history - both remote and recent - without which the words of Irish commentators cannot be understood. Much of this history has been shared with Britain, the main language in use in Ireland is English, and many Irish citizens have lived for many years in the UK: but these apparent similarities are only superficial, they are indeed illusory and can become dangerously misleading. The tenor of the comments made by British media upon Ireland, whenever Ireland takes a different political line from Britain, suggest that a large number of British journalists (or, at least, editors) are constantly being misled.

There was an item early this year in the Sinn Fein paper *An Phoblacht/Republican News* which well illustrates an (extreme) Irish view of the South Atlantic war. Readers will remember (or will they? it is hard, writing in Ireland, to understand just how much in the way of Irish news is in fact remembered in Britain) the Ballykelly explosion, when the INLA claimed the bomb which killed a number of soldiers and civilians in a public house frequented by the British Army off-duty. It was something of a prestige claim for the INLA - the bombers had penetrated what ought, by all the rules of counter-guerilla warfare, to have been an impregnable location. Off-duty troops in the Six Counties are only very rarely allowed recreational venues where they can mix with civilians: and for obvious reasons these must be most carefully checked out before being approved. The British media generally reacted to the explosion with the sort of shock-horror headlines that suggest no-one has ever set off a bomb in the north of Ireland before. The media of the Twenty-Six Counties followed suit, though with rather more awareness of the reality of the situation - criticisms of armed republican groups in the Dublin press are not usually founded upon the assumption that all such groups must consist of criminal psychopaths *per se*: and, of course, the whole affair ended with the Home Secretary (Mr Whitelaw as he then was) denying entry to the UK to Gerry Adams and Danny Morrison, the two Sinn Fein N.I. Assembly representatives who had been invited to London by Ken Livingstone.

Sinn Fein has its connections with the IRA Provisionals, not with the INLA, which is the military counterpart of the IRSP - a rival organisation to Sinn Fein. The rivalry has recently been notable, as Sinn Fein is taking part in elections, whereas the IRSP not only refuses to do this (except at local government level) but also speaks of carrying out policies of 'destabilising' the Twenty-Six Counties, a course the Provisionals have not found it necessary to adopt. Again, I explain all this at some length because it is not always understood in Britain: the ability of the British media and British MPs to suggest, for example, that all republican bombs are the product of *one* centrally-directed strategy needs constant correction. I perhaps should not have written 'strategy': a better description for the concept regularly presented to the British voter would be something like 'one centrally-directed force of evil' - the analysis is often as simplistic as that. The point here is that an *INLA* bomb, neither more nor less atrocious in its intention than many others, but one which happened, almost by chance, to hit the security forces more severely and humiliatingly than usual, became the pretext for magniloquent denunciations of the *Provisional IRA*; and a first-rate pretext for refusing permission for dialogue in London between an elected leader of the GLC and elected members of the N.I. Assembly.

The ironies of this development were not lost on a writer in *An Phoblacht/Republican News* (I have now extricated myself from my digression, but the digression is very much part of my theme): in a mordant paragraph he affected to have forgotten the name of the bombed pub in Ballykelly - could it, he queried vaguely, have perhaps been called *The General Belgrano* ...? It was not necessary for Irish republican readers to have the point amplified any further. It should, however, be noted that this macabre little joke was made quite a time before Tam Dalyell MP had really got going on his revelations about the sinking of that warship, and all the material about the sinking which has since appeared in the *New Statesman* and other journals had not yet been put before the eyes of the British public.

The *Belgrano* incident was not seen in Ireland as anything other than - at best - a fearful disaster. Within weeks Irish journalists were writing of it as a regular war-crime. The old adage - 'Britannia rules the waves because Britannia waives the rules' - was quoted in more than one article. That there might have been more to it than this, that the torpedo might in fact have been deliberately authorised from London in order to compel a military solution to the problem of the islands even as possible negotiations were just possibly about to be seriously undertaken by the Argentinians - this was not, to my knowledge, suggested in the Irish media: but the general run of comment on the incident was such that, had there been to hand any of the evidence that has more recently come to the surface, the Irish journalists would not have had to eat any of their words on the subject. It will perhaps be remembered that it was the *Belgrano* affair which prompted a minister of the Dublin government to an angry denunciation of British policy, and eventually caused the withdrawal of total support by Ireland from the EEC's general commitment to Mrs Thatcher's war. This in turn sparked off the sort of response from the British Tory press alluded to in my preliminary quotation.

Now, before I offer any more quotes from the Irish media of the period, I should perhaps give my own interpretation of Irish views towards Britain in 1982. The country had undergone a devastating psycho-political experience, throughout the previous year, from the H-block hunger-strikes. These do not seem - to my own imperfect perceptions - to have made very much impact on British opinion, except in certain comparatively small areas where there was already a keen interest in Irish matters, often because of some Irish family or political connection with particular individuals. The Irish, however, were appalled, at almost all political levels (even those most vehemently opposed to armed republicanism: ie the Fine Gael party led by Dr Fitzgerald, the business classes from which it draws its chief support, the Labour Party in its strange political alliance with Fine Gael; and the Workers' Party which used to be the Official Sinn Fein and, before the split in the late '60s, had made up, with the Provisionals, the old united Sinn Fein).

'Appalled' can be taken in several senses. There were those who felt that men deliberately starving themselves to death for an issue of principle demanded public support as a matter of principle - one might say that this was the ancient more-or-less irrational attitude which has been held in Ireland about hunger-strikes ever since the Iron Age Celts made use of them as a means of political and moral pressure, a 'cultural institution' with possible anthropological connections to traditional Hindu India. There were those who felt, more simply and with more partisan sentiment, that these hunger-strikers were good republicans and should have all good republican support. There were those who were furiously resentful of them, who hated the entire Provo campaign, but who were also very frightened of the consequences of such an emotive issue in the deeply-divided society of modern Ireland - so much unemployment, so much 'street-crime', so little respect for conventional bourgeois politicians and the system which they operate.

All these areas of public opinion were deeply angered by what was seen as the total incomprehension of Margaret Thatcher and her ministers, by the duplicity whereby the first hunger-strike, in the late months of 1980, had been apparently solved by an offer of unwritten concessions - the 'wink-and-the-nudge' technique, the tacit agreement - an offer which was immediately denied and withdrawn as soon as the prisoners began eating again. The election of Bobby Sands to the Westminster parliament made things much worse - it seemed as though the British government refused to recognise the very democratic process which they had been urging for so many years on the nationalist population of the North ... 'if this sort of man gets elected, then we must alter the constitution so that it cannot happen again' - once again, Britannia waiving the rules.

It was very soon realised in Ireland - except perhaps in those political quarters so hostile to Sinn Fein and the Provos that hawks and handsaws are no longer distinguishable, still less wood and trees - that Bobby Sands MP had achieved a degree of world-wide fame and admiration comparable almost with that won by a Che Guevara or a Lech Walesa. Opposed to this: the perceived personality of the British Prime Minister fell very neatly into a certain atavistic category for British heads of state - her Caligula-like 'immovable rigour', cultivated deliberately as a display of public virtue - 'resolution', 'the lady's not for turning', and so forth - impressed itself as a disagreeable reminiscence of the Irish image of Queen Victoria ('the famine queen'), or of Queen Elizabeth I (who was referred to in a primary-school history book my children studied in Galway a few years ago as 'a cruel and selfish woman' who sought only to punish the Irish for not wishing to obey her). Mrs Thatcher herself, of course, is clearly enthusiastic for both of these historical archetypes: but her view of them is the British bourgeois view, an entirely different thing. Even the 'radical' British view of them does not contain the profoundly resentful and personal undertones which their policies, utterances and presumed motives bred in the Irish mind, bourgeois *or* proletarian.

But, all emotion and historical prejudice apart, the hunger-strike of 1981 was a very adequate ground for Irish resentment of British policies. The intervention of H-block candidates in the Dail election towards the middle of the year lost the contest for Fianna Fail and its leader Charles Haughey. Fianna Fail had been more inclined to condemn the British government for the H-block impasse than was Garret Fitzgerald's incoming coalition: and yet it had failed to secure any change in the immovable rigour. So the H-block candidates took votes away from Fianna Fail, and also - to a surprisingly large degree - from the Labour Party, an indication of the extensive working-class sympathy for the hunger-strikers, even from people who would normally have voted for a party strongly opposed to republicanism. The huge marches in Dublin and elsewhere, the demonstrations, road-blockings, occupations of buildings (radio/TV offices, railway stations, the Dail itself upon one occasion), the vigils, the black flag displays that occurred all over the country to mark every death in Long Kesh, were principally the efforts of the working-class: often, observably, the working-class at its most deprived level.

A relevant quotation from the more recent Dublin press about the possibility of Britain reintroducing the death penalty:

> Clive Soley of the British Labour Party argued this week
> that there were those in the IRA who actively wanted to
> see the return of the death penalty, and who might set off
> a bomb or two sometime before the Commons debate to boost
> the hanging lobby. Not all MPs, however, would read the
> situation that way. This is because they have not worked
> out who actually won the hunger-strike. It wasn't the SDLP,
> who have been under pressure ever since; it wasn't the
> British Government, which will have to come to terms with
> a rising Provo tide; it wasn't the image of Northern
> Ireland, which became ever blacker in the eyes of the world;
> it wasn't Bobby Sands, who is dead. The IRA won the
> hunger-strike. (2)

Even after two years that is not a point of view likely to be accepted very generally in the UK: but it is now almost what one might call 'received wisdom' in the pages of the highly respectable, constantly anti-Haughey *Irish Times*, a paper whose overall political and social centre-of-gravity sways somewhere half-way between those of *The Guardian* and the London *Times*.

Now when the Falklands/Malvinas crisis erupted, Ireland was being governed once again by Haughey and the Fianna Fail. There had been another election early in 1982 after two independent deputies (one of them a left-wing socialist but hostile to republicanism and hunger-strikers), who had previously supported Fitzgerald and in fact had held the balance of power, defected because of the Coalition's budget-plans - specifically the demented notion that children's shoes should be taxed at the same rate as adults' because, if they were exempt from tax, women with small feet would buy them for their own use and thus defraud the exchequer. This had been the Fine Gáel's equivalent of Thatcherite immovable rigour and on this occasion it reaped its due reward. But Haughey's total victory was itself a very narrow one - he too became dependent upon the votes of the three Workers' Party deputies (left-wing socialists hostile to republicanism and hunger-strikers), and also of one independent left-wing socialist (Tony Gregory) who had once been a member of the IRSP and was still of overt republican sympathy. Moreover Haughey was dependent upon another independent, Neil Blaney, a formidable figure from Donegal, who had been involved, with Haughey, in the arms trial crisis (Fianna Fail ministers accused of supplying weapons for the Provisional IRA) in 1969, and had left the Fianna Fail at that time. Blaney is a Euro MP, and sympathetic to republicanism. Now, shortly before the hunger-strikes began, Haughey had had a meeting with Mrs Thatcher in Dublin (following an earlier visit by him to her in London, when he presented her with a silver teapot, a gesture dangerously reminiscent of the Dauphain's gift of tennis balls to Henry V), and some sort of arrangement about deals between London and Dublin had been hashed up. I write in such vague terms because the whole thing had been so very vague and contradictory.

Haughey had said afterwards that regular talks would take place between representatives of both governments in which the 'totality of Anglo-Irish relationships' would be discussed. He put this out in such a manner as to imply that he and Thatcher were already half-way to agreeing the constitutional arrangements for a united Ireland. Mrs Thatcher, for her part, said that nothing of the sort had been decided upon, and that there would be no change in British policy toward the North. She proved that this must have been the correct version by her attitude over the hunger-strike: thereby deflating most of Haughey's political pretensions. But there does seem to have been one thing talked about, upon which no-one was officially prepared to enlarge because of the extremely delicate implications in Ireland - I mean, the possibility that a deal for Britain's withdrawal might just possibly be contingent upon Ireland's eventual willingness to abandon her traditional neutrality and to join NATO, or at least to accommodate her defence activities so closely to those of NATO that, in the event of war between the two great power-blocs, Irish bases, communication facilities, airfields, and so forth, could be used by NATO forces. Much of this is alleged to be under way as it is - the speed with which Garret Fitzgerald (once again in power) has moved in the summer of 1983 to join in the Aeroflot boycott at considerable loss to the national revenue, and also to expel Soviet diplomats accused (probably by British Intelligence) of spying, would certainly suggest as much.

But it is doubtful whether the erosion of Irish neutrality is yet sufficient to satisfy the British government that Ireland might not, in the event of war, once again prove a sort of military vacuum just behind, as it were, the British shoulder-blades. This has throughout the centuries been a permanent neurosis of British (earlier, English) strategists. In the sixteenth century it was the Catholic Spaniards who were liable to use Catholic Ireland as a base for attacks upon England; in the seventeenth century it was the Catholic French monarchy; at the end of the eighteenth century it was the revolutionary French who did in fact send some soldiers to aid the revolutionary Irish; and then, in the two twentieth-century world wars, the fear was of the Germans. The Kaiser misled the Irish volunteers of 1916 into believing he might send troops, or at least sizeable quantities of arms and ammunition to their aid: and in the 1940s the Nazis were making all manner of indecisive arrangements with the then right-wing orientated IRA, while Churchill was obsessed by the notion that U-boats at large in the Atlantic were using the west coast of Ireland for refuelling and refitting between attacks on allied convoys (the convoys themselves suffered greatly, it was held, by *not* having the use of Irish ports to supplement their defence).

At the present time, the left-wing ideology of the republican movement, its proclaimed solidarity with the PLO, various central and south American liberation groups, and other freedom-fighting organisations in different parts of the world, and its alleged arms purchases from nations inimical to Whitehall (Libya, Czechoslovakia, etc), have all made it appear to the British government that the north of Ireland, if vacated by Britain (a NATO power with a NATO army actually fighting on that NATO territory), would certainly cease to be what it now is - a firmly held part of the western military bloc. A united Ireland which would include this vacated territory (where, it is presumed, a degree of civil war would inevitably be in progress), would not only continue the traditional Irish neutrality but would be in severe danger of becoming a Soviet satellite. That this is indeed Whitehall, and presumably Pentagon, reasoning, was spelt out very clearly in a speech made by Mrs Thatcher's confidant Airey Neave shortly before his assassination by the INLA in 1979. If my memory serves me correctly (I cannot find the reference), he indicated that it would be militarily impossible for Britain to withdraw from Ireland - a point of view normally not emphasised by politicians (Tory or Labour), who prefer, as a rule, to speak of Britain's moral responsibility to the northern loyalists, the moral responsibility of 'peace-keepers' to the minority northern catholics, and the vast sums of money contributed by British taxpayers to northern Irish people in general for *purely altruistic reasons*. The 'what we have we hold' argument is cruder but, I suggest, much more honest.

Of course, neither Haughey nor Fitzgerald is the sort of politician who has any great desire to lead the electors into a position where a Soviet alliance can even be thought of as a serious possibility. Neither of them wishes to rock the NATO boat at all. But, at the same time, both of them have a political interest in solving the 'northern question' - *provided* the price is not one that will be perceived by the voters as a total sell-out of the country's allegedly sovereign independence. Haughey's Fianna Fail has stronger 'republican' claims than Fitzgerald's Fine Gael, which is after all descended from those Irish freedom-fighters (Michael Collins being their leader) who signed the partitionist Treaty with Lloyd George over sixty years ago. A left-orientated IRA is a threat to both main parties: but Fianna Fail is more inclined than Fine Gael to solve its problems by stealing the IRA's republican clothes and securing a British withdrawal.

Given all this, it will not be hard for British readers to imagine the state of mind of the Fianna Fail government only a few months after the hunger-strike, when its *allegiance* was suddenly demanded by Britain over the sovereignty of the Falklands/Malvinas.

At a level less personally concerned with political wheels-and-deals - ie among people in Ireland who are not professional politicos, but who do feel that their country ought to be as independent as it claims to be, and who (other things being equal) would use their votes to this effect, the resort by Britain to extremely heavy military force in order to expel the Argentinians from the islands was frequently seen as only part-and-parcel of the British policy towards the north of Ireland. That is to say, as a compound of the following ingredients:

(1) A desire, as a member of NATO, to exert power for the defence of NATO to such an extent that other NATO countries, in particular the USA, would continue to accord Britain her proper place in the alliance. The South Atlantic/Antarctic needs to be held as a NATO dependency just as much as does the North-east Atlantic in the region of Ireland. Britain did not plant a flag on barren Rockall some thirty years ago for nothing - Rockall could equally (and perhaps more justly) have been claimed by Ireland, had Ireland thought of it ... An Argentinian thalassocracy in the waters off Cape Horn could never be regarded as 'stable', given the bankrupt instability of the Argentine republic itself.

(2) A desire to present to the British electorate an image of 'protection of kith and kin'. The Falkland islanders have something in common with Rhodesian whites - who had been 'betrayed' by the Thatcher government in the eyes of many British Tories, and also in the eyes of northern Irish loyalists, who are always accusing Westminster of being about to betray them. Such base slurs conflict with the 'Great-Britain-great-once-more' slogans so essential to current Tory propaganda.

(3) A need to intimate to such dissident groups as northern Irish nationalists the impossible barrier they will be up against if they continue to challenge Britain's right to ignore their aspirations. 'If the IRA thinks it can *use force* successfully to challenge Mrs Thatcher's policies, then let it see what happened not only to its own hunger-strikers but also to the vainglorious Buenos Aires Junta'.

(4) Finally, and perhaps most importantly, a deep-seated hypocrisy, whereby anyone who *uses force* against the UK and its legitimate aims and purposes is to be regarded as immoral, cruel, treacherous and thoroughly criminal, while any use of force by the UK against such people is not only justified without further analysis (no subtlety here please about doctrines of *just war* or anything like that with all sorts of loopholes in it!), but is actually *beneficial* to the human race in general. The

benefit is not gone into in any great detail: it may be assumed simply by recalling Dunkirk, Trafalgar, the Spanish Armada - any historical occasion when Britain stood alone, or almost alone, against some foreign tyranny. Emotive signals for the British - at any rate, the English - chauvinist mentality: but carrying very little weight for the Irish, who have developed a rather different historical attitude to such episodes.

A quotation from the Irish *Sunday Press* (Fianna Fail orientated with a largely catholic readership): it illustrates the kind of writing on *war* and *just war* to which the Irish public is accustomed:

> It must now be obvious to everyone that the Catholic Church no longer has any coherent teaching on the use of physical force, but that every bishop from the Pope down is condemning, approving, or remaining silent according to his personal beliefs and inclinations and his judgement of what is expedient. How often have we heard from bishops in these last years in Ireland that the use of force for political ends is immoral. Yet no Catholic bishop has condemned the use of force to retake the Falklands, while Cardinal Hume has expressly approved of it. When the Pope was in Ireland, he voiced the hope that 'nobody may ever call murder by any other name than murder' ... I was inclined to agree that ... he was preaching pacifism as Christian doctrine. However, the Pope has by now spoken several times about the Falklands conflict without once using the word 'murder'; nor has he gone down on his knees to appeal to the Argentinian and English [*sic*] men of violence to desist for Christ's sake. (3)

The final paragraph of a leading article in the *Irish Times*:

> Washington is becoming more and more worried about the geopolitical consequences of the large-scale alienation of Latin America ... The strategic aspect of the South Atlantic war is of considerable concern to the British, too - that is, if Mrs Thatcher is as sincere about her NATO commitment as she so recently has been insisting she is. She cannot maintain that the re-possession of the Falklands is an isolated event of no concern outside Britain and Argentina. Yet, that is how it often seems in her speeches, with their ghostly and entirely inappropriate vocabulary of 1939. But Mrs Thatcher is not Churchill, any more than General Galtieri is Hitler. (4)

The above 'ingredients', summed up, amount to a portrait of an imperialist nation. There have been various arguments put forward at length, from both right and left points of view in Britain, that the South Atlantic war was not really imperialist at all, because there was no subject population involved. The Falkland islanders were incontrovertibly British, and they had no equivalent of the blacks of Zimbabwe or the Six-County nationalists to oppress. Had there been a clearly-defined group of islanders demanding 'enosis' with Argentina, the situation would have been quite different. So: if anyone was imperialist, the argument runs, it was the Argentinians, who came to the islands to dominate the people, oppress them, exploit them, destroy their culture, and so on. This is all quite true. But it is not to the purpose.

Imperialism and colonialism, as seen from a country which has been subject to them for centuries, have other characteristics as well. Two large powers quarrelling over a piece of territory, which originally was inhabited by citizens of neither of them, is in itself a colonialist phenomenon. It is not a practice which the Irish - as a nation, or conglomeration of nations or tribes - have indulged in since the days immediately sequent to the fall of the western Roman Empire, and inherited guilt-feelings cannot be expected to go back as far as that. It may be objected (it *was* objected by one person who heard me read this paper at Essex University) that millions of Irish people helped colonise the nations of the British Empire, depriving and exploiting the native inhabitants. But their need to emigrate had been compelled upon them by British colonial depredations in Ireland itself; and insofar as they became colonialists and imperialists, they were being used by Britain as part of the regular divide-and-rule system upon which empires are nearly always built up. Britain, in spreading herself across the world, planted her own people and her subject-people in so many territories in order to hold those territories for British advantage. The present British establishment will today not scruple to create both bloodshed and death in order to retain as much as possible of that severely-diminished world-wide advantage. Whether in the South Atlantic or in Ireland, this is a colonialist, an imperialist activity. As long as it is tolerated in the north of Ireland by 'progressive' British opinion, the 'Falklands Factor' will always remain powerful in national politics.

When the *Sun* shouted 'Stick it up your Junta' at the Argentinians, 'Gotcha' at the drowning men of the *Belgrano*, and 'Traitor' at any journalist disposed to remonstrate; and when the Prime Minister gave this species of controversial polemic her smiling approval; it was obvious to anyone watching and listening from Ireland that the message being conveyed across a much narrower stretch of water was exactly the same. The apparent collapse of the British Parliamentary Labour Party in the face of atavistic nationalism was noted without surprise. In Britain, I understand, there was surprise, consternation, anger. Had it been remembered that Roy Mason introduced the criminalisation in the H-blocks which brought about the hunger-strike, had it been remembered that Merlyn Rees and Harold Wilson caved in when the British Army repeated its behaviour of 1914 (at the Curragh) and refused to tackle the 'Loyalist Workers' Strike', had it been remembered how left-wing hecklers against Callaghan's election campaign of 1979 who called him to account for the tortures in Castlereagh were bundled out of the meeting-halls like objectors to Oswald Moseley in the '30s (and all this *is* remembered in Ireland), the atmosphere and events of 1982 could have been better comprehended.

In June 1983 Michael Foot was shown on Irish TV 'going walkabout' among the voters of some English country town: the Irish reporter asked him about possible changes in Labour's policy toward the north of Ireland. He was answered with what can only be described as a blatant brush-off - its general effect: 'Oh no no, all our policies on Ireland are well known, all decided long ago by the Party - I must take questions now from all of these people who are anxious to know about their *own* affairs ...'. A simple proposition in elementary logic: *if* the north of Ireland is British, as both Labour and Tory in Parliament maintain, then its affairs *are* the British public's own affairs. If, however, they are *not* the British public's own affairs, then the north of Ireland is *not* British and should be treated accordingly. The Tories under their present dispensation are not concerned with such logic: to them the north of Ireland - however it may think of itself - is a subject territory and its people either obey or they do not and if they do not, then ... remember the *Belgrano*. It is finally up to the British Labour Movement to decide how far they wish to acquiesce in this concept of subject territories: it may well seem to them that it is perfectly compatible with 'broad-church socialism', in which case we can expect Thatcherite triumphalism with its Task Forces, its calls to 'rejoice,

rejoice', and its deification of the SAS, to continue as long as the money lasts. On the other hand, another view may yet prevail ...

Some more quotes from the press in the country where I live:

A letter to the *Irish Times* (excerpt):

Dr Dairena Gaffney makes a mean attack on Charlie Haughey for his policy on sanctions against the Argentine. Let me say: Goodman, Charlie Haughey! The Argentines have never done anything to us. The English [*sic*] have 841 years of brutality to us to explain away. If Dr Gaffney is ashamed of being Irish, good riddance. She can easily become a naturalised Englishwoman, and the English need people like her in their propaganda machine - yours etc., Eoin MacNeill. (5)

From a report by a correspondent in Buenos Aires:

They thought the British wouldn't fight. They actually believed that Britain, like a tired old aristocrat with encumbered estates, would heave a sigh of relief when her ramshackle island property was taken over ... Not only were they wrong - they presumed, and being presumptuous, had to be put in their place. As the British Ambassador declared, withdrawing from Buenos Aires: 'They must learn that they cannot treat a major power like this.' (There is the principle that 'armed aggression must not succeed', and there is the principle that 'armed aggression against a major power must not succeed'.) (6)

From a letter to the *Irish Times*:

It is very disheartening to note the attitude of certain British politicians to the neutrality of this country ... When one considers how lightly the Irish Government let Britain off the hook over the sinking of the *Sheralga* [an Irish trawler sunk by a British submarine in the Irish Sea, 1982 : J.A.] ... they are hardly in a position to castigate this country's attempts to ensure a peaceful solution to the present conflict in the South Atlantic. It seems that Mrs Thatcher is intent on open confrontation with Argentina and needs the moral support of her EEC partners to help justify her: yet the same woman denies her same partners the same solidarity over farm prices. (7)

From a letter to the *Irish Times*, attacking the then leader of the Irish Labour Party, Michael O'Leary, for his support of Garret Fitzgerald in the latter's criticism of Haughey's Falkland/Malvinas policy:

No doubt Dr Fitzgerald with his tradition in the Irish counter-revolution of 1922 should feel perturbed at disturbing his masters in the European counter-revolution of ex-colonial powers which we know as the EEC. However, if Mr O'Leary were to act in the Connolly and Larkin tradition of the Labour Party he would be more concerned at what the Third World thinks of Ireland in the present crisis. (8)

From a report by a correspondent in Buenos Aires:

Observers at the United Nations believe it is British intransigence rather than Argentine stubbornness that threatens the peace talks. USA officials fear that their support for Britain has opened the door for the Soviets in Latin America who have now begun to take advantage of that opportunity. (9)

Nearly the end of the fighting: a headline expresses priorities:

Civilians killed in British bombardment: STANLEY - THE BATTLE IS ON. (10)

FOOTNOTES

1. Michael Maguire in the *Sunday Tribune*, 30 May 1982.
2. David McKittrick in the *Irish Times*, 1 July 1982.
3. Desmond Fennell in the *Sunday Press*, 16 May 1982.
4. *Irish Times* editorial, 14 June 1982.
5. Letter to the *Irish Times*, 15 June 1982.
6. Olivia O'Leary in the *Irish Times*, 17 June 1982.
7. Letter from Leo Traynor in the *Irish Times*, 15 May 1982.
8. Letter from Derry Kelleher in the *Irish Times*, 15 May 1982.
9. Neil Wallace in the *Sunday Tribune*, 16 May 1982.
10. Headline in the *Sunday Press*, 13 June 1982.

SOME NOTES ON MEDIA COVERAGE OF THE FALKLANDS
Or: "The Soviet Union Could Teach Us a Few Lessons"

Anthony Barnett

Even a few partial observations on British media coverage of the Falklands War such as those which follow, should begin with the reality of the war itself: it was brief and it was won by Britain. An overall judgement of the way the war was projected in the UK and how that projection was largely accepted by public opinion, is necessarily constrained by these two facts. The *realities* of the war greatly favoured the British authorities - from the government of the day to the military. The media "reflected" this faithfully enough. Yet it would also have reflected unfavourable developments in the war *if* these had gained the upper hand.

For example, when the military experts argued that the Task Force could not be kept at sea for six months, they mentioned the physical and logistical problems. But in the back of their minds, or perhaps in the front of their minds when talking privately to one another, there was the political problem: they doubted that popular support could be retained for a long war. They feared the political consequences of becoming "bogged down" in the South Atlantic, and that means that they feared that eventually the media would allow opposition to be articulated with conviction to a mass audience. Certainly, if Britain had begun to lose the war, and if, therefore, further support for the conflict in the Falklands would have meant endorsing an accumulating loss of British lives in a manifestly futile cause, then much of the 'loyal' media support for the Task Force would have turned into opposition.

So it is not sufficient to say that the role of the media was predominantly short-sighted and craven. Most reporters and editors in the press and television are under pressure to accept (and begin by accepting) the official version of events. The first official facts denote objective 'News'. Only when unofficial opinion becomes strong enough will it also become 'newsworthy', i.e. worthy of being considered as news. This takes time, if it takes place at all.

Thus the brevity of the war and its success functioned to confirm the initial, official British attitude and hence the initial, accepting and supportive, media coverage. Yet had the war become protracted, had the casualties mounted, had the Task Force been defeated, then the media coverage would have turned, perhaps even sharply. This phenomenon was witnessed in Vietnam, where the American press and TV networks became critical of the US role after the Tet uprising in 1968. In large part this was due to the way it became manifest that the US media had allowed itself to be duped by President Johnson and the Pentagon. For years its reporters had gone along with their own manipulation to the point where their professional self-esteem could no longer tolerate continuation. Thereafter, there was an effort by some in the US media to regain their credibility. (1) A similar development would have occurred in the UK, had the outcome seemed in doubt. Ashamed of its own responsibility for the War, the media would then have sought to wash its hands of it. In other words, if Britain had lost the war we can be sure that we would have had a proud (if belated) record of media opposition to the conflict.

It is important to register that although the media did actually play a subservient role to the country's political masters, and was in fact their servant, there were muted signs of rebellion and the *possibility* of a revolt.

II.

There is a further reality that must be emphasized at the outset of any discussion of British media coverage of the Falklands War. The conflict was confined to a remote and isolated spot entirely defined by military parameters.

Perhaps the most dramatic, if not necessarily the most accurate, way of grasping the consequences of the last point, is through a comparison and contrast. One occurred to me when I was watching television film of Margaret Thatcher's visit to the Falkland Islands in January 1983. The visit was a complete 'surprise' - for security reasons. Naturally she was greated with a kind of incoherent gratitude by the islanders, who tried to express their enthusiasm as best they could. The Prime Minister went to Fitzroy, with its 27 inhabitants. She then told the TV reporters: "They're spirited people. They really are. When they heard the Task Force was coming, they never lost faith." And she addressed the following words to the Falklanders themselves: "You have always had a total belief in freedom and justice. We've not let you down, you'll never let us down." It was absolutely marvellous television: the sovereign with grateful subjects; the victorious war leader with her liberated victims (and grieving widow who paid her tribute to the fallen at their war graves). The utter banality of the sentiments expressed were thus transformed by the circumstances.

Quite a few people felt that whatever the risk involved, the visit was a cynical exploitation of the islanders for party ends. Indeed, Conservative popularity rose sharply after the Prime Minister's visit; which with hindsight can be seen as an electioneering stunt. But what could the media do? None of the party opponents of the Prime Minister were willing to attack the trip. When interviewed about it themselves on television they appeared in the main to be jealous. And on the Islands themselves the camera crews were obliged to follow the leader, and film the small knots of grateful compatriots and cheering troops. While watching this hallucinating coverage, I suddenly thought: "It is like Nixon in China"; which was also an early move in an election campaign.

The comparison is worth pursuing briefly, even though Nixon's visit to China was an important world event, while Britain's Falklands War was an improbable epicycle in the history of a declining Empire. The two events were quite different. Nonetheless there was a similarity in the way they were covered by press and television. In at least three respects:

1) A combination of geography and state power meant that communications were sharply confined. In addition, the press corps was restricted and monitored, independent investigators had no place. Thus the news of the events turned into a news coverage of them and they became a 'spectacle', just like a formal dinner or a wedding, and hence 'unreal'. Yet they remained really real - actual history. For the Falklands the element of 'contrived reality' was more true of Thatcher's visit than

the war itself. Nonetheless, the outcome of the war lent its retrospective victory gloss to coverage of the fighting not least because much of the actual film arrived in the UK only after the war was concluded. In other words, quite apart from and much more important than any censorship, both events were 'controlled ones' as media projects. They *were* history (hence objective news) whose outcome was open, yet they were also staged.

Remoteness was crucial to this combination: one of the globe's smallest island communities in 1982, and the world's most populous country in 1972, were comparably 'remote' from the TV capitals of the West.

2) Each of the two real/media events took place in the context of an extended national crisis. This was clearer for the US because of the Vietnam war. Yet it was no less true for the United Kingdom. In Britain, the national passion invested in the Falklands campaign was rooted in the immense, cumulative and widespread sense of frustration with the 'decline' of Britain. The dispatch of the Task Force was greeted with a kind of excitement and relief by a 'national psyche' starved of decisive drama that was similar to the response aroused by Nixon's announcement that he would visit China.

In both cases the reaction of press and television commentators helped to create and confirm this state of affairs, but it was not *responsible* for it.

3) The general mood meant that hostility was muted to a whimper while scrutiny of what was actually going on was minimal. We will see below how far this went in the case of the Falklands. But for the sake of this comparison it should be recalled that the Taiwan lobby was swamped in 1971-72, while much more went on in the discussions in China than we were led to believe. It was only long afterwards that Hanoi denounced the 1972 Shanghai Communiqué for being the outline of a deal in which the US would loosen its hold on Taiwan provided that South Vietnam remain in the Western sphere. Kissinger's memoirs confirmed that there was indeed 'linkage' between Taiwan and Vietnam in the Communiqué. (2) Yet at the time there was virtually no probing of the political realities that were the skeleton within the flesh and fashionable display of the media realities.

III.

Two aspects of military events receive the most attention in terms of the media: the first concerns the action itself, "What is actually happening?"; the second, the speed with which the information can be transmitted, "How quickly can we inform people of what has happened?". There are good reasons why these questions are so attractive. They are asked constantly by journalists on the spot - that is their job. Large sums of money and considerable prestige are at stake in the answers, for those who syndicate them. More important such questions tend to presume that people have a *right* to know what is going on. As the media becomes more globally instantaneous, and as the world becomes a more risky place, the notion of a popular or citizen's right to know also expands. The technical development and international reach of the media, especially of television, extends the idea of free access to news across national borders to take in mankind itself.

Thus these two questions:

1) "What is happening?", asked with the *presumption* that as a citizen of the world one has a right to know;

2) "How quickly can I tell and show everybody who is concerned?", asked with the presumption that *they* also have the right to know.

These two questions pose both the most practical, technical difficulties of reporting and, at the same time, the most general right to the *freedom* of information.

But there is more to the media than straightforward reporting, hard though that is especially when it reports the truth. For in addition to the facts and immediate consequences of actions, the media in its different forms may, or may not, cover arguments over the reasons for a conflict, the principles at stake and the consequences of any likely outcome. In other words, the media covers *purpose* as well as the deeds themselves. Often it does so implicitly while in editorials there is a tendency - doubtless a very human one - to assert polemically that there can only be one major purpose. It is somewhat rarer to find 'purpose' actually investigated at the time of a conflict. However, if the *reporting of deeds* raises the principle of the *freedom* of the media to gain and disseminate information, the *investigation of purpose* poses the nature of the *independence* of the media from party, state and vested economic interests.

In the case of the Falklands War there was plenty of time to test the independence of the British media. Taken as a whole, it has little to be proud of (the main exception being the *Daily Mirror* followed by *The Guardian*). The editors at home had the opportunity to probe the causes and purposes of the British side in a way that the reporters, who were virtually imprisoned in the fleet, did not. Yet the front line reporters put up a better fight despite their adverse circumstances, demanding their rights to know and transmit news of events, than did their editorial colleagues at home, who had the luxury of being their own masters.

For example, take the question of the ownership of the islands. This matter is pretty basic. There is no doubt that the Argentine Junta should not have ordered the invasion of the Falklands as they did. But should the islands be under British sovereignty? There are two aspects to this. One is legal - the nature of British possession in terms of international law - the other more practical, namely the history of British policy on the question over the years. The fact is that the Foreign Office has long recognized that Britain's legal claim to the Falklands is weaker than Argentina's, while the policy of successive governments in London since 1965 has been to concede the principle of nominal sovereignty to Buenos Aires, while trying to postpone this eventuality at any particular moment.

The Task Force was launched on 5 April. The first clashes over the Falklands did not take place until 1 May. Thus the media had a month before the fighting began, and *seven weeks* between the announcement of the dispatch of the Task Force and the landings on the Falklands, in which to probe the question "Whose islands are they?" and "What had British policy been hitherto?".

Now Port Stanley was retaken on 14 June, when the forces on the Islands surrendered, a Monday. On the Friday, four days later, the *Economist* published a five-page analysis called "Origins of the Falklands War". It was a splendid piece of inside research and of course it showed how weak was the British case. The next day *The Guardian* carried a similar but even more massive examination of the causes of the conflict, which also revealed that it had been British policy not to keep the Islands. Again the exposé was a remarkable effort which clarified much that had been murky up to that time. On the Sunday we were treated to a third and even more devastating background analysis, from the *Sunday Times* 'Insight' team. It had acquired material from the researches of Dr. Peter Beck, who had gone through Foreign Office archives on the Falklands that stretched back to 1910 (when one document stated, as categorically as only internal memoranda can, that Argentina's claims seemed legitimate). Thus only *after* the fighting stopped were we told that British troops were fighting for something that, well, something that might not actually be 'ours'. Yet this information could easily have been uncovered and published before the killing began. Why wasn't it? We know in the case of the *Sunday Times* that the 'Insight' journalists were overruled when they sought earlier publication of Beck's findings. (3)

The press took its cue not only from the government but also from the senior benches of the opposition. On 20 May during the final Parliamentary debate just before the landings, Andrew Faulds spoke against military action. (4) In the course of his speech he made the point that "for twenty years we have been trying to withdraw from this outpost of Empire if we could decently concede sovereignty". He was then interrupted by James Callaghan, who was Labour Prime Minister from 1976-79. "I completely deny that myth", Callaghan said, "Certainly the administration with which I was connected ... never made any such proposal or had any intention ... Such a proposal was never made, nor was it thought of so far as I am concerned." (5)

However, when the lamentably feeble Franks Report - the official inquiry into the conduct of the government in the run-up to the Falklands crisis - was debated in the House of Commons seven months later, Callaghan could not avoid a different partisan point. The war was won; now Thatcher had landed the country with an unsustainable 'Fortress Falklands' and it was safe to play party politics again. So Callaghan attacked her by asking:

> On the *major* question, doesn't it really come down to this - that all parties for *many years* ... have been prepared to give up sovereignty of the Falklands provided we can get a substantial period of lease back? (6)

So we find that something which in May, when the Task Force was at sea, Callaghan claimed that he had never even thought of, turns out seven months later to have been the policy not only of his own administration but that of all others over 'many years'.

It was not perfidy that led to this contradiction, you understand, but patriotism. Nothing was to be said in the course of the conflict which might encourage the enemy or defeat our side. The leading politicians of *all* parties laid down the line, which the media followed.

But it was not only the matter of sovereignty that was left uninvestigated during the long pause between the dispatch of the fleet and the fighting. The party motives of the government and others were put into cold storage to await the outcome. We now know for sure that it was due largely to the intense pressure of the Royal Navy that the Task Force was assembled and sent to war. The Navy prepared for a massive fleet some days before the Argentinian invasion. The book by Max Hastings and Simon Jenkins shows how the Navy saved itself by its 'foresight'. The Falklands provided the excuse needed to save the Navy from extinction; it seems that almost every ship that was under threat of redundancy was dispatched to the South Atlantic to prove that the country needed to keep it. As Christopher Booker pointed out in the *Spectator*, in his review of the book, this "gives new colouring to the real motivation behind Britain's decision to send the task force. It is obviously too cynical to suggest that it was just to 'save the Royal Navy'. But it certainly makes all the self-righteous rhetoric about 'sovereignty' and 'the principles of international law' ... look even thinner and more like *ex post facto* justification than it seemed at the time." (7)

Actually, even at the time it was obvious that an intense Naval lobby was at work. (8) Yet no section of the mainstream media launched any effective research into this aspect of the war.

Alistair Hetherington, a distinguished ex-editor of *The Guardian* and now at work on media studies at Stirling University, made a very interesting radio programme with many interviews with editors of press and television, about the coverage of the Falklands War. He concluded with these words:

> Why was it being fought at all? Perhaps that is the question we should be asking now. And that is one question which newspapers and broadcasters did not ask clearly enough at the beginning. (9)

Precisely.

IV.

How do the British authorities look upon the media? When Rear Admiral Woodward was asked by a Parliamentary Committee what he thought about the qualifications of the press 'handlers' sent by the Ministry of Defence to censor journalists, he replied, "I am a great believer in setting a thief to catch a thief." He then went on to comment about Mr. Hammond, who was one of the Task Force PR men. Known as 'minders', they had the job of looking after and monitoring, i.e. controlling so far as it was possible, the accompanying journalists. Hammond gained brief notoriety for having told the journalists, "You knew when you came you were expected to do a 1940 propaganda job." (10) Admiral Woodward thought that perhaps Hammond was not sufficiently 'a thief in press affairs'. But there was no doubt that Michael Nicholson of ITN - of whom more below - was seen as a skilled and determined robber. The commanding assumption here, in other words, is that information even of the most public kind, really *belongs* to those who direct events. (11)

When Hammond himself was questioned, he said he found the journalists with the Task Force to have been "very responsible in the way in which they treated the stories, and when their misdemeanours were pointed out to them they were suitably contrite and resolved not to let the situation occur again." (12) This captures the attitude perfectly.

There are many other examples which reveal this underlying presumption: that what the press says and does should so far as possible be decided by those in power, and that a good journalist is one who knows how and when to doff his cap and touch his forelock. There is almost no registration in Britain of the notion that the press has the right to investigate the truth, including the alleged truths of national policy, and that this right rests upon its obligation to the citizenry as a whole, whatever the government might think. Rather the editors and owners of most newspapers feel obliged towards the ruling strata to which they themselves are so ambiguously attached: guests of the club rather than members. (13).

One set of exchanges *between* members of "the club" took place on the Defence Committee, and captured the mentality I am trying to convey. Sir Frank Cooper, the permanent under-secretary at the Ministry of Defence during the war, gave evidence alongside John Nott, Secretary of

State. Cooper argued: "You cannot, I now believe, simply have a situation which may be totally right in terms of our own public without looking at what is going on in the opposition." He then referred to the lack of coverage from Afghanistan. Chris Patten MP asked him, "It is more difficult *running* a democracy?" (my emphasis) and Cooper replied, "Yes it is." (14)

Later in the same session, Sir Patrick Wall MP had the following exchange with Nott:

Wall: You still consider psychological warfare has a part to play and had the campaign been longer it would have been successful?
Nott: Yes, certainly.
Wall: The Soviet Union could teach us a few lessons?
Nott: Certainly.

Who, we must ask, does the 'us' refer to in this question?

To underline the point, look at the character of the Parliamentary Committee from which I've been citing. There were sharp complaints during the war about the way news was released; vividly captured in the *Daily Mirror* cartoon of 27 May 1982, reproduced here. It shows a predominantly black TV screen with the words 'part of the story, some of the time' on it. The caption reads: "Here isn't the news". Then there was the nauseating jingoism of some of the papers, such as the *Sun*, and the failure to ask the question that Hetherington put. More than sufficient grounds, in other words, for a public investigation. It is striking, then, that this review was held by the *Defence* Committee of the House of Commons. Their report is titled "The *Handling* of Press and Public Information during the Falklands Conflict". Their major concern throughout was how in future to 'handle' the media in any war. The word sums up the basic attitude of the British authorities. 'Handling' means manipulating, massaging, even manicuring, press and broadcasting, and through them public opinion itself. There was no investigation of the war's coverage from the citizen's point of view.

V.

What problems did the authorities have, then? For in general, as Robert Harris has pointed out, there is a "ready connivance of the media at their own distortion" in normal peacetime conditions. (15) How much more so in times of war. One can see this in the evidence of the Press Association, which was actually one of the more aggressive elements in seeking news stories. Its chief editor demanded better centralization of news and information and complained about the embarrassing inconsistencies in the release of information - there was in particular a conflict between the Ministry of Defence and the Prime Minister's office. The PA's Defence Correspondent, who was based in London, complained that after his seven weeks' experience during the actual fighting, he no longer 'actually believed' what Defence spokesmen said. One of the MPs pretended to be affronted by this, and demanded to know whether if you do not believe a word he says, it could be inferred that he was a liar. (16) But what is really surprising, surely, is the idea that any professional reporter would *presume* the truthfulness of British Defence officials.

Perhaps the overall nature of British press coverage was summed up best of all by the plea from the *Daily Star* to the Prime Minister when it seemed that the paper might not be given an accredited reporter on the Task Force. "Please help us to be there when Britain's pride is restored by the armed might which you have promised the nation". (17)

Fig. 1 *Daily Mirror*, 27 May 1982.

That was at the very beginning of the crisis. At the end of the war, the BBC demonstrated its responsible approach. The Glasgow 'Bad News' group have acquired a number of the internal minutes of the BBC News and Current Affairs. On 15 June, i.e. the day *after* the victory, Mr. Wilkinson, Director of Public Affairs, apparently told his colleagues that he sensed that "public opinion remained volatile, and he suggested special caution in the weeks ahead, over the question 'has it all been worth it?'". No government could ask for more than that. (18)

Why, then, was there so much argument about media coverage? The key objection on the part of, say, the BBC was that the Ministry of Defence was attempting to decide how the war would be presented. There was never any question of any reporters or commentators wishing to reveal information that could directly threaten the operational security of troops fighting on the ground. Here, they were willing to accept direction but not deception, especially not deception that would make them appear to be ignorant stoodges of the authorities. There is all the difference between being put in such a role and that of being a privileged collaborator. Indeed, one could say that many editors were hurt that they were not taken into the *confidence* of officialdom. They did not object to the manipulation of the news in principle, but rather to their own exclusion from deciding how it would be done.

VI.

But perhaps government officials were right to remain suspicious of the media because of a deeper, structural conflict of interests that no amount of goodwill could overcome. Take the dramatic and now well-known picture of the Antelope blowing up, taken by PA photographer Martin Cleaver. This was not released by Downing Street for three weeks after it arrived in London because the Prime Minister's office felt that "enough bad news pictures had come out". (19) Such an attitude could hardly appeal to any journalist.

One reason for the tension that arose between government and the media was that the war was more closely run, in terms of domestic opinion, than it now seems in retrospect. There was a basis for public opposition to the war. The editorial line of the *Mirror* was evidence for that, as was the public opinion survey which showed a majority against the loss of any British life in regaining the Islands, just prior to battle being joined. (20) The authorities had the task of manoeuvring public opinion into accepting the scale of the losses which would be involved, because opinion would not have found them acceptable beforehand.

In addition, there was widespread scepticism about the war within the upper levels of the so-called establishment. Many were waiting for military failure to reveal their views, a form of opportunism justified by the notion that no-one should 'stab the boys in the back'. (One should only speak against their sacrifice if they are shot in too large a number from the front.)

Hence the alarm when it seemed that *Panorama* (an authoritative programme, unlike *World in Action*, which comes from the north and is therefore relatively marginal) began to give the case 'for and against', as if these might be equal. Although it followed a long, exclusive interview with Thatcher herself, and despite the fact that nobody doubted majority support for the adventure, the *Panorama* programme of 10 May allowed two Conservative as well as two Labour MPs to articulate a degree of scepticism. Whereupon Conservative Party pressure on the media peaked with a virulent attack on the BBC. The *Sheffield* had already been sunk and the War Cabinet was concerned to keep a grip on public opinion. The result was a tremendous blast of fury directed at the BBC and triggered by Thatcher herself, who watched the programme from Downing Street. You can see one aspect of this in the *Sun* front page of 11 May, where the BBC is traduced for its "despicable Argie bias". Another assult on BBC personnel can be seen in the *Sun* editorial of 14 May, which attacks Richard Francis, a senior BBC official, who had the temerity to claim that "the widow of Portsmouth is no different from the widow of Buenos Aires".

The intimidation worked, it seems. It stopped editors asking 'is it all worth it' in a way that might have opened out public opinion, at the crucial juncture of the conflict. (21)

Perhaps there is a further aspect which helps explain the pressures that built up so rapidly, in addition to the tension created by the risks being taken, and the heavy breathing of Thatcher's many opponents. It involves the potential professionalism of the media and its capacity to work by rules that have not been written by, and are not the same as, those of the political and military establishment. The best illustration of such a tension is to be found in the evidence of Michael Nicholson. Its significance lies in the fact that as an individual it appears that he supported the dispatch of the Task Force. Yet although he felt that Britain was right to fight, nonetheless *he* wanted to cover the action and do his own job, rather than be told what he could show, or have obstructions placed in his path by the Navy. His experience of the way the press can be treated elsewhere made his patience with the benevolent despotism of the Navy all the shorter.

In his verbal evidence before the Committee, Nicholson was asked: "Can you think of any way in which one can overcome that individual suspicion which you talked about earlier, between officers on board and members of the press? Is there anything in preparation one can do for that?" He answered: "I think they just have to realise we are on the same side." (22)

But are they on the same side? Not if Nicholson is trying to become a *member* rather than merely a guest of the club. In any crisis, naturally, a club expects guests to do what they are told, or leave; certainly they are not expected to express their views on the proceedings. It is an irony of Thatcherism that her opposition to the cult of amateurism, and to gentlemanly, British ways, and her celebration of professional independence, in fact contradicts her use of the tight machinery of government that is the British state. But television in particular represents a challenge of a kind to an operation like the Falklands one, at the time or afterwards, to claim the professional independence of the television eye and voice. But those who rule are on permanent look-out for potential sources of trouble and rebellion. Although they had almost nothing to fear from what actually happened during the War, they were right to sense a potential danger.

The risk came from the possible combination. If the media had been under firm central control, and propaganda certain to be transmitted, in other words if Sir Frank Cooper, John Nott and all the others, in particular the military commanders and the Prime Minister, *had* the capacity to discipline dissent that exists in Moscow, and from which they are so keen to learn, *then* the existence of dissent amongst the population and within the establishment itself would not have been a serious concern for them. On the other hand, if the genuine and significant dissent and scepticism had not existed, then the government would not have been too bothered about the independence of the media.

Tuesday, May 11, 1982   14p   PAPER THAT SUPPORTS OUR BOYS

Maniac is hunted as 2 women are knifed to death

TWO women were savagely stabbed to death as they walked their dogs yesterday.

The double murder came only hours after an 18-year-old girl was slashed by a crazed knifeman 15 miles away.

And detectives believe they are hunting the same maniac.

By ANDREW GOLDEN and MIKE SHANAHAN

The scene of yesterday's gruesome murders is only four miles from where the body of schoolgirl Marion Crofts, 14, was found last summer.

Guard

She was raped and battered to death. Her sadistic killer was never found.

The dead women, one married and the other single, were found in woodland used by courting couples near an army firing range outside Aldershot, Hants.

Their two dogs were standing guard near the bodies when a passer-by made the discovery.

The teenage girl was stabbed in the stomach earlier at Bracknell, Berks.

The fiend dragged the girl into a wooded glade, stabbing her frenziedly.

He used two blades to slash her face and arms before plunging a knife into her.

She lost consciousness and when she came round the man had gone.

The attack happened on a deserted cycle path and the girl, who has not been named, had to drag herself up a steep bank to get help from passing motorists.

Police later discovered two weapons, a potato peeler and a knife, near the scene of the stabbing. The attacker was described as aged between 20 and 25, about six feet tall with dark curly hair.

Savage

He was wearing a dark brown anorak and blue jeans.

The girl, who lived with her parents on the town's Wildridings Estate, was not sexually assaulted.

Det Sgt Bob Stevens, who is leading the hunt, said: "It was a savage and terrifying attack."

OUTRAGE OVER THE BEEB!

Storm at Panorama's 'despicable' Argie bias

By ROGER WARD

ANGRY viewers jammed BBC switchboards last night to protest about a Panorama programme on the Falklands.

Dozens more patriots called The Sun, and branded Panorama a "bloody disgrace."

They complained that the programme was biased towards Argentina.

And former Cabinet Minister Geoffrey Rippon called it "one of the most despicable programmes it has ever been my misfortune to witness."

ANGER

Premier Margaret Thatcher is expected to receive a full report on the programme today from party chairman Cecil Parkinson.

And Foreign Secretary Francis Pym made it plain that he shares the anger of The Sun and Mrs Thatcher at the over-

Continued on Page Two

Di picks modern Miss as nanny

★ PRINCESS Di has chosen modern miss Barbara Barnes to be her child's nanny.

Barbara, 39, refuses to wear a uniform. She is at present nanny to the children of Princess Margaret's lady-in-waiting, Lady Anne Tennant.

Full story—Page 3

Barbara . . . a thoroughly modern nanny

£50,000 BINGO! *Those lucky numbers are on Page 21*

But the co-existence of the two spelt danger, especially over time. The moment that an authoritative voice of dissent was raised, the professional criteria of the media could possibly have been used to ensure its public registration. In other words when *neither* the media nor opinion (especially 'senior' opinion) are fully under control, a government that is at war cannot be certain that its legitimacy of purpose will not be exposed and found wanting.

VII.

Another aspect of the censorship that worked concerned pictures of the fighting. The British military believe that the United States lost in Vietnam because of TV and press coverage. Somehow, they think that the reality of war was too much for softy civilians to take, and thus support waned. The evidence for such a view is very weak. But it made its impact on the Falklands coverage. During the fighting - and after - there were no press pictures of British dead in battle or being taken from the field, and almost no pictures of the badly wounded. Not only at the time of the fighting itself, but even afterwards. Now whatever the case may be with Vietnam, I myself think that this did have an effect on British opinion. The war was sanitized in terms of images and this helped to anaesthetize opinion. I'm not saying that the sight of the casualties would have put many against the war: it would have deepened the feelings of those who were opposed just as it would have strengthened the commitment of those who favoured the war. It might, therefore, have encouraged the polarization of opinion.

The argument used by the Army against such actuality pictures was best put by Major General Jeremy Moore:

> I think that had these sort of gory pictures - and I can only say that perhaps to some extent we can pay tribute to the good taste of our journalists that they did not show anything as unpleasant as could have been available - been shown, it would have had a very severe effect on relatives and I think it brought forcefully home to me the problem that the Americans had during the Vietnam conflict as a result of that. (23)

But by making war appear kinder than it is, by manipulating the images of war so that they are sensitive to the feelings of relatives and stress only the heroism of the ordeal, war itself is justified, and tomorrow's conflicts are prepared.

In a related move the media was barred from transmitting the views of the families of servicemen engaged in the conflict. The BBC imposed this through an internal order. Phone-ins had problems getting relatives of servicemen off the line. This was not therefore an instruction whose only aim was to stop the bereaved from being harassed by snooping reporters. Those who wanted to speak and who offered their views were silenced. Why was this? Almost certainly because many were against the conflict, and they would have spoken with all the moral authority of those who would have to pay a full price.

Relatives' opinions were silenced. Pictures of casualties were censored, avowedly for the sake of the loved ones. With a macabre twist, the family ideology of right-wing conservatism, gave the manipulation of information its moral righteousness. So far this theme has not received, to my knowledge, any extended examination or analysis.

THE SUN SAYS
Lost heroes

FAR AWAY in the South Atlantic, 20 seamen of the destroyer Sheffield died for their country.

We wish to honour their memory. We wish to show in tangible form the nation's gratitude.

We would like to write about them and about how their families are trying to rebuild their shattered lives.

But in our way stands the Ministry of Defence. It is not merely being unco-operative.

It is doing everything possible to prevent The Sun and other newspapers even talking to the widows.

In heaven's name, why?
No security is involved here.

We regard the Ministry's attitude as unacceptable and an insult to the sacrifice of brave men.

'B' for what?

IF YOU imagined the first 'B' in BBC stood for British, you could not be more mistaken.

Far away in Madrid, where perhaps he thought he was less likely to be reported, Richard Francis, one of the more arrogant of the Beeb's mandarins, betrayed his contempt for the people who love their country and believe in the justice of her cause in the Falklands.

Mr Francis is above patriotism.

For him, "*the widow of Portsmouth is no different from the widow of Buenos Aires.*"

Risk

In his view, "it is not the BBC's role to boost the morale of Britain's troops."

After all, they only stand ready to risk their lives so that he can sleep safely at night!

On the day that Mr Francis's remarks were reported, the Argentine authorities showed their own attitude to TV journalists.

Three Britons were kidnapped, terrorised and beaten and then dumped practically naked.

Smug Mr Francis should be down on his plump knees, giving thanks that he is privileged to live in a country where this could not happen to him.

Privilege

IT IS unjust for the Government to sanction massive pay increases of 14.3 per cent for top civil servants and service chiefs and even more for judges.

They may well have fallen behind in the wage race.

So have workers in the manufacturing industries.

The Sun has accepted that there have to be sacrifices.

But they must apply to everyone.

Above all, to top people.

They are supposed to set an example, and they can best afford to tighten their belts.

Fig. 3

VIII.

The authorities, however, are working hard to absorb the lessons and 'do better' next time. They are conducting internal enquiries, considering means of centralizing news information, developing better techniques for 'handling' the media and opinion. One example: experts pontificated about the military options confronting the Task Force as it sailed. This irritated the government as something that might help the enemy. Thus as the war progressed the pool of experts were themselves drawn into confidential briefings, so that, although they might *appear* as independent specialists, in fact they would actually be licensed informally by the Ministry of Defence.

Next time, doubtless such a system will be put into effect immediately. A similar approach may be taken with the journalists. It looks as if the armed forces in the United Kingdom will seek to train and familiarize themselves with a corps of journalists accredited to them not as 'defence correspondents' but as military reporters. The military will seek to professionalize the subserviance of journalists. Then, when a conflict comes along, instead of accreditation being offered to the newspapers, who then choose their own correspondents - as happened in 1982 - the forces will offer accreditation to individual reporters they already trust, and who are therefore unlikely to 'make waves'. This would be one way of weeding out such professionals as Michael Nicholson. The military will justify such a course on straight technical grounds, of course, that so-and-so is familiar with gear and procedures, will be less of an imposition during the crisis, that as he knows the ropes he will be better able to work on the spot, etc.

Ideally, such a licensed corps of the 'free press' will compete amongst itself not to get back the strong news first but for the medals that the Army has in its patronage to offer after every campaign. In the Falklands, the BBC radio reporter Robert Fox was proposed by the Army for an MBE - to become, in full title, a member of the Order of the British Empire. He accepted the honour. Wouldn't any soldier who so fought for truth?

What are the lessons that we should learn? However much we condemn the Junta's invasion, we need to ask, about the British response to the Falklands just as with the Israeli invasion of the Lebanon, "How is it that democratically elected governments can get away with aggression?" The central part of the answer is that the sword is mightier than the pen. That the deployment of military force itself, with all its accompanying images and meanings, has a massive effect upon opinion. The surprise at the outbreak of the fighting, the intimidation of those who are concerned about the consequences and want to say so, the opportunism of many politicians and many journalists alike, the dependence of the media upon the authorities in the first place, for something as basic as accreditation, all this combines to deliver the media into the hands of those who decide on war and peace.

Can this state of affairs be opposed successfully? Only when newspapers and broadcasting stations insist upon their independence when it really matters and the heat is on - when, in other words, the nation is at war. For this is when the 'unity' of the nation is most strongly claimed and when a challenge to that unity is most ferociously condemned for its treason. It was a positive aspect of the Falklands War that opposition to it, whether in the stifled voices of some BBC officials or the editorial stance of the *Daily Mirror*, was attacked *unsuccessfully* as treason. The pressure worked in a conflict of short duration, but the charge never struck. In retrospect we can see that critical questioning of the war and its motives not only could have been stronger, but also that it was desired and would have been respected by a substantial segment of the population. The media largely failed to exercise its editorial independence during the Falklands War. Yet without a vigorous and lively scepticism at such times of crisis, when it really matters, the 'pursuit of truth' by the press and television is just another chimera.

FOOTNOTES

1. Hence the irony of the Pentagon's complaint that the Tet Offensive of 1968 had been a defeat for the National Liberation Front, but that the media had failed to report and publicize this. For insofar as this was true, it was due to the way that the US media had transmitted so many Pentagon falsehoods in the past.

2. Henry Kissinger, *The White House Years*, New York, 1979, p.1077.

3. See his recent article which also discusses the British claim to the Falkland Islands in detail; Peter J. Beck, 'The Anglo-Argentine Dispute Over Title to the Falkland Islands: Changing Perceptions on Sovereignty since 1910', *Millenium: Journal of International Studies*, Spring 1983, pp.6-24.

4. Faulds was the Labour opposition spokesman for the arts; Michael Foot sacked him from his post after he voted against the war at the end of the 20 May debate.

5. House of Commons Official Report, Parliamentary Debates (Hansard), 20 May 1982, p.511.

6. Hansard, Official Report, Sixth Series, Parliamentary Debates, Commons, Vol.35 (1982-3), 18 January 1983, p.178.

7. *The Spectator*, 12 March 1982. The relevant part of Max Hastings and Simon Jenkins, *The Battle for the Falklands*, London, 1983, is Chapter 4, which ends by pointing out that the Task Force was sent "covertly" towards the Falklands, when "such an expedition had been approved by neither the British cabinet nor the British Parliament", p.71.

8. See, for example, the essay I drafted during the war; *Iron Britannia*, London, 1982, p.90.

9. 'Covering Our War', a BBC Radio 3 broadcast, transmitted on 3 November 1982; I am grateful to Professor Hetherington for allowing me to see a transcript of the programme.

10. Minutes of Evidence taken before the Defence Committee, Memorandum submitted by Michael Nicholson, ITN correspondent with the Task Force.

11. House of Commons, Defence Committee, *The Handling of Press and Public Information During the Falklands Conflict*, Vol.II, Minutes of Evidence, HMSO, December 1982 (hereafter 'Defence Committee'), p.280.

12. As above, p.380.

13. I take the analogy from Sir John Hoskyns, former head of Mrs. Thatcher's Policy Unit at 10 Downing Street. In his recent attempt to wake the rulers of the Kingdom from their conservatism, he told the Institute of Directors that: "The possibility of change lies in the hands of a small club of Britain's political establishment. I define this as the top 3,000 civil servants and, for the Conservatives, an average of 300 to 400 MPs. The commentators, who try to interpret their thoughts

and actions, are guests rather than members." *The Times*, 29 September 1983. Of course, Hoskyns was not interested in the guests, and if the *only* possibility of hope lies in the "3,000", we can surrender it immediately.

14. 'Defence Committee', pp.440-441.

15. Robert Harris, *Gotcha: the Media, the Government and the Falklands Crisis*, London, 1983, p.151.

16. 'Defence Committee', pp.321-323.

17. Harris, as cited, p.20. "Please help us to be there"; this, surely, is the apotheosis of non-investigative journalism.

18. The Glasgow 'Bad News' Group are planning to publish their material shortly; I am grateful for their supplying me with this quotation.

19. 'Defence Committee', p.318.

20. I have discussed some aspects of the press and public opinion with respect to the *Daily Mirror* in the *New Socialist*, Sept-Oct 1983, in which the *Mirror*'s editorial at the beginning of the war, 'Might isn't Right', is reproduced in full.

21. See Peter Beck's rueful discussion in his article cited above, p.7.

22. 'Defence Committee', p.179.

23. As above, p.300.

THE FALKLANDS WAR: TRIUMPH OF AN IDEOLOGY

Christopher Hampton

The Falklands War was at once a triumph and a disaster. It was a triumph considered in terms of military organisation, with a massive force of ships and men equipped with the most sophisticated weapons ("a task force of prodigious power") (1) dispatched across 8,000 miles of ocean in a slow-motion show of national will - male, iron-fisted, stiff-lipped - which was carried to victorious conclusion to a rising crescendo of acclamation as a Just Cause. And it was a disaster because it embodied recourse to the most primitive male instincts, coldly and calculatedly applied; a response to a territorial dispute in the worst spirit of aggressive nationalism, asserting the murderous logic of war as an instrument of policy, in clear contempt not only for the authority of the United Nations, but also for the civilising principles of international law and justice without which all nations must sink back into barbarism, and in a world context already deeply threatened by the irresponsible and indeed unprecedented confrontation-politics of the nuclear arms race.

Above all it was Mrs. Thatcher's war. Not for her, reason against fury, civilised restraint. For her, it was the sense of outrage that counted, a cold, steel-hard sense of righteousness and an instinct for self-aggrandisement: determined to avenge national humiliation against all counsel. "She held us to it. She never seemed to flinch from her conviction about its course. She took the risks on her shoulders and she won." (2)

And there were handsome dividends to be gained from that victory and from the opportunist methods by which it was engineered and exploited. In the recent General Election, Mrs. Thatcher - having fully digested the lessons of the Falklands War and perfected her command of the simplistic dogma she had employed in her appeal to the people of Britain - was once again able, apparently without effort, to seize the initiative and ride home in triumph. It might have seemed inconceivable, considering what her Government had done to the structure of society and the expectations of ordinary working people over the previous four years. But in the event, her arrogant imperiousness, together with the suave packaging of the Tory publicity machine and the media, proved irresistible and left the Opposition demoralised and impotent.

No doubt the ineptitude of the Labour Party and its failure to argue the imperative issues of its manifesto with any conviction had much to do with the scale of the Thatcher victory. But there was little serious chance of debating such issues as nuclear disarmament or unemployment; for the strategy of the Tory party was to reveal as little as possible. And there seemed no need to: all the evidence was there on the record, it was implied. The Resolute Approach had been triumphantly vindicated in the Falklands War, and hardly needed to be emphasised, because it was so clearly embodied in the Woman Herself. As one constituency leaflet at Beverley had it: "Even her enemies respect Mrs.

Thatcher's determination. Given another five years the Falklands victory will be repeated on the home front". (3) That is the significance of it.

And there must be few who would now question that the key to Mrs. Thatcher's victory in the election was what she made almost a year before of her opportunist gamble over the Falklands crisis - the single-minded conviction with which she invoked and exploited dormant tribal sentiments in the people, their nostalgia for a past greatness at a time ripe for such an appeal, in a country faltering, its wealth contracting, its territories gone, and the future appearing to offer such bleak prospects.

We all know what it felt like to be caught up and dragged along in the path of that outburst of rampant nationalism and of war hysteria so ruthlessly orchestrated by Mrs. Thatcher and her War Cabinet. We were immobilised by the speed with which the Government seized its advantage and managed to upstage almost everyone - even to the point of getting the Opposition (with the honourable exception of a mere 33 MPs) to support the Task Force and thus reducing the Labour Party to a position of sycophantic and servile acquiescence. This is an object lesson in tactics and manipulation and ability to command the terrain, which Socialists are going to have to learn if they are ever to have the opportunity of building for a progressive future.

It is on these grounds, recognising the conditions which dictate the nature and direction of state power, that the crisis has to be confronted. There was the enemy suddenly ranged in full battle array before our very eyes - there, daily supported and acclaimed on television screens and in newspaper headlines in a ceaseless flood of propaganda. This blunt fact registers the ease with which the institutionalised forces of capitalist state power can organise and take control in an emergency, commanding all the channels of public opinion to silence opposition. And it was not a palatable experience; for it demonstrated beyond doubt where the real power lay - as those of us will know who went through those ugly weeks of preparation, trying to make our voices heard above the clamour, writing letters, speaking, joining rallies against the war, being spat on and vilified as 'traitors'. There we were plunged against all reason and every civilising impulse, up to our necks in war and a climate of rabid enthusiasm for the heavy pride of revenge. And in that clamping down upon debate, with the D notices out and the Government imposing a rigid censorship on the news (cynically sweeping aside all pretence of democratic procedure), inevitably the first casualty was truth. Given instead the inane presence of Ian MacDonald treating us in his excruciating enunciation as if we were some species of deaf-mute, and belated, mangled reports from correspondents on the spot, all dissent was immobilised. We were expected to 'rejoice' that 'our boys' were out there defending the 'self-respect' and the 'glory' of our heritage - Boy's-Own stuff, a debasement of all that harsh and futile bravery.

Mrs. Thatcher, in Dr. Johnson's words (referring to a previous Falklands crisis - incidentally dealt with in a recent television play by Don Shaw which made trenchant parallels, though these were mutilated by the censors), "snatched with eagerness the first opportunity of rushing into the field". (4) After the Government's initial confusion in face of the proofs of ineptitude and culpable negligence, you could sense it. You could hear it in her voice, gratefully accepting her clean sheet from the scapegoat Carrington. You could see it in her eye. And there it was in the blatant presence of the Task Force, steaming inexorably towards the South Atlantic, the presence on the High Seas of a huge and growing armada of death-ships that neutralised and derided the legal restraints and injunctions of the United Nations. For it was obvious by the end of the first week that the Government had no intention whatsoever of obeying Resolution 502. Peace was out; armed force was the law; Mrs. Thatcher had chosen her course - to bludgeon the 'enemy' into submission perhaps, or to break him ("Stick it up your Junta!") ("Smash the Argies!").

It was a unique opportunity - return to the spirit of 1940 and 1945, the Churchillian option (a new "Ministry of the Deed") - infinitely more attractive to her and her Party (if she could pull it off) than the unsensational bureaucratic alternative of working through the UN - though *that* route, as Johnson put it in 1770, would have enabled Britain "to obtain by quiet negotiation all the real good that victory in war could have brought us". (5) Her confrontation-politics no doubt made this (for her) the natural choice. It needed courage and audacity, of course, together with a supreme insensitivity to the possible consequences - a personification of Task Force Resolution. And she couldn't have organised a *better* opportunity. To be daily witnessed (and presented on the media) commanding the Task Force from 10 Downing Street or Chequers or Northwood made a focal point for all the drama and sensation of war and of war's pressures, absorbing the attention of millions as the War Cabinet hastened in and out of the limelight, with the Government in complete control of communications and timing pronouncements to maximum effect in the context of a machinery of censorship which virtually blocked all inquiry and thwarted all forms of criticism.

It was a masterly and chilling performance. Though she could not have known the outcome, she and her 'campaign' managers were clearly intent (once the bombing of Stanley airport had begun) on engineering from the ritualised murder of this war and its rousing of a nationalistic populism the momentum of support which would enable them to silence criticism and to pursue with impunity their repressive anti-democratic policies against the community at home - with the consent of its victims. Indeed, afterwards, in her triumph, the campaign show continued to squeeze every drop of political capital from events; and people were invited to join the victory feast for days and weeks, as ship after ship (in what seemed like a staged re-entry into British ports) returned home to the waving of countless flags by people now thoroughly drunk on the jingoistic propaganda that was everywhere, and backed with elation by the forces of the competitive market and their money. (One recalls that the Falklands Islands Company donated £250,000 to the families of the War Dead - as well they might, having gained a great deal from the publicity, at least in the short run.)

The Falklands War came, so it seemed, at exactly the right time for the flagging fortunes of the Tory Party, deep in mid-term unpopularity. One might even be forgiven for believing that the breakdown of relationships with the Generals - already for months restive and threatening over a profoundly emotive and popular issue (the 'Malvinas') - had been deliberately incited, though that would be to credit Thatcher's instinct for things with Macchiavellian powers of calculation. But anyway it served to affirm her policies at every level - her combative strengthening of the intimidatory powers of the police, her virulent anti-Soviet posture, the raising of the stakes over the escalation of nuclear arms, her independent deterrent, the attack upon the labour movement and the community services.

During the War we were constantly being urged to applaud the Justice of the British Cause. Suddenly, the Islanders' interests, which nobody had shown the slightest concern for in the months and years preceding the crisis, had become 'paramount' (the word was used like a refrain), and the Generals we had been selling arms to as 'friends' of the militarist confraternity but weeks before were reduced to a 'tin-pot Fascist Junta'. But with the scandalous evasion of the conditions of UN Resolution 502 and the sinking of the *General Belgrano* with the loss of 368 lives on the direct orders of the PM at the very moment when the negotiations of the Peruvian peace initiative seemed delicately balanced on the verge of success, justice was sunk beyond recovery ('Gotcha!' sneered *The Sun*). And as the Task Force went on from that infamous episode - the first act of murderous aggression in the war - answering violence with violence in cynical defiance of the UN, the Government set about 'tightening the screws', as John Nott put it, both at home and abroad.

That, one might say, is the Tory answer to confronting crisis - what they would call getting down to business and cashing in on the market in hardware. For though we may temporarily have lost the Argentinians, there would be other and bigger buyers for the weapons being tried out in the South Atlantic, on display to the world as at some vast Aldershot Arms Show, such as that which actually followed up on the War. (As one British Conservative, Alan Clark, commented: "The only world opinion that counts is the one that queues up to buy the kit you've won with"!) (6) Forget the deaths, the loss of ships and equipment (machinery is easily replaced, no matter what the cost), forget the unemployed, the wrecked communities, the repression of democratic rights, the terminal dangers ahead. It was competitive success that mattered - and in that area, for ideological reasons, most of all. Hardly surprising, therefore, that Defence should be identified as having the fastest growth-rate in the economy. It is no accident, one feels, that on the same day (29 April 1982) that Admiral Woodward was reported predicting "a long and bloody campaign", Philip Smith, Manpower Consultants, should have placed an arms sales advertisement in *The Guardian*. "This", it announced, "is an opportunity to join one of the fastest growing companies in international defence sales - part of a large UK group and the world leader in its sphere ... The establishment of a virtually new international sales organization has created the need for several sales managers and assistant sales managers who ... will identify and pursue specific sales leads in the field of communications, command and control and military information systems ...". (7)

No doubt those who were qualified to do so would have answered this advertisement, and will now be reaping the most lucrative benefits from their work. For who cares about *democracy*? It's the competitive monopolies that count, the kit you've won with. Let BL, steel, shipping, coal, education, health and social services go to the wall. 'We're for High Technology. People? Scrap them. Let's have a leaner, fitter Britain for the rich to profit from.' Though they with their hardware may go down in history as the killers of community, they will at least be making Britain Great again as she sinks below the waves. Which once more recalls the 1770 Dr. Johnson: "These are the men who, without virtue, labour, or hazard, are growing rich as their country is impoverished"; who "rejoice when obstinacy or ambition adds another year to slaughter and devastation; and laugh from their desks at bravery and science, while they are adding figure to figure, and cipher to cipher, hoping for a new contract from a new armament, and computing the profits of a siege or tempest." (8)

There are ominous signs (which have to be faced and made public) that the reckless investment in and profit from the defence industry are absorbing a growing proportion of Britain's scarce resources, and slowly but surely throttling the rest of the economy. As Malcolm Chalmers, of the Peace Studies Department of Bradford University, has declared, there is a direct relationship between rising defence expenditure and economic decline. But it is no surprise that an increasing proportion of our private industry is turning towards the defence market and the arms trade; for there is guaranteed growth and profits to be had from military business, with the MOD's spending on equipment rising from 31.3% of its budget in 1974-5 to 46.4% this year, and preferential terms on offer which make pretty reading when set against the Treasury's constant lament (as the Chancellor starts on yet another round of vicious spending cuts) that we cannot have what we cannot afford; with 360 defence contracts out of 594 involving excess profits. (9) And the Minister of Defence announces a *one-fifth* increase in overall defence spending as a first priority (now greater than the whole budget for education and against a background of over a £1,000 million projected cuts), to make Britain the second largest arms spender in the Western World, with £640 million ear-marked for the Falklands alone.

And who is to pay for this? Why, the people of course, with their social and living standards, the wealth of the community - the cultural, educational and health rights fought for in the long struggles of ordinary men and women over generations and now to be stolen from them to furnish the Falklands with its fortress hardware. The argument is that "if we were to sacrifice defence to the needs of the welfare state, the day might come when we should have neither peace nor freedom", as Mrs. Thatcher said at the North Atlantic Assembly. Thus Cruise and Trident are more important, and the MX Missile is unilaterally confirmed as "the final guarantor of European liberty"! (10)

It is startling enough that the Government has been able to get away with such daylight (and midnight) robbery over the last four years - the irresponsible anti-democratic game it has been playing with the fabric of society and the basic rights and freedoms of the British people. But even more startling is the scale of Mrs. Thatcher's victory this June. How could it have happened? For it is true, as Gerrard Winstanley wrote so long ago in the upheaval of the Civil Wars: "If we lie still, and let you steal our birthrights, we perish". (11) If, that is, we do nothing, "Shall not the councillor", as Blake put it in his anger, continue to
>throw his curb
>Of poverty on the laborious,
>To fix the price of labour,
>And invent allegoric riches?

>And the privy admonishers of men
>Call for fires in the city,
>For heaps of smoking ruins
>In the night of prosperity and wantonness? (12)

For that is what the Thatcher regime is moving towards - fires in the inner cities, riots on the streets, confusion in the home, heaps of smoking ruins against the future - even while "the actors for freedom are oppressed by the talkers and verbal professors of freedom", (13) till the very idea of freedom becomes a sick joke and Britain itself a fortress of reaction and intolerance dominated by the militarists and drifting closer and closer to the holocaust.

This *is* a disaster; and clearly the Thatcher ideology, with its divisive prescriptions for cure, deserves to be condemned for the direction it is taking us in. But the Thatcherites did not bring it *about*. It was the underlying conditions of a contracting economy, declining rapidly under pressure from negative interactions on the capitalist world market that made possible the rise of Thatcherism. And these conditions had already seriously eroded the foundations of the 'consensus-politics' that had held Britain steady for years, which were further weakened by the irresolute policies of the Callaghan Government, throwing aside all conviction in its miserable attempts to maintain some sort of balance and to accommodate the increasingly strident forces of the market. The polarisation that occurred between 1974, the year of Heath's downfall and the 1979 defeat of Labour, was dominated not by the Left but by the sharp rightward swing of the Tories, which brought the hidden forces of the money-system out into the open and onto the attack. This, together with Labour's internal squabbling and disarray, the defection of certain of its leading members, and the incessant vilification of the Left by the press and its unseen persuaders (thus isolating its power to influence the electorate) gave the Right its chance. With the ground nicely softened and all the signals right for anyone prepared to take risks and to move 'forward' with conviction, Mrs. Thatcher seized her opportunity and exploited it for all its worth - and at no time with more belligerent assurance than when the Falklands crisis was handed to her; conjuring up that species of "rampant and virulent gut patriotism" (14) which unleashed the frustrated longings and disappointed hopes of the people, and harnessing it to her own perverted vision of society.

What Mrs. Thatcher has done, finding herself in the right place at the right time, is to drive home the callous logic of the competitive market economy which controls British society; and in doing so with such inflexible commitment, she has changed the climate of opinion. By correctly gauging the prevailing moods and attitudes of the people at a time of crisis and by the special instinct she has developed for appealing to a divisive individualism and self-interest, she has induced them to put their trust in a firm authoritarianism rooted in the values of the past, and thus to acquiesce in the demolition of their own community institutions, those which encourage people to think forward.

This indeed is a phenomenon. But in getting at the unexamined patriotic assumptions and prejudices that lie repressed and twisted out of shape at the roots of our aborted cultural life, with its dislocated and insulated elements and its 'satisfying repressiveness', it is also a nightmare - the nightmare of our conditioning, which deprives us (even the poets among us) of the power to see through it or beyond it, or to recognise what it is *doing* to us.

Not that everyone is being taken in; for we are not all so myopic that we cannot see what is going on around us. But there seems to be little anyone can do at the moment (beyond generating ways and means of resisting this conditioning) to combat the ideology of the Right or its power to take hold of the popular imagination. Mrs. Thatcher's invocation of the individualistic virtues of Victorian capitalist initiative and self-help has been all too successful, politically, socially and psychologically. But then she has a rich groundwork to tap, with an affluent working class responding to her lead, and an ingrained submission to custom and tradition, which is anyway being ceaselessly drummed into us by the institutions of British society, so many of which are the creation of the ruling class.

Thus it was that Mrs. Thatcher could declare, in her Cheltenham Racecourse speech, that the Falklands triumph had proved Britons were the same people who had built an empire, and ruled a quarter of the world. No matter that this should be stated against a background of vicious cuts in social services, and the struggle of the NHS workers for just conditions - though in the context of the dead and wounded and the £1 billion so freely spent on sending her armada to the South Atlantic, such cuts in fundamental social lifelines are an obscenity. We are informed over the heads of the deprived, and as the Government's relentless attack upon the poor goes ahead, that "we have ceased to be a nation in retreat" and "have instead found a new confidence, born of economic battles at home, and tested and found true 8,000 miles away". (15)

What kind of confidence is it that, openly equating the calculated violence of the Falklands conflict with Government domestic policy, can prosper on the dispossession and despair of the most vulnerable? It is a confidence based upon a creed of competitive war, the domination of 'free' market forces and the ruthless exploitation of the weak by the strong. If the market needs a pool of the unemployed to make its profit, so be it. If poverty and bad housing are a consequence, that's too bad. A thousand Argentinian dead do not matter; even the hundreds of British soldiers maimed and mutilated for a Cause which is not theirs don't matter - and anyway they'll get pensions. The UN doesn't matter; starvation and famine in the Third World do not matter. What matters is competition - the triumph of the strong, what she calls the 'wealth-creators', the men of enterprise and initiative, the sellers of arms, the exploiters and expropriators of capitalism who are daily making millions out of other people's misery.

Mrs. Thatcher has persuaded people that *her* conviction, *her* belief in the rights of the hidden minorities who control the sources of wealth, are to our benefit, though palpably they are *not*. The tunes she has got us to listen to are the old nationalistic tunes of militarism, of imperialist glory, of charity, pride and independence played to seductive harmonies. They are false, they contort reality, they leave most of us only with our fantasy world of dreams; and they cheat us of our rights, as the private monopolists take over. But, like the monarchy and the advertising barons, they thrive. And perhaps I may here be permitted to define the style of it all in terms of my own kind of tune - a poem I wrote back in 1981, which I called *Tunes from the Thatcher Songbook*:

> The mode is rigid, four-square,
> Unaccommodating, radical-reactionary;
> The presentation jingoistic, British, white;
> The sound a re-hash of the Thirties -
> Tunes of glory and hypocrisy;
> The lyrics redolent of after-empire
> Arrogance and militant appeal
> To all who serve the economic status quo.
>
> But this performer outshines all
> Her background managers in zeal,
> And sings the tough line without guile,
> Apeing the obtuseness of the male.
> No hint from her of hope for the poor.
> Her battle-cry's to the market war -
> Repressive competition, order, law,
> A strong police force and a hotter
> NATO - all to stop the Socialist rot.
>
> And in her anti-Soviet stance
> You hear her at her best: she rants.
> Intoxicated by the Reds that blind her,
> With all the business world behind her,

> Jubilant as they sense their chance,
> She leads the chorus to the market-place
> Where, armoured for the great crusade,
> Her chanting Britons, pride of their race -
> This Better-Dead-Than-Red brigade -
> Acclaim her great Valhalla serenade. (16)

As with Valhalla - consumed in flames as a result of the arbitrary exercise of power and the lust for gold - so with this malign crusade, which Mrs. Thatcher, in the service of the interests of international capitalism (what she calls 'freedom and the rule of law' against the 'evil ideology' of socialism), invites us to join her on. In these terms, as Winstanley observed of *his* world, her callous market philosophy of control by the rich "is a breeder of wars", and would turn England into a prison again, as it was for him and his fellow labourers, with "the variety of subtleties in the laws pursued by the sword" becoming the "bolts, bars and doors of the prison ... and poor men (and women) the prisoners". (17)

Witness: in the South Atlantic, the authority of law was brutally overwhelmed by the incompatible argument of force - an argument legitimised by the House of Commons, which put the Government itself above the rule of international law and enabled it to demonstrate that the answer to aggression against the law is another (and more vicious) act of aggression. So much for our vaunted system of democracy, breeding violence and tyranny in the name of legality.

Apparently the sinking of the *Belgrano* - which was clearly outside a unilaterally imposed 'exclusion zone' and moving away from it - was a means of proving that 'aggression doesn't pay'. This, it seems, was the Cabinet's way of indicating that Britain had (in contrast to Argentina) "shown all the restraint of a strong and civilized nation" (18) - though the death of 368 men is a strange way of showing restraint; especially when measured against the three Argentinians who died in Galtieri's invasion.

Those lives and their blood are on our hands as a consequence of Britain's 'representative' acquiescence in the Government's refusal to comply with the UN's three-part resolution, which was totally misrepresented in the press. And as John Nott made it clear, the Government did all it could to counter the influence of the UN and to hold off world opinion. In Nott's words, the overriding need "was to get our people there", onto the Islands, against "this Haigery going on, and the United Nations, and the clash of opinion among us". Apparently the censure of the world - the Security Council had called for an immediate ceasefire and the implementation of Resolution 502 in its 'entirety', with nine in favour, four abstentions, and only Britain against - counted for nothing. Nott even admits as much. "When we got ashore", he says, "and the United Nations *was out of the way*, we had a clear objective again." (19) In other words, the United Nations was just one more obstacle to be overcome, and finally they brushed aside all its injunctions, and got down to business.

That business, which it had been the imperative aim of the UN to stop, ended with a death-count and a mutilation-count of upwards of 2,000, the majority of them Argentinian, which British news programmes only incidentally revealed, no doubt on the assumption that the deaths of Argentinians were of no interest to the British public.

In these circumstances, when the process of representative democracy is permitted to serve such ends and such interests, which demand that the public be lied to and kept ill-informed, and which in their resort to the barbaric rule of war are so palpably an outrage against the principles of international (let alone national) justice, how is the citizen to act in defence of that justice? Through the House of Commons? But the House of Commons condoned and confirmed these actions. Through the ballot-box which has given us such representatives? But the electorate itself (complacently defined as "the most sophisticated in the world") has voted back the most callous, divisive and anti-democratic Government of the century. By obedience to 'the rule of law'? *Whose* law? Tebbit's? Howe's? Lawson's? The law of the multi-nationals? Heseltine's law, legitimising the terminal arguments of the nuclear arms race? Thatcher's Task Force law? The law of the gun and the nuclear weapon? The Northern Ireland law of confrontation and murder? The law of the open market, which permits the selling of British weapons for use against the repressed people of the world and the British themselves? The law of the police against the citizen - of arbitrary stop and search and of secret grillings and racial discrimination? The law of the unelected profiteer who steals our birthrights?

These are questions we have to find answers for. Because we cannot protect our rights or act in defence of our rights by silently permitting ourselves to be stripped, as Thatcher's war-policy stripped us, of the protection of the fundamental laws of justice, or by rejoicing with her in extolling the barbaric values of armed force. Under such conditions, we have no choice but to act in defiance of a process which demonstrates such contempt for the interdependent rights and interests of the people, whether British or Argentinian. In the past, when the land was hedged round with barbaric laws to enforce conformity and obedience on them, the people had to stand up against authority and fight for their rights. And we are going to have to do the same today.

For Mrs. Thatcher's victory in the Falklands was a victory for the enemies of the British people, for the militarists and the arms merchants everywhere. Either we stand for internationalism, world peace, cooperation and disarmament in the interests of social progress both in this country and among the dispossessed millions of the Third World, or we surrender our rights and freedoms to the laws of armed force and repressive order which at present dictate the policies of the dominant powers, and which - in the name of reason, at immense cost to the productive resources of the world - are turning that world into an arsenal of genocidal weapons for the destruction of humanity.

Though the choice is not yet ours, we have to be doing all we can to make it ours. For the alternatives are terminal.

That is the lesson of the Falklands war, and it is a lesson no-one can afford to ignore. If socialists are to have any hope of answering the challenge it puts before us, they are going to have to provide a vision of society and a sense of purpose at least as convinced (and as convincing) about socialism as Mrs. Thatcher is about the Free Market. And it is only when this conviction is harnessed to a sustained and compelling programme of social activity at every level that it will be possible to counter the seductive appeals of the bankrupt materialism that dominates our lives and break the power of the reactionary institutions which are constantly being manipulated to their own advantage by the killers of community.

FOOTNOTES

1. Cecil Parkinson, Tory Party Chairman and member of the War Cabinet, in *The Guardian*, 14 July 1982.
2. From an article by Max Hastings and Simon Jenkins; *It Was Mrs. Thatcher's War*, in *The Observer*, 7 November 1982.
3. Reported by Alan Rusbridger in *The Guardian*, 7 June 1983.
4. Dr. Samuel Johnson, *Thoughts on the Late Transactions Respecting Falkland's Islands* (1771), in *Johnson: Prose and Poetry*, ed. Mona Wilson (London, 1969), p.643.
5. *Ibid.*, p.643.
6. Reported in the Terry Coleman interview with Alan Clark, *The Guardian*, 12 June 1983.
7. Advertisement in *The Guardian*, 29 April 1982.
8. Samuel Johnson, *op. cit.*, p.643.
9. Martin Walker, *Britain's Self-Inflicted Wound*; article in *The Guardian*, 25 April 1983.
10. Mrs. Thatcher, speech at the North Atlantic Assembly, Westminster Hall, 17 November 1982.
11. Gerrard Winstanley, *A Declaration from the Poor Oppressed People of England* (1649), signed by 44 comrades; in *The Law of Freedom and Other Writings*, ed. C. Hill (Penguin, 1973), p.104.
12. William Blake, *The Song of Los*, in *Complete Writings* (Oxford, 1966), p.247.
13. Gerrard Winstanley, *A Watchword to the City of London* (1649), in Hill, *op. cit.*, p.129.
14. Stuart Hall, 'The Empire Strikes Back', in *New Socialist*, July/August 1982, p.7.
15. Mrs. Thatcher, at Cheltenham, 4 July 1982.
16. This poem was published in the issue of *Tribune* (25 September 1981) immediately preceding the start of the Labour Party Conference. It has not yet appeared in a volume, though it is to form part of a new book nearing completion, to be called *The Fruits of History*. For my view of the place of poetry (and literature) in society, see my article 'Poetry and Commitment', printed in the February and April issues (1983) of *The Ethical Record* (published by the South Place Ethical Society).
17. Winstanley, *A New Year's Gift for the Parliament and Army* (1650), in Hill, *op. cit.*, p.170.
18. Cecil Parkinson, in *The Guardian*, 14 July 1982.
19. John Nott, *The Guardian*, 13 September 1982.

THE GOVERNMENT AND INFORMATION IN TIME OF WAR: THE FALKLANDS AND THE MEDIA*

David Morrison and Howard Tumber

One overall aspect which has emerged and governed the debate about the media coverage of the Falklands conflict is that the attempts to regulate, monitor and manage the news were fully orchestrated by the Government, and further that it did so to prevent information from reaching the public. By so conspiring the Government was able to mobilise and maintain support for its actions in the South Atlantic throughout the two and a half months of the crisis and consequently was able to strengthen its position nationally, culminating in the huge parliamentary victory gained at the 1983 June General Election.

Whilst such a view may be ideologically appealing to some sections of the political left, there is no evidence from our research that there was any overall co-ordinated control warranting notions of conspiracy or even planned management. The fact, however, that something is not planned does not mean that the results in terms of desirability could not have been better if they actually had been planned. It is intellectually slip-shod to mistake function for purpose. Our research, which besides a content analysis of the main evening news bulletins and current affairs programmes during the conflict, a national survey of viewers' perceptions of the news and attitudes towards a variety of related questions, also included interviews with the Task Force journalists, the Ministry of Defence Information Officers (minders) responsible for vetting copy, MOD and military personnel in London, Government figures, editors, defence correspondents and media technicians, the results of which suggest not orchestration and symphony but disharmony and cacophany.

Much of what occurred both in Britain and the South Atlantic involved far more complex relationships between troops and journalists, ministers and the press, the media and the state, than the simplistic myths that have evolved. For example the fact that Margaret Thatcher's political star rose due to the events in the South Atlantic, the Falkland Factor as it has been called, there is no doubt. But the achievement is one based on the rubble of disagreement, stress and strains between the War Cabinet, the military and the Ministry of Defence, not on the solid platform of a planned harmonious design. We can do no more here than briefly examine four aspects of the conflict to illustrate that matters were not as the myth would have them appear; namely, the experiences of the news-gatherers themselves, that is, the journalists who sailed South, the logistics of communications which resulted in the lack of immediate TV pictures, Information Policy, and fourthly the political attacks made on the BBC, in particular Newsnight and Panorama.

---

* Research undertaken at the Broadcasting Research Unit, 127 Charing Cross Road, London WC2H 0EA.

The Journalists with the Task Force: Why Me?

Whatever one thinks about conspiracies there is one thing for certain, they do require planning and the Ministry of Defence was certainly not up to that task in any grand sense. Not only could the MOD not get its act together, it could not even get the show on the road.

For example, on the Sunday afternoon of the Task Force making ready to sail the MOD phoned the Director of the Newspaper Publishers Association, John Le Page, at his home and requested him within two hours to select four newspapers to be represented on the Task Force. This hardly conjures up the image of a slick high-powered machine gearing up for sophisticated censorship and control. It borders on farce when in the true tradition of the garden party raffle, not even Le Page, but his wife, drew the four lucky winners to go with the Task Force from a hat. From then on things went from bad to worse. Not renowned for their spirit of public school boy fair play the rest of Fleet Street contested the selection results. It was hardly surprising. Even *The Times* had not been selected. Without the prestigious *Times* a war cannot be official! In fact *The Times*, like the rest of Fleet Street, put pressure on Number 10 to have the numbers increased, which they dutifully were, since Number 10 was also far from happy that so few journalists were going. For example, Witheroe of *The Times* was contacted by the First Lord of the Admiralty saying he could not go, only to be phoned later at nine o'clock Sunday evening, following pressure from Number 10, to say that he now could go. The permission was begrudging and the only help he got in terms of instructions was, "Bring a dark suit". Gareth Parry of *The Guardian* was only given twenty minutes to prepare himself; he packed a pair of swimming trunks. Tony Snow of *The Sun*, however, beat the lot: a virtual modern-day William Boot out of Evelyn Waugh's classic novel on journalism, *Scoop*. The only instruction he got that Sunday was the vague one from his news desk of, "Head in the direction of Portsmouth". This he did on his motorbike with a suitcase strapped on the back. He stopped ten miles outside Portsmouth, made a hurried call to his office and received the further instruction, "Proceed to Portsmouth, you're on". This scrabbled confusion although bizarrely amusing, is instructive of the lack of a planned media policy. For example, when Mick Seamark of *The Star* and Tony Snow of *The Sun* arrived in Portsmouth and were allotted ships, they could not believe their luck when both were placed on the carrier *Invincible*. Not only was it thought that *Invincible* would be the flag ship, and thus carry the overall commander, Sandy Woodward, it possessed an even more attractive journalist gem for these two papers, Prince Andrew. Both these papers it will be remembered had only recently fallen bitterly foul of the Palace for publishing pictures of a very pregnant Princess Diana in a swimsuit.

Both Snow and Seamark informed us that they thought that there must have been some mistake. As good working journalists, however, and realising the value to their papers of a figure such as Prince Andrew, they kept quiet and took their places aboard. The point about this is that the notion of mistake is in the context wrong, since mistake carries with it the idea of policy or ruling against which one can be wrong or get wrong. Nothing existed, it was a shambles, and it was this shambles which was responsible for many of the complaints which the journalists made on their return and which are well documented in the Defence Committee.

However, as stressed, just because something appears ramshackle and a shambles in fact does not mean that it may not, despite everything, work, in terms of ends, in the manner hoped for. If that hope was that the journalists in the Task Force would be closely supervised and controlled, then in the situation existing on the Task Force it was unnecessary to have a very elaborate or sophisticated system of checks. Basically, the journalists' copy was going nowhere unless it went through the Navy's signal system. And to those who have argued that it would have been a much more openly reported war if foreign journalists had been allowed along is to misunderstand that basic fact. Foreign or not, they would still have had to go through the military signal system. It wasn't a Hershey Bar war like Vietnam, where the journalists could return to the Inter-Continental or whatever, and file their copy through a commercial communications system, it either went through the military system and military/political control or it did not go at all. And this still stands true for the commercial marisat satellite, because the terminal was still on ship. In a secondary sense it might have made a difference in the margins to have had the foreign press corps on board, particularly the aggressive Americans who would not have put up with the type of conditions the home press did, but then again if they had been around there is every reason from our research to consider that everyone would have been thrown off at Ascension anyhow. As it was, Captain Black of the *Hermes* had wearied of the British journalists and, to put it politely, invited them to leave at Ascension, of which there is some evidence to believe that a signal was sent from England advising against this. But this illustrates a basic problem, especially insofar as the Navy was concerned: namely, that the journalists were seen by them as there as their guests, and not as of right. For example, Kim Sabido of Independent Radio News, who after the *Sheffield* went down tried to do a reaction piece in the Ward Room and was told not to in a very heated exchange, which supposedly included the threat of being thrown overboard. The gist of the altercation was that they saw Sabido as a guest and therefore had to behave like a guest, whereas Sabido saw himself as a working journalist.

By and large, apart from initial suspicion the journalists and the troops got on very well indeed, one might even say too well. One of the problems which certainly influenced the structuring of the news, the press most of all, is that the journalists began to identify with the troops. Some more than others. Some became full 'troopie groupies', as Robert Fox of BBC Radio mockingly used to refer to his colleagues. The structural fact of life of reporting the war meant that there was simply no bolt-hole, no retreat, no escape, day in and day out, week in and week out, even month in and month out, from the very men the journalists were reporting on and about. They lived with the troops, they ate with the troops, they drank with the troops, they took fitness exercises with them, they attended unarmed combat and weapon training lessons with the troops, but above all they faced the same danger together. Furthermore, the journalists depended on the troops for food, clothing and most importantly physical protection. It was inevitable that there would be a process of assimilation. They became not so much observers but participants. It is here that the presence of other correspondents of other nationalities might have had some effect by offering a reminder of the journalistic principle of observation. As it was, it was an all-British affair of which there was little possibility of emotional removal.

The Logistics of Communication: I Can't Get the Picture

The lack of immediate television film of the war has provoked enormous debate with allegations that there was a deliberate attempt to prevent the public from seeing the real horrors of the conflict.

Whether seeing pictures would have turned majority support for the British action into opposition is a separate debate - but purely on the ability to get pictures back to Britain from the South Atlantic it was, only in the most academic of fashion, technically feasible: operationally and logistically it was impossible.

It is worthwhile going into this in some detail, not only to clear up much nonsense that has been spoken in this area but also, by understanding the unfeasibility of picture transmission, help collapse any myth that the lack of pictures was a political decision. It may, after Vietnam and the Middle East conflicts etc., have become almost a political law in some quarters that wars ought to be shown nightly in the living rooms of the world, but physics also has its own laws. To put it bluntly, in terms of a television war the Falklands conflict was fought in the wrong place and that is a geo-technical fact totally removed from any political engineering.

There were three possibilities of transmitting pictures during the conflict. The first was to transmit pictures from terminals on the aircraft carriers and larger Navy vessels via the British Military Satellite SKYNET. The first problem here, however, was that the terminals on board *Hermes* (the carrier where an ITN engineer was present attempting to get picture transmission) are designed to carry communications not television pictures. The satellite link is designed to carry either voice encrypted or teleprinter messages encrypted. For sending these type of messages far less bandwidth, i.e. far less information density, is needed than that for television. Consequently the Navy communications was designed to carry many channels all at once between the ships themselves and between the ships and Northwood, the fleet command centre in Britain. The total bandwidth of the satellite was not adequate for a full colour television signal, although it was sufficient for black and white pictures.

However, to use the whole bandwidth of the satellite would have meant commandeering every available channel. There are approximately twenty to thirty channel links available on the satellite for communication between the various vessels and Northwood. To have transmitted black and white pictures would have involved taking over all these links at once. But these links were the Navy's only secure communication between the Task Force and Northwood. For outbound communications from Northwood to the Task Force there was not too great a problem, it being possible to use High Frequency radio. The reverse was not the case. For if the Task Force had attempted to transmit an ordinary HF radio it may have been possible for the Argentines to 'Direction Find' (DF) them. In other words, their position could have been charted very accurately and from a military stance it was essential that the fleet remain hidden. Consequently radio silence was maintained the entire voyage South. The only communications from the Task Force to Northwood was via the SKYNET satellite. The reason for this is that it is virtually impossible to 'Direct Find' the satellite signal unless you are in possession of the relevant sophisticated technology such as that held by the US and USSR. It was, it must be pointed out, unclear how much assistance the Russians were giving the Argentinians. Nevertheless it has been claimed that there were moments when the Task Force was not using this satellite communications link and that therefore the television companies could have transmitted film during these moments. To do this, however, all the terminals throughout the Task Force would have been required to shut down completely, closing all the Navy communications. It still, though, would have been possible in the event of an emergency for the Navy to immediately have reacquisitioned the use of the satellite link from the broadcasters. But the logistics of doing so was a problem. Somehow the ships in the fleet had to be informed that the satellite was operational again and thus to wind up their satellite terminals. To circumvent this problem, one possibility was to inform the fleet that during a specified period each day the broadcasters would transmit. This is not dissimilar to the standard commercial practice of buying and booking satellite time. The difference was of course that it was not a commercial or civilian situation and thus the problem still remained of what to do in an emergency if the Navy had to 'crash in' on the satellite whilst the broadcasters were using it. The old problem therefore returns of how to inform other ships without breaking radio silence by broadcasting it on HF radio at a crucial moment when the Navy would least wish to be tracked by the Argentinians. In short, there is no escaping the vast logistical problems which severely restricted the possibility of the Falklands ever becoming a television war. In this light it must also be noted that because the SKYNET satellite was only of use up to South Georgia, the broadcasters, even if the military had given their blessing, could only have transmitted up to that point and not beyond, and much of the operations would still therefore have gone uncovered. The only possibility of using SKYNET was to have stationed a ship within the 'Footprint' of the satellite. But that would have required the diverting of much needed escort ships to protect it from possible attack. Once the Task Force had moved on from South Georgia the only option remaining was to use the American Military Satellite DISCUS. That was not without its own attendant, although admittedly different, problems. For example, as normally operated the DISCUS satellite is technically not capable of sustaining television transmission. To do so would have required a tilting of the satellite. But even then it would still not have been possible to transmit from the ships' terminals. A land-based terminal could have accessed the right channels and thus sent pictures, but the reason it was impossible for ships of the Task Force to relay them was because the signal was incompatible with it.

It is not as if a great deal of effort was not expended exploring various avenues to overcome the technical difficulties faced in transmitters from such a far-flung outpost. At one point hopes did rise when tests in Britain involving the MOD, the BBC and ITN engineers demonstrated the feasibility of sending pictures and sound from a mobile Army earth terminal. Prompted by both BBC and ITN, the three American TV networks approached the Pentagon to explore the possibility of tilting the American satellite so that it could be used. The television companies were not alone in this endeavour and according to the MOD informal approaches were made at *desk level*, but they proved so negative that no higher or formal attempt was made.

Although matters are not entirely clear about DISCUS, it would not seem surprising that the Americans showed a reluctance to alter its footprint and tilting. At the time of the request, DISCUS was covering central America which was in a state of political tension with the US; it is unimaginable that the US would have fired rockets to alter its footprint just for the convenience of British television.

Once the Task Force had reached the Falklands and established a landing, HF radio could be used for communication because by then the Argentinians would know, only too painfully, the location. For this reason it is debatable if even the military themselves bothered to use DISCUS.

The final possibility for receiving pictures was by use of the commercial satellite system INTELSTAT. Yet again nothing was straightforward. Although capable of carrying communications and pictures, for the purpose of television it needed an extremely large dish terminal with a lower frequency and more power than military terminals. Whilst mobile stations do exist in Britain, those available to the BBC and ITN do not have the appropriate frequency for use with INTELSTAT. In order to use that system what is required is a 40-foot dish terminal. Such enormous mobile dishes are available only in the US. They cost, furthermore, approximately £1 million, but more serious than that they can usually only be used on land. Only occasionally are they used at sea, as when for example the US did so for the Apollo splash from one of their aircraft carriers. In the context of a war it is highly improbable that the Navy would have released space on either of its two carriers to accommodate such a massive dish and thus interfere with the landing and lift-offs of the much valued and prized Harrier jump jets. Once the landing was recorded such a dish could have been mantled on the Islands but the problem of transportation and the enormity of the cost made any attempt unfeasible. It was not resolved, and is still not really resolved. Who should pay for war coverage - the television companies themselves or the Government? Even in this case, for example, if the Navy had been willing both the BBC and ITN were unwilling to commit £1 million to such a venture. The military, however, did take with them a smaller mobile ground station of about 15-20 feet, but that was for communications only, not pictures.

What especially needs stressing from all this is that it required no human conspiracy to prevent the transmission of pictures of the war; the technical problems alone conspired to take care of that.

Information Policy

Similarly the MOD was slow in co-operating with the BBC and IBA over the possible technical means of transmitting pictures, but as political pressure mounted co-operation increased; all, however, to no avail as the logistics of doing so proved insurmountable. The military, but particularly the Navy, were never keen on having television along, but despite the occasional hindrance and once or twice outright refusal to allow filming, they philosophically accepted its presence. Despite the willingness and desire of the government to have pictures, there is no doubt that their absence has resulted in some embarrassment as if it were planned and deliberately engineered. Victory, however, is its own celebration, only failure requires profound explanation. Nevertheless, despite political will, ministers and civil servants now frankly admit that there is worry about the televising of military conflicts. Thus in future any embarrassment that not having pictures may have caused could well be outweighed by the thought of having them. Our interviews with senior civil servants suggest that there was no contingency plan for handling pictures in the event of such a possibility and that had pictures arrived back it would have presented a very serious problem of knowing what to do. The question of censorship therefore was never in its fullest extent ever raised: television was the nightmare that never actually manifested itself. Information policy was never therefore really tested; that is, the contradiction within liberal democratic society of political/military desire to withhold information and the public right to know. Caught unaware in the Falklands crisis, contingency plans for future military operations have now been drawn up.

Both General Sir Hugh Beach's study group on censorship, set up by the Ministry of Defence, with the task of examining whether "any new measures are necessary in order to protect military information immediately prior to or during the conduct of operations" and which has produced a 92-page report, details certain conclusions and recommendations and the regulations issued in October 1983 by the Ministry of Defence for correspondents accompanying an operational force and participants in Exercise External Triangle (NATO) underline the dissatisfaction over the *débâcle* which occurred during the Falklands. It also illustrates a serious desire to get it right the next time.

However, the Falklands conflict was a unique situation for all involved including the media. Not surprisingly many of the news organisations have compared their experiences in Vietnam and Israel unfavourably with the Falklands and consequently severely criticised the facilities and information procedures provided by the British Government. The fact, of course, is that Britain has not been involved in conflicts even approximating the Falklands for many years. The Whitehall information machine was rusty and hardly up to the task of what was a very difficult and demanding situation, much less so to control information smoothly in any articulated fashion. Although much has been trumpeted about the Army's successful handling of information in Northern Ireland, it must be remembered that it has had twelve years with which to do so. The Royal Navy has hardly any experience of an information war. Its last outing in the Cod War was lost miserably to the Icelanders. Insofar as the Government is concerned and the question of the control of information, there appears to be common consent that in the two areas of 'endangering British lives' and 'jeopardising the security of the operation', it had and does have legitimate reasons for not releasing certain categories of information. But the problem arises when defining these two categories. With the first one there appears little scope for ambiguity.

But the second category has a very wide definition with plenty of room for differing interpretations and not surprisingly, therefore, has generated the most debate. The Ministry of Defence has been accused in the media of using this all-embracing term as an excuse for delaying, censoring and misinforming them and, by extension, the public.

Whilst it is perhaps politically naive not to be sceptical of Government information during a period of heightened difficulties, it is nevertheless the case that part of the criticism which has been levied at the manner in which the Government handled information should be understood, not just in any simple terms of a desire to confuse but as a result of organisational confusion. There were conflicts within the Ministry of Defence, between the Services themselves and between the operational commanders with the Task Force and the Ministry of Defence. All these factors served to compound the already inadequate overall information policy. Internally it was difficult to get a clear understanding of what was going on and from where the sources of intelligence and policy were coming. The lack of an organised information system for dealing with the situation meant that there was no centralised system of control. There was a marked lack of co-ordination between all departments involved. Indeed, since the ending of the conflict it has been revealed that there was a report made in 1977 on information procedures which has been lying on a shelf in the Ministry of Defence untouched for the last six years. The existence of these draft guidelines was not known to Ministry of Defence PR staff at the start of the conflict. Had these been known, then according to our sources it would still not have made any real difference. It does, though, serve to underline the woeful lack of preparedness that the existence of such contingency plans was not even known.

Given the furore which has resulted from the Government's considered mishandling of information during the war it is quite clear that existing procedures proved inadequate and that attempts to provide additional practices to normal services failed. However, in general during a crisis situation such as that of the Falklands the whole of normal parliamentary government itself is suspended. Existing politics are considered inadequate to the new demands. A whole new machinery takes over. A War Cabinet is set up and the Treasury, the central arm of British administration in peace-time, is mothballed. The country is run instead by five members of the War Cabinet, Northwood, the Ministry of Defence and Downing Street. Parliament and the Treasury become superfluous. Although supposedly synchronised, the problem was that during the Falklands there were considerable differences in strategy and tactics producing not inconsequential strains within and between these various administrative arms which rebounded as an incoherence of public information.

Within the MOD, for example, there were problems over personnel with differences of opionion between Sir John Nott and Bernard Ingham (the Prime Minister's powerful press secretary) about the suitability of Ian MacDonald (the MOD spokesman) and which had a great bearing on the type of information given to the media. The Services also continued to struggle amongst themselves and, in addition, put pressure on MOD civilian personnel not to give the Argentines accurate information about British losses. The military information side were much more keen than the civilian officers with the MOD to put out misinformation that they hoped might confuse the Argentinians. It is not surprising that these tensions within the MOD should frustrate the journalists and lead to doubts about MOD honesty as they attempted desperately to winkle out what was true, what was false and what was going on.

There is no more exact a science than hindsight, but even so, despite the ending of the conflict, a certain fog still exists about who was actually co-ordinating the information effort. Sir Frank Cooper, the permanent Under-Secretary of the MOD, John Nott, the Secretary of State for Defence, Neville Taylor, the Chief of Public Relations at the MOD and Bernard Ingham, the Press Secretary at Number 10, all have somewhat differing views on this matter. Without going into all the details of what each has since commented on the subject and our own interviews, suffice it to say there were considerable differences about what occurred. As the Defence Committee which reported on the handling of information during the Falklands conflict put it: 'Institutional incompatibility is a little unsettling'. The consequences of this lack of clarity, allied to the frictions within the MOD and between the MOD and journalists and broadcasters during the crisis, was little short of disastrous. It was hardly surprising that complaints came pouring in about the handling of information policy. But journalists on the whole tend to be a complaining breed when denied access to information; however, what marks this case from others is that the discontent spilled over and out into the public arena to become news itself.

If We are to Believe the Ministry of Defence: Whose Side is the BBC On?

If the media criticised the Government for its handling of information it was quickly returned by the Government lashing out at perceived disloyalty in a time of national concern. Within television the BBC felt the force most directly. Both charge and counter-charge did not take place *ex nihilo*, but against a background of worried assumption laid down by Vietnam. At the immediate level it was the chaos at the MOD which prompted John Snow of *Newsnight* to publicly cast doubt on the veracity of ministerial information. We had presumed at the beginning of the research that such outspoken questioning was meant as a warning shot to the MOD to start co-operating more honestly otherwise *Newsnight* was not prepared to go along with what was becoming a game of collusion by repeating dubious information. Snow himself, however, was adamant to us that his statement was an absolute product of sheer frustration at spending so much time at the MOD for so little reward in terms of reliable information. In other words, Snow's frustration was a product of MOD incompetence and lack of procedural skill. Snow was not alone amongst journalists in his anger. It was common to the defence corps correspondents in general. Neither ought it to be presumed that the blocking and refusal to keep the journalists adequately informed was a mark of professional skill on the MOD's part. A successful information policy is not one which upsets journalists especially at a time when their co-operation and goodwill is needed the most. Thus, for example, to give only on-the-record briefings as the MOD did is professional lunacy: off-the-record briefings to journalists whose confidence has been gained over a long period of exchanges can work both to the benefit of the journalist in that he knows what is going on, but also has an element of control attached. Not only is the journalist frustrated by on-the-record briefings, but in the absence of information from usual sources will attempt to turn elsewhere. This is exactly what happened. Control of information therefore had broken down all along the way and arguably to no-one's benefit, neither the Government, MOD, the Services nor the journalists.

It is not surprising, although professionally courageous, for Snow to go public and lay forth his concerned feeling that truth was not being served by the Government's information policies. The consequent attack on Snow and other programmes rests partly outside the morass of the MOD and within the prior historical event of Vietnam and the conclusions drawn from the American experience.

Historical alternatives must forever remain unknown but both the MOD and the military, drawing on US experience of Vietnam, were concerned about the possible effect that pictures might have on British morale. In fact, insofar as the military are concerned, there appears to be something of a consensus that the nightly pictures from SE Asia contributed to America's losing the war in Vietnam. Thus when asked by the Defence Committee what would have been "the effect on the morale of troops if television pictures of the sort of realism that the Americans had during the Vietnamese War had been shown during the Falklands conflict on British television screens and if the relatives of those men had seen those pictures", Major General Jeremy Moore, the Task Force Land Commander, replied unequivocally, "it would have had a very great effect". It may have had an effect but it would be absolutely wrong to consider that the relay of pictures from the Falklands, no matter how harrowing, would have resulted in the political effect such scenes from SE Asia wrought on the American public. It was analysis not gore which led the Americans to embark home: it was the increasing awareness that the war in Vietnam could not be won, and the analytical questioning of America's whole policy towards South East Asia which provided the necessary frame which gave the pictures shape and power to touch liberal American consciousness. No similar framework of analysis existed in Britain during the Falklands conflict; there was no heart searching question of policy by which pictures of corpses, no matter how delivered, could have moved to challenge and to say something other than offer the sentimentality of death and age-old comments about war and war's futility.

Historically there is no evidence to suggest that pictures of war carnage alone can promote a lack of resolve to fight: quite the contrary.

In fact it makes good propaganda so long as the case is believed. Nothing is static, however, and one is not arguing that interaction between pictures of slaughter and questions of policy can never occur. Historical evidence shows that for pictures to work to any real effect it is questions of policy in the first instance which is the prime mover. By understanding this, it is easier to understand the outrage over current affairs programmes rather than the news during the Falklands because that is the area where policy is so much more readily under the analytical microscope. Thus the trouble began when, as mentioned, John Snow on *Newsnight* had the temerity to suggest that the Ministry of Defence were perhaps not always telling the truth. What caused an even bigger row was the *Panorama* film in which two Conservative MPs appeared to question the policy of the Government. They do nothing of the sort really, but there is an apparency of questioning. The criticisms show in a loose sense a Government losing its nerve, or more accurately perhaps an appreciation that it cannot afford to have any questioning of basic policy otherwise the news from the Falklands, all news following our argument, could become bad news. That is once the basics are challenged then even battle victories, since they entail death, become bad news. There is no doubt the Government appreciated that the war might get difficult. This meant that when bodies might start piling up on the beaches, it was expected, and desperately hoped for, that the country would stand solid, not waver, and accept such costs as the legitimate price for a right political policy. By looking at the dates of events it becomes clear to see this process of worry at work.

On 2 May the offending *Newsnight* programme went on. John Page MP then complained via the Press Association, and Fleet Street, ready as ever to criticise another medium, picked the story up and ran it for what it was worth. On 6 May, Margaret Thatcher attacked newsmen in the House of Commons for unpatriotic coverage. The 10 May brought the *Panorama* programme, a Commons motion attacking the BBC, and on 11 May further remarks by Thatcher in answer to Commons questions. The furore reached a crescendo on 12 May with Alistair Milne, the Director Designate of the BBC, and George Howard, the then Chairman of the BBC, attending the Tory Party back bench media committee. Interestingly the attacks lessened around 18 May.

The point to stress is that up until the end of April the conflict was still going well. The Haig shuttle, although still in operation, was breaking down, the Task Force had been successfully assembled and the 200-mile total exclusion zone established. On 25 April the Royal Marines had retaken South Georgia and Sandy Woodward, the overall Task Force commander, had said, although he later recanted, that it was going to be a walkover. On 30 April the United States formally sided with Britain. Also by this time Britain had pushed through the EEC boycott of Argentina and there was also the UN resolution 502 that had been passed at the beginning of April.

By the end of April, then, everything was not necessarily sweetness but there was room for confidence. At the beginning of May the climate changed and an air of nervous expectation took over. It was not the worst disaster time, Bluff Cove did not happen until 8 June, but what did occur was a realisation that the game was being played for real. On 1 May, Harriers and Vulcans attacked Port Stanley with the loss of three Harriers but without managing to destroy the runway. On 2 May, the Argentine ship, the *General Belgrano*, was sunk with over 300 sailors killed. The decision to sink the *Belgrano*, it has now emerged, was a decision taken by Thatcher at Chequers that weekend. On the evening of 2 May *Newsnight* went out. On 4 May the first British vessel, the

Sheffield, was hit and sunk by an Exocet missile. These two events, the *Belgrano* and the *Sheffield*, resulted in a great deal of questioning about how the conflict would develop. On 6 May, more Harrier planes were lost and on 10 May *Panorama* went out.

It was this initial nervousness, the dawning of realisation that battle was joined and that it was not going to be easy and that the fight had to be seen through, which forced the attacks on the BBC. One could not have current affairs programmes damaging the news, by which we mean not the specifics of content, but the framework within which the news was watched. In short, the pictures received would hang differently if the political policy was seen to be askew.

Conclusion

The coverage of the Falklands was structured by a number of factors some of which we have managed to highlight. What will not be found amongst the information *débâcle* are the workings of any skilfully prepared plan or even *ad hoc* conspiracy to account for the news as witnessed. The fact that Margaret Thatcher was returned for a second term on a massively increased majority might say something about the popularity of military victory to a populace robbed of confidence across a whole gamut of performances, but it can say nothing, and does not, about the way in which the *media war* was managed. The fact that victory was exploited after the war is not the same as having a high powered machinery working to that end during the conflict. Military events might have gone terribly wrong in the South Atlantic, bogged down in some frightful Crimea-like campaign, which would then have required an information machinery of greater sophistication than that which existed to explain events to the British public. Defeats, not successes, require explanation. In this sense it was the soldiers who took care of the information war by rolling on from success to success. Thus, the whole information apparatus was never really put under political stress. On the mechanical level of organisation though, the information service was put under considerable stress, requiring all its energy to be converted into efforts of information relay. Even at this level it had real difficulties in functioning. Undoubtedly, as our overall research shows, there were several instances of attempts at political management of the news. But these attempts were neither uniform nor consistent in purpose or direction. They certainly do not warrant the notion of a nation duped in any planned fashion.

In terms of an information war, the major battle defeat was in losing the confidence and trust of the journalists. Admittedly incidents can always be covered up by straightforward blanket censorship, but that is not ideologically easy in terms of liberal democratic theory especially when the conflict concerned does not threaten the very existence of the state, but only political careers and Britain's world standing. Effective news management requires something more subtle than that, and that subtlety and ability was not there in the Falklands.

TELEVISION NEWS AND THE LABOUR MOVEMENT

Antony Easthope

> 'There could be no question about our
> supporting the Government in general ...'
>
> Lord Reith

During the early 'eighties, as the Great Britain Limited ploughed ever deeper into crisis, the plates of the old ship began to buckle and rivets started to come out. One small symptom that the crisis of the present British political economy is terminal rather than just chronic may be the way the phrase 'media bias' acquired journalistic currency from around 1981. In April that year a letter complaining of broadcasting coverage of trade unions was sent to the BBC and IBA. It was signed by 74 MPs, 23 trade union general secretaries and 20 academics (including 14 professors). It requested programmes to examine the whole issue in detail with broadcasters having the opportunity to respond to criticism. For the IBA Barbara Hosking simply denied the accusation; the BBC maintained an Olympian silence.

Besides such interventions from the Labour movement, there has been important work on television bias from the Glasgow Media Group. However, this work has taken place mainly on the basis of a reflexive problematic: that is, by measuring television news as a truth against the reality it purports to reflect. Another approach, one which may in some ways have more actual leverage, would emphasise the television text as a *production* of meanings and criticise these by putting forward alternatives within the domain of what is offered. The text I shall analyse is the BBC's coverage of the TUC's Day of Action on 14 May 1980. I shall go on to suggest some ways to confront and oppose media bias in television.

Institution

The BBC is a state institution. Its paymasters are ultimately the government of the day since parliament annually approves the rate of the BBC licence fee. Established by Royal Charter, the Corporation is required as part of its Licence 'to broadcast an impartial account ... of the proceedings in both Houses of Parliament' (Clause 13, 2) and to refrain from editorialising. The principle is glossed by the BBC *Handbook* for 1978 which says: 'For the BBC to take sides in any controversial issue would in any case be contrary to its own long-established policy of impartiality'. On 30 January 1983 the *Sunday Times* carried a long report about the BBC coverage of the South Atlantic war under the headline 'BBC toed the official line on Falklands'. When I wrote to Alisdair Milne drawing his attention to this report and the BBC's duty to be impartial, I got a reply from the Secretariat which began acidly, 'Thank you for your letter of 1 February, reminding the Director-General of the BBC's responsibilities'. But it is important

that the Corporation has a statutory obligation. They should be made to
live up to this prescription and it is something they are rightly sensitive about.

As far as I have been able to discover - for this is not a topic
the BBC publishes a fact sheet on - the organisational hierarchy is as
follows: the Queen in Council (that is, the Privy Council, that is, the
government in effect) appoints twelve Governors of the BBC. The Chairman
of the Governors (I don't think even on paper its Chairperson yet) is
appointed on the advice of the Home Office (that is, the government).
The Governors appoint the Director-General, the General Advisory Council,
the Board of Management and the top 30 management positions (the Board
of Management appoints all the others). The BBC as an institution is
far from being an example of workers' control, exhibiting as it does the
typically British formation of the state as an informal annex to the
dominant class. It is centralised and hierarchic but with considerable
delegation of authority relative for example to French television. It
ensures that no one will get promoted unless they spontaneously generate
versions of the dominant ideological consensus. This has the advantage
that directors of programmes can write perfectly sincere letters to the
Guardian - as did John Wilson, BBC News Editor on 21 February 1981 -
defending the impartiality of the institution that made them because they
are not aware of any pressures on them. I shall later be analysing the
discursive effectivity of television news format but in doing so I shall
not forget Nicholas Garnham's remark that the most powerful discourse
deciding what gets said in BBC news is the discourse of unemployment (as
the BBC career of Jonathan Dimbleby neatly illustrates).

But the hierarchic institutionalisation of power is insufficient
to contain what it deploys - it has to be supplemented by a secret committee for fixing the news. Once again this has the apparently decen-
tralised informality of that very traditionally British ruling class
form which Edward Thompson likes to refer to as 'old corruption'. Censorship at the Corporation seems to work like this. First of all every
sensitive decision has to be 'referred up' the hierarchy. Making a programme that said the wrong thing about Northern Ireland, for example,
could lead to loss of contract not because you had said the wrong thing
(which would raise the issue of bias) but because you had shown insufficient work discipline - you had failed to refer the matter up. But
how are you to find out what to refer up since you can't keep asking all
the time and since new problems keep coming up (Mugabe suddenly ceases
to be a terrorist guerilla and becomes a Prime Minister)?

The answer is DNCA or 'Duncan', the Director News and Current
Affairs Committee. This is said to meet every Tuesday in the Shepherd's
Bush centre in Room 7082. It discusses news matters in a general and
academic tone - how the Metropolitan Police or the CIA feel about their
recent coverage, who is given a 'hard' interview (Benn) and who is given
a 'soft' one (Hattersley). The Minutes of DNCA find their way into
every news and current affairs studio in the Corporation. There is no
diktat, nothing which says what you should or should not say. It is
all gentlemanly and very British, and makes perfectly clear to any
ambitious reporter what the current 'line' is. But then history sets
people no problems people cannot solve. The informal system for the
distribution of Minutes, even the very Xerox machine on which they are
copied, means that some copies find their way beyond the Corporation to
less reverent ears outside. The DNCA Minutes often speak with the
authentic voice of old corruption. When the Glasgow Media Group first
published its account of television news the Director-General of the
time said he saw 'no sense in attacking *Bad News* in detail' but thought

'the ideology of sociologists was a subject which would repay a little study'. And on 27 January 1981 when DNCA discussed an article by the same Group it accepted that 'there was something in what the Glasgow Group was saying' but since the analysis had appeared in the *New Statesman* 'the BBC could therefore ignore it'.

The BBC has always been structurally and institutionally predicated on the state, though not always the government of the day. Its relative autonomy makes it more, not less, effective in the transmission of the dominant ideological consensus. As John Reith, 'father' of the BBC, explained during the General Strike in a memorandum to senior staff dated 15 May 1926:

> There could be no question about our supporting the Government in general, particularly since the General Strike had been declared illegal ... we were able to give listeners authentic impartial news of the situation to the best of our ability ... if commandeered or unduly hampered or manipulated the immediate purpose of such action would not only have been unserved but actually prejudiced.

In other words: in the conditions of liberal democracy we can represent the interests of the state *more* effectively if we are not openly and directly controlled by the state.

It is not so much that the BBC is against socialism, CND or trade unionism; it is rather that it is structured so that it *cannot* speak well of anything outside or against the state. In 1977 I wrote complaining about coverage of the British Oxygen strike and got a reply from a Duty Editor saying that 'the British Oxygen strike could well have put the entire British industry out of work', a point of view identifying state, nation and economy. It is not accidental that a similar complaint to ITN in November 1980 should get a reply from a producer of *News at One* that 'Any strike is a threat to the economy'. This kind of thing reminds you of Althusser's analysis of ideology as a form of subject position in which people are produced so that they think they work all by themselves.

Text

On 14 May 1980 the TUC Day of Action against Conservative government policies took place. That evening the BBC 9.00 p.m. news gave 11 minutes and about 1,460 words to coverage of the strike. Because of a quite separate strike (over pay) there was no ITN transmission that day. In the 11 minutes' worth, which drew on the *Nationwide* format to cover the whole country, there were nine main speakers: Kenneth Kendall the newsreader, Martin Adeney the industrial correspondent, five reporters in different places, Bill Hamilton in Barking (he also interviewed Len Murray), Len Murray himself. Minor roles were taken by two Leeds busdrivers and a local Conservative; there were also the chanting voices of the demonstrators ('Maggie, Maggie, Maggie - Out, Out, OUT!').

It is very unusual for a news report of Labour movement activity to be so long and so these 11 minutes constitute an exemplary text. In this range and depth it is possible to analyse a full deployment of the forms for constructing truth that enable the BBC to attach an authoritatively pejorative rather than honorific meaning to such trade union activity, to bad-mouth it while appearing to report it fairly. I shall point to three main strategies depending on: (1) genre; (2) denotation and connotation; (3) a regime of truth.

1.   Genre

Like all television the news is a serial - a constant updating of a story without beginning and (we hope) without end. Each new item has to be folded into the serial and made sense of in the form of genre. Some means to reduce difference into repetition is ineluctable (the alternative I suppose being psychosis) but the generic modes currently dominant work against the Labour movement, not for it. That made available for the Day of Action was the strike genre. Like football, this turns on victory or defeat, and this is a question of numbers (what percentage of the work force struck, what didn't). Hence, inserted into the genre of the strike story, the Day of Action became *ab initio* a failure *unless the whole British working population (or most of it) had taken the day off.* Just as in the conventional strike genre the issue for which the action is taken gets lost amid the day to day reporting of events, so the political significance of the Day of Action was invisibly set aside. The General Strike was industrial and not directly political. The Day of Action had been the first national call for a political strike since the Chartists' Holy Month of 1839. The BBC's use of the strike genre turned it into a dull and repetitive report about the numbers of trains running in Glasgow.

Genre also determines that certain items should be taken together, and often whether they should go in at all. A nuclear accident at Sizewell might well guarantee inclusion for a report of CND activity somewhere else that otherwise would get ignored. But the tendency towards what we might call *generic condensation* often has pejorative effects through juxtaposition. The 11 minutes conclude with Kenneth Kendall reporting under industrial news figures showing that wages were rising faster than prices. The implication was clear: why should anyone be discontent if their pay was going up?

2.   Denotation and Connotation

Barthes has taught us to contrast denotation with the ideological connotation which, in realist representation, nestles all but invisibly inside it. In television news this is a matter both of words and images. The innovation of the personally 'present' and visible newsreader that developed from the early 'sixties means that face and voice inevitably attach connotation to what is said. Thus, Kendall is manifestly uneasy during the early part of the report, his tone of voice registering his *effort* to speak impartially about the most massive, organised and widespread defiance of state authority since 1926. By the end he has relaxed and is positively jubilant about the rate of pay in the subsequent item. In Jonathan Dimbleby's film about newsreels in the 'thirties, *Before Hindsight*, Leslie Mitchell speaks about - and dramatises - his deliberate use of tone of voice to stress the threat of fascism while sounding unenthusiastic about the Chamberlain government's response.

There are linguistic methods for annotating English intonation but it would be hard to bring these into play over newsreaders. It is easier to demonstrate that the words chosen have connotations that others of equal brevity do not. Throughout the 11 minutes the word 'normal' is used six times; it denotes that which happens by routine but connotes that which *should* happen. Used for continued production ('Most of industry except some mines and ports carried on normally'), it renders industrial action as *abnormal*. Industrial action was also implicitly referred to as some kind of bomb damage ('The only major casualty was one tin-plate works closed for the day' ... 'Scotland and West Region were badly hit'). Passages for which one could most obviously find a less partial alternative were Frances Coverdale's conclusion in reporting from London:

> ... as drivers made the slow journey home Scotland Yard praised them for their patience. And the verdict on the Day? Bad, but not as bad as expected ...

and Martin Adeney's summary which began by comparing the Day of Action to some kind of satanic birth: 'The Day of Action was conceived in the dark days of winter in the steel strike ...'. He could easily have said 'The TUC decided on the Day of Action during the steel strike last winter', saved two words and been fairer.

Images have even more connotations than words. One sequence in particular showing a city gent cycling to work with a briefcase in the basket of his bike was notably polysemous: holiday, a break from mental into manual labour, cycling as healthy outdoor activity, cheerful British amateurism and improvisation, the underlying humanity of the British middle class (as celebrated in Ealing comedy), war memories of 'Britain can take it', a pragmatic rather than rationalist tradition. Every image connotes but again as Barthes argues the image is likely to be so open to meaning that it must be closed down with words. Images therefore are hard to examine apart from the particular regime of truth in which they figure.

3. <u>Truth</u>

Within its specific effectivity as a televisual form, the news conforms to the dominant mode, which is classic realism: that is, while being news it aims to disavow the means of its own production and offers itself only as a transparent window onto a supposedly pregiven truth. The attempt to efface the process of signification is brought about particularly via three formal strategies: the relation of image and word, the effect of 'presence', the hierarchy of knowledge.

(a) <u>Image and word</u>. The realism of television news aims to hold and contain image by word, to make the image merely an evidential support for the word: 'Throughout Yorkshire the majority of bus services were running normally' is spoken over shots of green buses driving through Hull. But the intended homogeneity which would fix image in subordination to word can never be achieved. What for example is the photographic equivalent for 'throughout Yorkshire'? And if the word has no visual equivalent, similarly the image always tends to exceed the verbal closure imposed on it. The photographed stillness of factories, shipyards, train stations became incrementally more eerie and alien, connoting some sci-fi film of the 'fifties (*The Day the Earth Stood Still* perhaps?). The repeated insistence on normality became ever more surreal. 'London Underground was running normally' intones Bill Hamilton as a tube train processes slowly past trees in the middle-distance and one wonders exactly what Magritte-like transposition he was expecting. Further aleatory effects can be remarked in the images, those surrounding the figure of Len Murray for example. What of his resemblance to Eric Sykes? His smoking a Hamlet while being interviewed, however consonant it might be with his general air of lugubrious stoicism? His tapping of an off-camera book ('to the extent as which [*sic*] is reported here')? His sudden incapacity to speak prose? His green shirt, whose tone coincided exactly with the greens of a map on a wall behind him? The purpose of the regime is precisely to exclude such play of the visual signifier. 'Good' television means television that works hard to fix image onto word in the name of truth.

(b) <u>Presence</u>. The specific mode of television, as Stephen Heath and Gillian Skirrow argue in their *Screen* analysis of a *World in Action* programme, seeks to express truth as presence. We look up and out to the film screen in a public auditorium; we look down and in to the television screen in the domestic audience (hence its infantile narcissism caught in the pet names, 'telly', 'boob-tube'). Television is structured for such presence in a double sense: presence in that the dominant position is that of a talking head in direct address to us (the shot forbidden by classic Hollywood narrative); but presence also in that television, that small intimate screen, always surrenders narrative for actuality. Both constraints inform the truth of television news: the personalised newsreader seemingly present as the voice of the Father (even if it's Jan Leeming), the making present of immediately contemporary footage from everywhere in the world (in the case of the Day of Action from every part of Britain).

(c) <u>The Hierarchy of Knowledge</u>. For this text it can be set out as follows:

1. Kendall (in the studio: face and voice)
2. Adeney (in the studio: face and voice)
3. Five reporters (in the field: voice over)
4. Len Murray (formal interview)
5. Leeds bus-drivers (informal interview)
6. Chanting demonstrators (non-speaking people)
7. Bus stations, steelworks, etc. (inert matter)

The hierarchy is erected via a series of oppositions: subject/object (from Kendall to the steelworks); inside/outside (from studio to streets); centre/margin (from London to Yorkshire); word/image (from voice speaking to voice replying to thing seen). The movement is between knowledge penetrating down through the hierarchy and evidence passing up. It would, I suppose, be Derridean to remark that the hierarchy presumes knowledge as intuitively present to itself *before* the evidence 'confirming' it arrives and to wonder then how it got to be knowledge in advance of this arrival. It is certainly important to note that the hierarchy is temporal as well as spatial since the sequence opens with Kendall, moves on through the five reporters down to the marching demonstrators (non-speaking parts these) and back via the Len Murray interview to Martin Adeney and thence to Kendall himself. The hierarchy and its progress towards closure seek to interpellate the viewer into the position of an all-knowing, all-seeing subject in identification with the presence of the newsreader. In turn this renders the marchers as a mere brute object of knowledge, lumpenly *there* like the silent yards and railway stations.

<u>Interventions</u>

There are a number of things to be done about television news. The institution, the site for the practices and discourses, needs to be changed, most obviously in the first instance by some democratisation. In the longer term it might be desirable to split the channels into 'right' and 'left' news programmes, as with RAI 1 and 2 in Italy (RAI 1 being mainstream Christian Democrat and Communist, RAI 2 being for everybody else). God alone can view reality in total objectivity so that to have the partiality of news put up-front rather than effaced would be a definite step forward. Greater regionalisation of news, possibly in association with local authorities and trades councils, is another possible structural change. But of course these could only be brought about by a political party, and so the issue returns to the manifestly political arena where it's a question of ensuring that the party of your choice has a progressive policy for the media.

In the meantime the Campaign for Press and Broadcasting Freedom is an important vehicle for expressing opinion and exerting pressure for change. Set up in 1981 as the Campaign for Press Freedom, it took on Broadcasting as well in July 1982. It has considerable support in the media unions in London, the NUJ for example. It publishes a bi-monthly journal, *Free Press*, as well as pamphlets, such as that on *The Right to Reply* (it encouraged Frank Allaun's bill in the last parliament). It organises conferences, such as that on 'The Media in the Eighties' held in London in May 1983. It slid into the BBC's Open Door slot in February 1983 when Julie Christie and Julie Walters presented a half-hour programme called 'Why their News is Bad News'. You can hire the programme from CPBF at 9 Poland Street, London W1 3DG. You can also join CPBF as an individual member for £5 at the same address.

It is worth writing letters to the BBC and ITN, an exercise which is more than just personally cathartic. Letters are effective if they are polite, rational, specific, factual, suggest practical alternatives to offensive material and remind the authorities of their statutory obligation to be impartial. Write to the Director-General or ITN on general issues but to producers and senior editors (names publicised in *TV Times* and *Radio Times*) about more specific issues (they don't often get fan mail). The occasional phone call also keeps up the pressure.

I don't know how long they'll go on writing replies if they begin to get a lot of tightly argued dissident correspondence. I certainly do value a letter from a Producer of *News at One* which says 'I totally agree that the phrase "the likes of Arthur Scargill" is perjorative'. But I am not surprised there was no answer to the letter I wrote which began 'I wish to complain about the use of the phrase "bitch and counter-bitch" by Ian Smith to describe different views in the Labour Party on *Newsnight* on Monday 8 June 1981'. I don't think any reply was possible.

THE VERBAL ARSENAL OF BLACK WOMEN WRITERS IN AMERICA

Melissa Walker

In 1974, Harvard University Press published a book entitled *Black Fiction* in which only three of the thirty-nine writers the author considers are women - Zora Neal Hurston, Paule Marshall and Ann Petry - all of whom came of age as writers before the sixties began. (1) I mention this book not as evidence of the author's sexist bias, but rather to suggest that as late as the first years of the seventies, few black women were receiving any serious consideration by literary historians and critics. And this was at a time when the works of black males - James Baldwin, Richard Wright, Eldridge Cleaver, Claude Brown and Leroi Jones - were widely read and admired.

A decade later that has completely changed. Black American women writers are assuming leadership in publishing, they are winning the prestigious literary prizes in the United States, and they are forging a large and varied body of significant literature. To begin to appreciate this powerful new literature, we must try to see how it, to use Terry Eagleton's words, "is rooted in, without being reduced to, specific social conditions". (2)

Raymond Williams in *The English Novel from Dickens to Lawrence* speculates about the "pressing and varied experience" (3) out of which a new society and new kinds of novels evolved and flowered in the late 1840s:

> The first industrial civilisation in the history of the world had come to a critical and defining state. By the end of the 1840's the English were the first predominantly urban people in the long history of human societies. The institutions of an urban culture ... were all decisively established in these years. There was critical legislation ... [affecting the everyday lives of common people] But the sense of crisis, of major and radical issues and decision, was both acute and general. It is then not surprising that in just this decade a particular kind of literature - already known and widely read ... should come to take on new life, a newly significant and relevant life. (4)

Much of what Williams says about the English at that time was true of black Americans in the 1960s. They had become a largely urban people. Critical legislation had been passed to effect changes in their education, medical care, housing and voting rights. There was a widespread sense of crisis in the society at large with particular intensity in the black community; and by 1968 the violent upheavals that were so dreaded in England in 1848 were regular occurrences in American cities. And there was a new literature about to be born in response to what Williams calls "new and varied but still common experience". (5)

The civil rights movement was in significant ways over by late 1968. Richard Nixon, who was at best indifferent to the plight of minorities and the poor, had defeated Hubert Humphrey, who had long been an advocate for racial equality. There had of course been victories: black Americans could now sit in the front of the bus, they could buy a hamburger at any lunch counter, they could use public facilities - parks, restrooms and water fountains - and they could send their children to integrated schools if they lived in the right neighborhood. If they had the courage to register, they could vote; if they had the money they could eat in good restaurants, buy a drink in a bar, stay in a luxury hotel, and even rent or buy a home in an affluent white neighborhood.

There were still many obstacles to true equality, however. Many school children were locked in ghettos, millions of black Americans had not registered to vote, and only a small percentage could afford decent housing. Poverty was widespread, huge resources were being drained into the war in Vietnam, and the national conscience had shifted from civil rights to the anti-war movement. The last major legislation to affect black Americans was passed in August of 1965, and five days later one of the worst riots of the decade broke out in Watts, a black district of Los Angeles. The next three years were marked by acts of violence, growth of the black separatist movement, and decreasing hope that the dream of integration and equality would ever be realized. In 1968 President Johnson's Commission on Civil Disorders reported that "Our Nation is moving toward two societies, one black, one white - separate and unequal". (6) Not only were blacks and whites becoming increasingly alienated from one another, but the rifts within the black community had widened to chasms.

There were, however, other forces at work in the society at this time, forces that were to energize the literature of a whole generation of women. The women's movement had attracted the attention of a significant number of black women, who had begun to identify those issues that were unique to them. In 1968 Frances M. Beale, a black woman and a Civil Rights activist, wrote an essay entitled "Double Jeopardy: To Be Black and Female". Frequently anthologized and reprinted, this essay serves as a starting point for much thinking about the black woman's place in society and her role in the process of social change. "Double Jeopardy", which was adopted by the Student Nonviolent Coordinating Committee (SNCC) as that organization's official position on women, can be summarized in the following four points:

1. People need to be led to understand that their roles in an exploitive society affect the way they behave to each other. There is inevitable conflict between men and women in a society in which exploited males are often out of work, females are retained indefinitely as low-paid domestic servants, and neither group understands the plight of the other. Women often assume that their men are lazy; men respond with rage and sometimes abuse.

2. Black men and women must not imitate their white counterparts - the women staying at home and avoiding involvement in social change, the men excluding them from active roles in the greater world.

3. Black women must take responsibility for changing society by first changing how they structure their lives and relate to their husbands, lovers, parents, children, friends and co-workers.

4. Black women must take active roles to envision the kind of society they want to create and to work to bring it about so that *all* people can live decently, free from oppression and exploitation.

That Frances Beale's manifesto was endorsed by an organization dominated by militant males is evidence that a new alliance was taking place between members of the waning civil rights movement and the growing women's movement. Among those who responded to the urgent imperative of this document were a number of black American women, who seem literally to have risen phoenix-like from the ashes of the urban riots, to ask questions and to begin to answer them in a new and compelling literature. Perhaps black women like Maya Angelou, Toni Cade Bambara, Toni Morrison and Alice Walker asked themselves this question: how can we help people understand that social forces push them to behave in destructive ways, that they can choose to act differently, and that they can change themselves and in the process, change society? For these and a number of other women, the answer was plain: they could help people understand the relation of their own lives to society through stories, plays, novels and poems. They could create a literature that responds to the need of black people to understand the social conditioning that leads them to pursue destructive behavior.

Women who looked around them in 1968, who were conscious of the intensity and number of crises of the time, who responded to the particular urgency of the condition of black women at that time, and who tried to address the crises through writing, did so with a sense of the difficulty and complexity of the task. How did they go about it? First, they formed alliances: they got together, formed networks, and committed themselves to helping each other. To understand what Guitar in Toni Morrison's *Song of Solomon* was to call "the condition our condition is in", (8) women writers looked at all the social forces that affect a given life. They looked around: at the home, the family, and the ways members of a family relate to each other. They looked out: at the neighborhood, and further out at the community, the nation. They looked backwards: at history, at events that have created the present "condition". They looked ahead: to the kind of society they want to create. And they looked within: to the powerful negative emotions that debilitate them and to the positive feelings that feed their creativity and their capacity to survive. Black women's literature is not about fulfilment and success and easy victories: it is about work, struggle, pain, the defeat of many, the survival of some, the victory of the few, and success only after enormous effort.

In 1970, a scant two years after the SNCC manifesto, each of four black women who have achieved considerable stature as writers today, published her first book and each of the books demonstrates a determination to grapple with the complexity of that time. The books are Toni Cade Bambara's *The Black Woman*, Maya Angelou's *I Know Why the Caged Bird Sings*, Toni Morrison's *The Bluest Eye* and Alice Walker's *The Third Life of Grange Copeland*. Each represents a woman's attempt to look around, to look out, to look backwards, to look ahead, and to look within.

In the "Preface" to *The Black Woman*, the editor, Toni Cade Bambara, argues for the need to consider "what Blacks have done to and for themselves", (9) to acknowledge that "Black women are individuals" (10) who share many concerns but who also have unique and original perspectives, and to initiate a system of communication among black women so that they "don't keep treadmilling the same ole ground". (11) This important and unusual book, which has gone through at least sixteen printings, combines polemical political writings of social activists with selected poetry and short fiction by some of the best young writers of the time. *The Black Woman* is not only a record of involvement in and response to recent social changes, it is also an appeal to black women to join together, to write their own histories, to create and to maintain "a vision of a society substantially better than the existing one". (12)

I Know Why the Caged Bird Sings by Maya Angelou, who has been called "one of the best known black women authors in the world", (13) may be the book by a black woman with the widest audience. This best seller is the first of four volumes of her rather special kind of autobiography. In a recent interview, Angelou explains what she was trying to do in *Caged Bird*:

> I wasn't thinking so much about my own life or identity. I was thinking about a particular time in which I lived and the influences of that time on a number of people. I kept thinking, what about that time? What were the people around young Maya doing? I used the central figure - myself - as a focus to show how one person can make it through those times. (14)

Abandoned by her parents, raised by a loving grandmother, reclaimed by her mother, raped by her mother's lover, and rendered mute for five years by the experience, Angelou had bad times to get through; and she uses the story of her own victory over difficulty as an example to others of what is possible even in the face of extreme suffering. Concentrating on the victory of the few, Angelou attempts to counter the despair of the many. While she fully acknowledges the evils of racism and mourns its victims, she ultimately tells of strategies for survival and for positive, successful living. She celebrates the spirit that sings in the dark, in prison, and in a hostile land; and she writes to nurture that spirit in people who struggle to break out of the cage of oppression.

Toni Morrison's *The Bluest Eye* and Alice Walker's *The Third Life of Grange Copeland* explore the destructive forces at work in the black community. Both examine the everyday lives of poor, alienated black people, and both expose the nature, causes and results of the pervasive suffering that is inherent in those lives: the feelings of separateness and unworthiness; the cruelty and violence that emerge from poverty and the consequent self-hatred; the transformation of love to hate between husband and wife, parent and child; the evil nature of a society that not only disenfranchises some of its citizens, but discounts them. In both books, the main culprits are the evils of racism and the economic structures that sustain it.

In *The Bluest Eye*, the accumulated suffering of generations of black Americans longing for a better life is subsumed in one little black girl's yearning for blue eyes. Her name is Pecola Breedlove, and Toni Morrison tells her story in a one-page prelude at the beginning of the novel: Pecola's father, Cholly Breedlove, rapes and impregnates her; she has his baby; the baby dies, and so does Cholly. "There is really nothing more to say," Morrison announces to the reader, "except why. But since why is difficult to handle, one must take refuge in how." (15) But the how is not so easy to grasp either, and Morrison proceeds to unravel the social conditions and events that lead to this little girl's ruin.

Violence is part of the daily life of Pecola's family: Cholly, suffering from bouts of drunkenness, periodically assaults his wife in his children's presence with feet, hands and teeth; she retaliates by throwing frying pans, pokers and an occasional flat iron. Mrs. Breedlove needs the fights to relieve the "tiresomeness of poverty" (16) and to reinforce her moral superiority over her husband; Cholly needs the fights to express his "inarticulate fury and aborted desires". (17) Pecola, however, does not need the fights, and she struggles to endure the violence that surrounds her by escaping into a fantasy that becomes an obsession and finally ends in madness. Pecola becomes convinced that if only she had blue eyes, her troubles would disappear. After the rape, the fantasy becomes a delusion, and she is convinced that her eyes have turned blue and that other people refuse to look at her because they are jealous of her blue eyes.

Pecola is only the most recent victim of a complex system of exploitation and oppression. Morrison takes care to show, if not why, then how Cholly is humiliated by white people and how he succumbs to fury and drunken rage; how, if not why, Mrs. Breedlove withdraws from this man she had once loved and attaches all her affection to the white people she serves; how the family is ostracized; and how the entire black community takes pleasure in the tragic tale of little Pecola.

While Morrison is looking around at the destructive behavior of the Breedlove family, she also looks back in history when such behavior was perhaps inevitable. The birth and death of Pecola's baby take place in the fall of 1941 - a year which is of course, for Americans, charged with significance. The fall of that year was the last time that most black Americans were unaware that they had options and that a better life might be possible for them. The war brought military careers for some and jobs in industry for others. In June of 1941, Roosevelt established a Fair Employment Practices Committee, which oversaw the defense-contract industries. (18) Further significant changes for black Americans began with Pearl Harbor, and accelerated after the war when Truman created a Commission on Higher Education, which condemned state laws designed to enforce segregation. Morrison explores black life before it all started, a time when "change was adjustment without improvement". (19) To understand the how, if not the why, of a race riot and the bitter hostilities within civil rights organizations, Morrison suggests that it is necessary to study the destructive behavior patterns that are passed from one generation to the next among oppressed people. *The Bluest Eye* may be seen as a response to the mandates of the 1968 SNCC manifesto composed by Frances Beale. By dramatizing the destructive patterns of everyday life, Morrison demonstrates the urgent need for people to work to change those patterns, to change how they relate to each other. She does not, however, directly address the issue of changing society.

Alice Walker's *The Third Life of Grange Copeland* shares with *The Bluest Eye* a vivid dramatization of the ways oppressed people, specifically black Americans, lash out in fury at those closest to them since they live in a society that makes it impossible for them to oppose those who oppress them, but her novel is more explicit about the social forces determining the personal responses. In both books the misdirected fury turns back and destroys those who indulge it.

The novel begins in the 1920s and ends in the early sixties, and Grange Copeland's three lives represent three periods in black history: the first, the rural period, from the end of the Civil War through World War I when the majority of black people lived much as they had as slaves on the Southern farms they worked; the second, the period of the northern migration beginning in the twenties and extending through World War II; and the third, the period of revolution initiated by the Supreme Court decision of 1954 that banned segregation in the schools and culminating in the civil rights legislation of 1964 and 1965. In all three periods Grange's existence was representative of the masses of black people. He, like many Americans of his race, was a social outcast, exploited by an economic system that used him and discarded him without regard for his needs. In his first life Grange is underpaid and deprived of decent shelter and food; like so many of his counterparts, he sinks into a pattern of inadequately rewarded, exhausting labor, followed by escape into alcohol and physical abuse of his family. His second life begins when he abandons his family and journeys to the North in the mid-twenties. There Grange fails even to find employment and soon resorts to crime to ward off starvation. Eventually he does come home and settles down with money acquired by mugging "old women and weak limbed students" (20) and by marrying and taking money from a resourceful old prostitute. His ill-gotten gain gives him a degree of prosperity and the possibility of a third life as he begins to develop moral concerns. Living in self-sufficient retirement with his basic needs taken care of for the first time, Grange is able to look about him and to note and respond to the needs of others. Free from the threat of starvation and physical abuse, Grange late in life develops a generous nature which he focuses first on all his neglected grandchildren and then on Ruth, the one grandchild who becomes his ward when Grange's son Brownfield kills her mother.

Release from poverty is only one factor in Grange's transformation. His moral awakening is further spurred by the rapid changes taking place in society at large, as his hope for a better life for his granddaughter expands with his growing awareness of the world outside. In the evening he and Ruth watch the news on television. They hear about integration of schools and public places; they see pictures of students marching, singing and praying; and they learn about a man named Martin Luther King, who soon becomes a hero for Grange and Ruth. As the old man and his now teenaged granddaughter talk about the possibilities for change, Ruth's hopefulness is countered by Grange's despair. Ruth becomes increasingly confident that she can join the age of choice, and Grange recognizes that he must free Ruth from the past - to insure her freedom, he must give up his. He must kill Brownfield - his own son and Ruth's deranged father - to sever Ruth from circumstances that would otherwise destroy her as they did her mother.

The Third Life of Grange Copeland ends with grief for the old man who sacrificed himself for the future and with hope for his survivor, Ruth, who represents that generation of young people who belong to the age of choice and in whose hands the future lies. *The Bluest Eye* does not move beyond a mournful sadness for the wasted lives of the Breedlove family. In 1970, Morrison looks back to 1941 on the eve of Pearl Harbor when black American men, women and children were dying and going mad because they lived in a society that was hostile to them:

> This soil is bad for certain kinds of flowers. Certain seeds it will not nurture, certain fruit it will not bear, and when the land kills of its own volition, we acquiesce and say the victim had no right to live. We are wrong, of course, but it doesn't matter. It's too late. At least on the edge of my town, among the garbage and the sunflowers of my town, it's much, much, much too late. (21)

In a subtle and indirect way Morrison leads her readers to see that what was happening in Europe on a large scale was happening in the United States. A spiritual and sometimes physical genocide was quietly going on in the hidden, isolated communities of black people.

Morrison leaves the task of translation to her readers who must feel that the hostility of the country to marigolds symbolizes the hostility of that same land to the lives of the black people it chooses to ignore and ultimately destroy. Walker, on the other hand, who is more overtly didactic, uses her characters to convey her message: "We keep killing ourselves" Grange tells his revenge-obsessed son, "for peoples that don't even mean nothing to us." (22)

The success of *The Bluest Eye*, *Grange Copeland* and *Caged Bird*; Bambara's appeal to black women to do what only they can do; and the urgency of the times may all have contributed to the substantial number of important books by black women published in the next few years. Alice Walker, Maya Angelou and Toni Cade Bambara regularly published short stories, poems and full length books. Audre Lorde and Nikki Giovanni published some seven volumes of poetry each in less than twelve years, and writers such as June Jordan and Gayle Jones wrote critically acclaimed books. The works of older more established writers - Gwendolyn Brooks and Margaret Walker - took a new turn. One unusual work, *For Colored Girls Who Have Considered Suicide When the Rainbow is Enuf* called by its author, Ntozake Shange, a Choreopoem - a mixture of poetry and dance for the stage - became in 1976 a Broadway hit, a successful book and a cultural phenomenon that is still provoking controversy.

Reading through the plays, poems and novels published by black women during this time, one is struck over and over with their overall quality and originality. Two works, however, stand out from the others: *Sula* by Toni Morrison, published in 1973, and *Meridian* by Alice Walker, published in 1976.

Sula is a highly personal story of Nel Wright and Sula Peace - their families, their growing friendship, estrangement and reunion, followed by Sula's betrayal of Nel, her death and Nel's grief. Nel and Sula represent the generations of black women who have lived out their lives in a personal sphere, unaware of the outside world and the forces of history that determine the nature of their lives. Nel, like her mother before her, spends all of her energy to maintain the semblance of a middle class life. Conservative, rigid and conventional in every way, Nel has no sense that her life might be part of a larger world than her own little community. Sula, rebellious and defiant of convention, is equally alienated from community by her wilful renunciation of responsibility for the consequences of her actions or for the welfare of others.

In this short novel, Toni Morrison explores another toll that racism takes on its victims. Isolated from the mainstream of society, kept on the fringes of the economy, used and discarded by history, many black people in the first half of this century lived without any consciousness of the possibility of change. Sula is a rebel without a cause; Nel a conservative with nothing to conserve. *Sula* then is a kind of elegy for the emotionally and economically impoverished people whose lives were discounted and wasted by a society that was indifferent if not openly hostile to them.

Sula is also Toni Morrison's response to the changes brought about by the civil rights movement. The last chapter, entitled "1965", begins with Nel, a sad and defeated woman in her fifties, meditating on the changes that have taken place in recent years:

> Things were so much better in 1965. Or so it seemed. You could go downtown and see colored people working in the dime store behind the counters, even handling money with cash-register keys around their necks. And a colored man taught mathematics at the junior high school. (23)

Change for Nel, however, has never meant anything but loss: she has lost her only friend, her husband, and what she thought of as the good domestic life. She has not been affected by the changes in society at large. She has not helped to bring about the changes, nor will she profit from them. What may seem like progress to the young people of the sixties, may very well be loss for the older generation who will have no part of it and who will lose their own children to the movement. All change has its casualties. "Hell ain't things lasting forever," Nel once told Sula, "Hell is change." (24)

In the sense that it begins historically where *Sula* ends, Alice Walker's *Meridian* is a sequel to *Sula*. The events of *Sula* extend from 1919 to 1965, the year of the Voting Rights Act and the riots in Watts; the main events of *Meridian* occur between 1960 and 1976, years of upheaval, hope and change, as well as war, violence and disillusionment. The young people in *Sula* live outside of history, or they are used and discarded by it; though the time of the action spans the Depression and World War II, these events never seem directly or explicitly to influence the lives of the fictional characters. The young characters in *Meridian* create history, and in the process they create their own lives.

Meridian, a novel about the civil rights movement, focuses on the lives of three young people: Meridian Hill, a naive but highly intelligent black girl from an isolated rural town, who in April 1960 "became aware of the past and present of the larger world"; (25) Truman Held, a pretentious young black man from an affluent middle class New York suburb; and Lynne Rabinowitz, a Jewish girl from the other side of the same community. These young people first meet through their involvement in the civil rights movement, and they soon become entangled in complex personal relationships. Meridian gets pregnant and chooses to have an abortion after her only sexual encounter with Truman; later, Lynne and Truman marry, have a child who is brutally murdered, become estranged and finally come back together as friends. These and other sensational personal events are set in the context of day-to-day political struggles. As the story of Meridian and her friends unfolds, the reader becomes increasingly aware of the intense physical suffering and psychic trauma endured by these young revolutionaries. Yes, Alice Walker says, change is possible. People can change themselves and society, but they do so at enormous cost. Those who fought the battles of the civil rights movement often did not survive as whole people to enjoy their victory. If *Sula* is an elegy to the discounted victims of an exploitative society *Meridian* is a memorial to those who dared to change it, and to the youthful energies that were spent in the effort.

As Alice Walker sees it, Meridian, Lynne - like their real-life counterparts - did make changes. In a 1973 interview, Walker talks about those changes:

> One reason I never stay away from the Southern Movement is because I realize how deeply political changes affect the choices and lifestyles of people. The movement of the Sixties, Black Power, the Muslims, the Panthers ... have changed the options of Black people generally and of Black women in particular. So that my women characters won't all end the way they have been, because Black women now offer varied, live models of how it is possible to live. We have made a new place to move. (26)

But the price of making that place was high. Many young people - black and white - like the characters in *Meridian* became estranged from their families; some lost their physical and mental health; others lost their jobs. All endured the daily stress of battle; some lost their lives.

In 1977 *Song of Solomon*, a prize-winning, best-selling novel, established Toni Morrison as a major novelist. *Song of Solomon* is about a middle-class black family in a Michigan city, and it focuses on the youngest member of that family, Macon Dead the Third, called Milkman. The son of a slum landlord - who was himself the son of a slave - and of a passive privileged woman - the daughter of a black physician who was the most respected man in the black community - Milkman is self-indulgent and uncommitted, with his father's greed and his mother's false sense of privilege. Working for his father and still living at home at the age of thirty-two, Milkman uses people for what they can do for him and discards them when they are no longer useful. Milkman's middle-class life is complicated by his involvement with his Aunt Pilate, an ignorant "conjure woman", who has no navel; her granddaughter Hagar, who sleeps with him for some years; and his best friend Guitar, who lives on the fringes of society and belongs to a secret gang of men dedicated to wreaking vengeance on white people. Finally, the consequences of his careless life begin to catch up with him - the discarded Hagar is trying to kill him, and he and Guitar have been arrested for stealing what they thought was a bag of gold but what turned out to be his own grandfather's bones. In the last part of the novel, Milkman leaves Michigan and heads south in search of the gold that he believes Pilate has left there. Though he fails to find gold, he finds, along with his own rich heritage, the power to love that his father has denied and his Aunt Pilate has nurtured all these years.

Morrison carefully sets this novel in history. References to World War I, the Depression, World War II, Franklin Roosevelt, Harry Truman and the Kennedys are carefully integrated into the narration, and a careful reading reveals that the options the characters have are directly related to their place in history. For example, Milkman's indulged sister, Corinthians, graduated from a prestigious girls' school in 1940, a time when the few middle-class black girls who did receive college degrees learned only what would help them to be "an enlightened mother and wife"; (27) when after some years it is apparent that she will not marry, Corinthians secretly takes a job as a maid, her only option in the early 1960s.

Milkman's entire adult life is marked by the years of racial unrest from the early 1950s to his death in the fall of 1963. The day when Milkman first asserts his autonomy, defies his father and learns why his father hates his mother is the day that Emmett Till, a young black man, is murdered in Mississippi for whistling at a white woman. Till's death, which historians frequently refer to as an example of the kind of violence which white people had earlier frequently inflicted on blacks with impunity, made national news and spurred considerable racial unrest. His boastful murderers were never even arrested. Milkman's awareness of the racial conflict in the country during these years seems to be limited to news of sensational murders and to the talk of the local barber shop. Yet "politics ... put him to sleep. He was bored. Everybody bored him ... racial problems ... were the most boring of all." (28) Morrison carefully dates the events that lead to Milkman's search for his heritage. He steals his grandfather's bones two days after the bombing of a Birmingham church killed four little black girls on 19th September 1963, a time which is sandwiched between two sets of events that most Americans who were old enough to remember will never forget: the famous civil rights march to Washington on 28th August 1963 and the death of John Kennedy three months later on 22nd November. The absence of any reference to the events in Washington in a book by a black writer can only be a case of conspicuous exclusion. By calling attention to the kinds of racial issues Milkman's friends are interested in - violent retribution and revenge - Morrison also suggests what did not concern them.

The march of Washington on 28th August, some three weeks before Milkman heads south, was a unique public demonstration in which harmony and peace reigned. The demonstration, attended by some half million Americans, was presided over by A. Philip Randolf, who had probably worked longer than anyone there for the cause of racial equality. The climax of the day was Martin Luther King's famous "I Have a Dream" speech. But there was an undercurrent of unrest on that day. John Lewis, the leader of SNCC, agreed at the last minute to suppress from his speech the militant language that was then dominating the goals of his organization in order to maintain for that day a facade of unity. (29) The march may have been the single most spectacular event to prepare Americans for change, but the many speeches of that day did not address a number of pressing problems such as black poverty, unemployment and living conditions in urban ghettos - the very problems that plague Guitar and the other self-appointed vigilantes.

Geography is also significant in Milkman's story. He grows up in an unnamed city in Michigan, the state which was to be the scene of the worst of the urban riots in the sixties. Guitar and the group with which he is allied represent the segment of the black community which was alienated from the civil rights movement and which was soon to fuel the fire of the urban riots.

If the August march on Washington marked the last truly successful demonstration of unity within the black community and between that community and its white allies, the death of John Kennedy three months later marked the beginning of a period of assassinations and violent upheavals as well as the beginning of the end of the hope that gradually diminished with each new eruption of violence. *Song of Solomon* is a complex book that explores the private lives of individuals in the context of complex social forces, historical events and the folklore of the black culture. To understand "the condition our condition is in" Morrison insists that we must try to see it whole.

That has been the function - if not the sole value - of black women's literature in the last fifteen years: to help us to see the condition of blacks, women, perhaps of modern capitalist society, whole, to both feel and think about what it means to be black and female in modern America. After the upheaval, the progress, and the violent aftermath of the civil rights movement, there has been not only betrayal of its achievements in Washington, but somehow an end to public action in the streets. The unfinished business of the civil rights movement cannot, it seems, be achieved by more marches - though demonstrations still serve to call attention to what remains to be done - and more civil rights legislation, but rather by something more effective, more sweeping, more permanent. During this pause, black women writers are preparing for what comes next by forcing their readers to look profoundly at contemporary life in the broadest possible context, to see "the condition our condition is in", which is of course where any change, for better or for worse, must begin.

FOOTNOTES

1. Roger Rosenblatt, *Black Fiction* (Cambridge, Mass.: Harvard University Press, 1974).
2. Terry Eagleton, *Myths of Power* (New York: Harper & Row, 1975), p.3.
3. Raymond Williams, *The English Novel from Dickens to Lawrence* (New York: Oxford University Press, 1970), p.11.
4. Williams, pp.9-10.
5. Williams, p.10.
6. C. Vann Woodward, *The Strange Career of Jim Crow*, 3rd ed. (New York: Oxford University Press, 1974), p.195.
7. Toni Cade [Bambara], ed., *The Black Woman* (New York: New American Library, 1970), pp.90-110.
8. Toni Morrison, *Song of Solomon* (New York: Knoph, 1978), p.222.
9. Bambara, p.8.
10. Bambara, p.10.
11. Bambara, p.12.
12. Bambara, p.9.
13. Amiri Baraka (Leroi Jones) and Amina Baraka, *An Anthology of African Women: Confirmations* (New York: Quill, 1983), p.401.
14. Claudia Tate, ed., *Black Women Writers at Work* (New York: Continuum, 1983), p.6.
15. Toni Morrison, *The Bluest Eye* (New York: Washington Square Press, 1970), p.9.
16. Morrison, *The Bluest Eye*, p.37.
17. Morrison, *The Bluest Eye*, p.37.
18. Woodward, p.135.
19. Morrison, *The Bluest Eye*, p.22.
20. Alice Walker, *The Third Life of Grange Copeland* (New York: Harcourt, Brace, Javonovich, 1970), p.157.
21. Morrison, *The Bluest Eye*, p.160.
22. Walker, *The Third Life*, p.209.
23. Toni Morrison, *Sula* (New York: New American Library, 1973), p.163.
24. Morrison, *Sula*, p.108.
25. Alice Walker, *Meridian* (New York: Washington Square Press, 1976), p.73.
26. Gloria T. Hull, Patricia Bell Scott and Barbara Smith, eds., *But Some of Us Are Brave: Black Women's Studies* (Old Westbury, N.Y.: The Feminist Press, 1982), p.214.
27. Toni Morrison, *Song of Solomon*, p.188.
28. Toni Morrison, *Song of Solomon*, p.107.
29. Milton Viorst, *Fire in the Streets: America in the 1960s* (New York: Simon and Schuster, 1979), p.299.

SOME BLACK WOMEN WRITERS: 1970-1983

Angelou, Maya, *I Know Why the Caged Bird Sings*, New York: Bantam, 1970. First of four volumes of autobiography.

Angelou, Maya, *Gather Together in My Name*, New York: Bantam, 1974.

Angelou, Maya, *Singin' and Swingin' and Gettin' Merry Like Christmas*, New York: Bantam, 1976.

Angelou, Maya, *The Heart of a Woman*, New York: Bantam, 1981.

Brooks, Gwendolyn, *Aloneness*, Highland Park, Mi.: Broadside, 1971. Poetry.

Brooks, Gwendolyn, *Beckonings*, Highland Park, Mi.: Broadside, 1975. Poetry.

Bambara, Toni Cade, ed., *The Black Woman*, New York: Doubleday, 1970. An anthology of writings by women.

Bambara, Toni Cade, *Gorilla, My Love*, 1972; rpt. New York: Vintage Books, 1981. Short stories.

Bambara, Toni Cade, *The Sea Birds are Still Alive*, 1977; rpt. New York: Vintage Books, 1982. Short stories.

Bambara, Toni Cade, *The Salt Eaters*, New York: Random House, 1980. Novel.

Baraka, Amiri (Leroi Jones) and Amini Baraka, *Confirmation: An Anthology of African American Women*, New York: Quill, 1983.

Jordon, June, *Civil Wars*, Boston: Beacon Press, 1981. An anthology of the author's essays written from 1964-1980, dealing with the complex interaction of a private life and the crises of those years.

Hooks, Bell, *Ain't I a Woman*, Boston: South End, 1982. Explores the relation of sexism to the history of black American women.

Hunter, Kristin, *The Survivors*, New York: Scribners, 1975. Novel.

Hunter, Kristin, *The Lakestown Rebellion*, New York: Scribners, 1978. Novel.

Hull, Gloria T., Patricia Bell Scott and Barbara Smith, eds., *But Some of Us Were Brave*, Old Westbury, New York: The Feminist Press, 1982. An introduction to black women's studies.

Lerner, Gerda, *Black Women in White America*, New York: Random House, 1972. A documentary history of black women in America from the early 1800s to the 1970s.

Marshall, Paule, *Browngirl, Brownstone*, 1959; rpt. Old Westbury, New York: The Feminist Press, 1981. Novel.

Marshall, Paule, *The Chosen Place, The Timeless People*, 1969. Novel. Out of print.

Marshall, Paule, *Praisesong for the Widow*, New York: Putnam, 1983. Novel.

Morrison, Toni, *The Bluest Eye*, 1970; rpt. New York: Washington Square, 1972. Novel.

Morrison, Toni, *Sula*, 1973; rpt. New York: New American Library, 1982. Novel.

Morrison, Toni, *Song of Solomon*, New York: Knopf, 1977. Novel. Winner of the 1978 National Book Critics Circle Award.

Morrison, Toni, *Tar Baby*, 1981; rpt. New York: New American Library, 1982. Novel.

Naylor, Gloria, *The Women of Brewster Place*, 1982; rpt. New York: Penguin, 1983. Novel. Winner of the 1983 American Book Award.

Shange, Ntozake, *For Colored Girls Who Have Considered Suicide When the Rainbow Is Enuf*, New York: Macmillan, 1976. A choreopoem.

Shange, Ntozake, *Sassafrass, Cypress & Indigo*, New York: St. Martin's, 1982. Novel.

Tate, Claudia, *Black Women Writers at Work*, New York: Continuum, 1983. A collection of interviews between the editor and fourteen black women.

Walker, Alice, *The Third Life of Grange Copeland*, New York: Harcourt, 1970. Novel.

Walker, Alice, *In Love and Trouble*, New York: Harcourt, 1974. Short stories.

Walker, Alice, *Meridian*, 1976; rpt. New York: Washington Square, 1977. Novel.

Walker, Alice, *The Color Purple*, New York: Harcourt, 1982. Novel. Winner of the 1983 Pulizer Prize.

Washington, Mary Helen, ed., *Black-Eyed Susans: Classic Stories by and about Black Women*, New York: Doubleday, 1975.

Washington, Mary Helen, ed., *Midnight Birds: Stories of Contemporary Black Women Writers*, New York: Doubleday, 1980.

OTHER BLACK WOMEN WRITERS ACTIVE SINCE 1968

Deveaux, Alexis. Poet, playwright, biographer.

Evans, Mari. Poet, musician.

Giovanni, Nikki. Poet.

Grimes, Nikki. Poet, essayist.

Jones, Gayle. Novelist, poet, playwright.

Lorde, Audre. Poet.

Meriwether, Louise. Novelist and author of children's books.

Sanchez, Sonia. Poet, playwright.

Walker, Margaret. Novelist, poet.

Williams, Sherley Ann. Poet, short story writer.

LITERATURE AND SOCIETY IN CRISIS

The Case of Israel

Nurith Gertz

In this lecture I shall address the complex relationships that exist between the sense of crisis in Israeli literature and in Israeli society. I will try to show how literature expressed fears and anxieties - even if only indirectly and unknowingly - which were not acknowledged by the Israeli public. I also intend to show that literature should not be regarded as all of one piece, and that even as the literature of the centre expressed a sense of power and optimism, a critical approach was expressed by marginal groups and authors. Finally, I shall try to point out parallels in Western society to the crises in Israeli society and their expression in Israeli literature.

In Amos Kenan's *Holocaust II*, written in part before, but completed after the Yom Kippur war, the refugees of a devastated Tel-Aviv live in an immense camp in a tropical region without sky, where there is no day or night, no bird or trees or nature, neither past nor future.

Yitzhak Ben-Ner's story "After the Rain" (1977), also describes Tel-Aviv after destruction - a lawless city where roaming street gangs rule, while frightened solitary people wander through the streets because they are afraid to stay at home, for there, too, fear lurks. All hope for a sudden miracle - the discovery of oil in the desert, a diplomatic breakthrough with China - anything to end the nightmare, to bathe them in a light that will suddenly beam on them all.

A. B. Yehoshua's novel *The Novel* (1977) is not about destruction. It concerns a young Israeli garage owner who has lost his capacity to function in a normal human way: Arabs work for him, others go to war for him, he needs someone to love his wife for him, someone to dream for him, to hope for him, while the real dreams in the story are those of an Arab boy who works in his garage.

Amos Oz's last story, "The Hill of Evil Counsel" (1976), does not contain a terrifying apocalyptic vision either, but it does portray the destruction of a family in Jerusalem prior to statehood in 1948. The account of this family's disintegration is also a description of the shattering of dreams about the establishment of the state, even before these began to be realized.

From the looks of it, it appears that Israeli literature is reflecting the fear of a new holocaust, or another trauma more devastating than the Yom Kippur war. What is the source of this sense of imminent disaster?

The ready explanation is that it was indeed the Yom Kippur war that shocked the Israeli consciousness out of its sense of inviolability. But this does not apply to the literary consciousness (world vision in Goldmann's terms), for in the six-year period between the last two wars, and even previously, when morale was at its peak, Israeli literature constantly dwelt on terror and destruction.

Until recent years this theme was either kept below the surface, treated metaphorically, or relegated to sub-plots. When it did appear undisguised, it was not recognized by critics or readers.

What could be clearer or more explicit than the story of the Israeli student who helps an Arab watchman set fire to a young forest in order to discover beneath it the ruins of a destroyed village ("Facing the Forests" by A. B. Yehoshua, 1965)? Or the story of a strange old man who goes from kibbutz to kibbutz warning the Jews of the Russian threat because he fears that the State of Israel stands on too flimsy foundations, like a cardboard stage set, surrounded by hostile forces ("Late Love" by Amos Oz, 1971)? Could there be a clearer socio-political measure than that of an ageing Bible teacher who, after the death of his soldier son, awakens to hopes for renewal, by discovering his son's faiths and beliefs as a source of meaning for his own existence?

These and other stories were seen by critics and readers to be not political but psychological studies in political settings. (The sources are critical articles and readers' letters sent to the authors.) When the politics could not be attributed to the psychology of the heroes the stories were criticized for resembling reality too closely.

In fact, then, it is precisely when Israel was strongest that its literature dealt with the fears of the persecuted Jew still without refuge, even in his homeland - either because past destruction and disaster must inevitably be repeated, or because in Israel past and future belong not to the Jew but to the Arab, or because 'this evil land' and its inhabitants, the jackals and the Arabs, are hostile to the Jews, or because the threat of war is ever present.

Few stories deal with these things explicitly, they only allude to them. In the early sixties Israeli literature began to evince two new traits: an attempt to avoid political involvement and the use of a symbolic allegorical style. This writing was influenced by Kafka and Agnon and came as a reaction to the political-social writing of the previous authors.

Nevertheless, writers of those years, most of whom were involved in Israel's political life (taking leftist positions), did not avoid grappling with national and social problems. In most cases their social meanings are conveyed by way of symbolic structures, images, allegory or by a world-view realized in personal situations weighted with social significance (drawing on leftist Zionist ideology). According to the world vision of those years all the trans-individual values with which the hero seeks to link up (another person, nature, divine mystical forces which govern the world arbitrarily, etc.) cán in fact be attained, but only through the destruction of both himself and his object. This formula is used in the story of a solitary, forsaken and estranged hero who tries (or, more accurately, is pushed, for these heroes are invariably passive) to establish contact with a woman, or man, or nature or mystical forces. As the plot progresses towards the moment of contact or fulfillment, it becomes apparent (more to the reader than to the hero) that the world with which the hero is trying to establish contact is a deformed one, that the hero himself is either warped or lacks the moral fibre to take a stand. Thus, the moment of attaining the goal is one of unleashed passion, destruction and disaster, in which the hero destroys either himself, the other or both. It is for this reason that the myth evoked by this writing is the sacrifice of Isaac. In modern dress this myth takes the form of the sacrifice or destruction of the sons' lives for the parents' dubious goals.

This structure is found in its purest form still without a clear political signification in the early stories of those writers. A good example is a story by A. B. Yehoshua, "Night Convoy to Yatir" (1959). It tells of an isolated mountain village whose inhabitants decide to establish contact with the world by derailing an express train that speeds past them twice a day. The insane decision is reached and acted upon without objection; neither from the station-master, who is likened to God, nor the hero who, although he feels that the act is evil, is attracted to the woman who proposed it. The train is derailed, by torchlight and amidst the screams of the dying and wounded the village reaches a moment of true spiritual elevation, the villagers achieve human contact and the hero lies with his love 'on the twisted rocky ground of a beloved country'.

In the early sixties the political content of this type of writing is not yet apparent. The problems are human and personal but even then they are laced with political meanings that will become more dominant later. The quest is for human contact, or contact with nature; symbolic allusions and secondary plots give this quest a national dimension, in which fulfillment can only be achieved through social destruction, i.e. war.

The elements of this world vision were taken from Western, mainly existential, literature, in order to express a similar historical situation, though in Hebrew literature they received significant new twists. Thus, for example, the futility of trying to make contact with an indifferent and alien nature here assumes national significance: nature is alien to a people who have not managed to become part of an alien land. Life appears to be a series of unrelated moments, the meaningless extension of a perpetual present, not only because of 'the dark wind blowing from the future' (in the language of Camus' *The Stranger*), but also because according to these writers past and future in Israel do not belong to them. The heroes move through their world alone and detached from each other not only because "one must die alone" but because there is no hope of contact between people who lack a common social past; they have no way of building a common future. The terror is not only the existential one of 'having been thrown into the world', but of finding oneself in a strange, rejecting land.

On the other hand, while the existentialist hero, on which the Israeli hero is based, discovers the possibility of union with nature through total renunciation and solitude (*The Stranger*), or through a common but hopeless social struggle (*The Plague*), the Israeli literary hero, influenced by Zionism's long and bitter struggle, achieves the longed-for union in destruction and war.

A vivid example of this mixture of existential and national themes, of social-political and personal-human situations, is Amos Kenan's *Holocaust II*.

The action is set in a camp, after the destruction of the world. This setting is described in existential terms, in Israeli political terms and in universal social terms. For example, there is a daily execution in the camp. But since neither the condemned man nor his friends know who the victim will be, every day may be one's last. As the hero puts it: "The truth is that I know that every minute is the last minute of my life. That's a strong physical feeling". This is the definition of an existential situation, in this case in a political-social setting: national holocaust. Moreover, since every moment is the final one, time is Bergsonian - a series of present moments without past or future. There are no hopes in the camp, but memory too is confounded. The hero repeatedly tries to recall the beautiful Tel-Aviv he knew, but his recollections give way to memories of death and destruction. He tries to remember the golden sands but instead recalls the zealots' last stand at Massada. He wants to picture a camel caravan but remembers the Ninth of Av (the day of the destruction of the Temple in Jerusalem) and the Spanish Inquisition and Expulsion. Where there is no hope, there is no memory, but that of death. The assumption is familiar although here a Jewish political variant has been added. The death of the individual represents national destruction and also worldwide destruction, for the Israeli holocaust is but part of a world ecological holocaust.

There is no escape through time or space. Dreams of distant, exotic places become thoughts of Massada; memories of pine forests, blue skies and snow-covered landscapes lead to visions of the transports to the death camps. It is almost like the Midas myth twisted so that everything turns not to gold but to blood, war and death. Even the moment of love becomes the moment of execution: a shapely woman opening a door, slipping off a shoe or a silk stocking, is transformed into a naked woman taking her last steps towards the extermination chamber. It is hardly surprising, then, that the intimate dialogue of a tryst is placed in the context of death. For example, the hero meets a pretty girl and asks her, "Is this your first time?" The conversation ends with her angry reply: "You men are all the same". The conversation is not about love but about execution, which this young woman has carried out.

In other words, the concentration camp is a focus of various themes: the human condition, Israel's present and future political reality, and the world political situation. To bind them together, the author employs a mixture of styles: journalistic, to describe Israeli life in almost documentary fashion; poetic, to add metaphorical meaning to the reportage; and fantastic, to heighten the imaginary reality of the story. This imaginary reality is itself composed of several imaginations: that of the author, who envisions the concentration camp of the future and that of the heroes, who envision their own enchanted worlds - two people who dreamed of building a new world, a magician who builds a golden city for children in the forest filled with dwarfs and fairies, people who build a kibbutz with ploughed fields and thick woods. The author apprehends these dreams at the moment of their collapse. The imagined kibbutz is slowly sinking into the mud, the two who dreamed of a new world become maimed, the magician's forest is surrounded by tanks and the procession of fairies, children, princes and gnomes begins to march towards death. The combination of poetic and journalistic prose tries to convey both a specific Israeli reality and its general universal significance as well as the connection between present and future and between legend and dreams, clashing with reality and shattering it.

Other authors achieve this blending of themes by attaching diverse meanings to metaphorical situations. Thus, the hero of A. B. Yehoshua's "Facing the Forests" who is sent to guard a national forest, has his private dreams of human warmth and light. These dreams are reflected in his attraction to fire. When he discovers that beneath the young forest are the ruins of an Arab village, the fire acquires a social meaning: the need to set the forest ablaze in order to discover the true past buried beneath it.

Israeli writing reflects Western literary trends in another way. The change it has undergone within two generations corresponds to developments in Western literature since the nineteenth century. When this transformation takes place over a relatively short time, as in Israel, the social factors that have influenced it are fairly easy to trace.

Israeli writers in the late forties and early fifties were influenced primarily by socialist realism and in their own way emulated American action literature of the twenties. Their heroes are not isolated individuals but members of society - usually a kibbutz - and they believe with their fellows in a common social national purpose. The dilemma is how to integrate two ideals - collective fulfilment (in society, work, war) and personal fulfillment (in artistic creation, love, the family). These two goals sometimes clash and the hero is often compelled to sacrifice his individual world for society, for the collective. But even such sacrifice represents a correct value choice, if only partially.

The world vision in these stories is homologous to that of the leftist Zionist parties within which these authors were active. (In the fifties leftist parties were revolutionary and fought for establishing a socialist society.)

An example of this is Moshe Shamir's story "Until Dawn" (1952). The hero, who is in charge of giving out work assignments on his kibbutz, is so totally immersed in this task that he forgets himself and his family. His wife leaves the kibbutz because it does not give her the freedom to find artistic fulfillment by teaching piano to the kibbutz children - and because her family life is crumbling under the burden of work. After some serious introspection the hero sees his error and goes to the city to regain his wife.

Other stories of this period deal with external not internal conflict, in which the enemy comes from without. The hero of these stories is a combination of Wild West courage and sabra doggedness. The plot formula is standard: a tremendous challenge is presented, which the hero meets with valour and resourcefulness. The threat to the kibbutz, the woman, the nation, is averted.

The world-view that emerges from these stories is homologous to that of the group to which those writers belonged, namely that the social Zionist dream, and perhaps all other dreams, can be realized by war, struggle and work. Ten years were to elapse before major Israeli authors considered the price paid for the fulfillment of this dream.

The poetics of this literature matches its world-view and sets it apart from the poetics of later writers. In these stories, the narrator is always reliable, and he is always in harmony with his hero; his attitudes are stated clearly and explicitly and always match his hero's values. The hero believes in the narrator's and the work's values and acts to realize them. At most, he is sidetracked by internal conflicts or by external obstacles placed in his path; but then too the values have a clear existence in the work, whether in his consciousness or in that of other characters. In *He Walked in the Fields*, Uri, the firstborn son of the kibbutz, knows that he can fulfill himself in love, in building a family, in work on the kibbutz, and if necessary in war. Only because of a weakness of which he is aware, and troubled by the stigma of his parents' failings (his father volunteers for the British army and his mother has an affair with another man), he is incapable of forming a loving relationship with a woman and indirectly this leads to his death in a military training exercise. Uri erred and failed. The work ethic prevails, personified by the parents who are finally reconciled, both with each other and with the kibbutz.

A hero and narrator of this sort is inconceivable to the next generation of writers. In their stories the narrators prevaricate to a degree that leaves the reader unsure where reality ends and distortion begins, and what, if any, is the moral position - either of the narrator, the author, or his characters. In Amos Oz's *My Michael* (1968), the heroine, who narrates her story, dreams of romantic love in faraway places, with strange men, but she does not know what love is. For her, love means domination, violence and hatred. This has been her experience in the past, and is the subject of her present fantasies, which include a pair of Arab twins, her childhood playmates. It governs her relations with her husband, a young neighbour and others. But there is no judging her for blocking out a reality which is unrelentingly miserable, empty and bourgeois, killing all dreams. There is no figure in the work who represents a sane alternative.

Since the values of the previous generation are clear and easily translated into action, the plot in these stories develops with evident causality. The hero faces problems, takes action to solve them, successfully or not, which accordingly creates a new set of problems, and so on. Such a pattern cannot occur in the following generation, where the stories are merely a succession of eruptions of inner passion and external disaster. The passive hero understands neither himself nor his world, and is propelled by fatal external forces and uncontrollable inner ones. The plot, therefore, is not constructed as a series of causal events but of recurrent outbursts of violence until the final eruption, at the climax of the narrative, or as an unlikely devolution of a destructive idea nearing realization.

Even the landscape takes on an altogether different aspect in the two generations. In the earlier generation it is beloved and familiar, the hero feels at home in it and the narrator describes it in colourful detail. In the later generation, the landscape becomes ominous, filled with threatening mountains where jackals, Arabs and other untamed forces lurk. Not surprisingly, this landscape is bare of concrete detail, serving primarily as a metaphor for savage forces operating beyond it.

The generation that fought to end the British mandate and to build a socialist society, created a literature in which the protagonist maintains a tie with the world. This tie is severed in the subsequent generation, when confidence in Zionist values and their fulfillment are in question.

It would seem that a complete reversal of world-view and literary poetics occurred over the last two generations. In fact, however, signs of this reversal could already be discerned in the earlier generation.

The outstanding example of this is a writer called S. Yizhar. Yizhar's hero is not the valiant sabra who plants himself firmly in the landscape of his homeland. On the contrary, his is passive, out of place in the toiling or fighting group (although he generally accepts its values). Unlike the heroes of the other writers of his generation, the medium of this type of hero is not action but the lyrical interior monologue. The accepted hero of that generation, the dauntless fighter, is here a secondary figure. He is often described with mocking disdain by the narrating hero, who wants to be part of the group, to be active like the others but whose longings for love, nature, and home set him apart. The author's beliefs are expressed in the contemporary structure: the struggle between two sets of values - the public-collective and the private-personal. But there is one small difference: both the hero and the narrator rather than feeling any ties with the values of the real world, long for contact with a strange land, of open spaces and undisturbed nature. They feel estranged from their group. Yizhar's two political stories, "Hirbet Hiz'ah" and "The Prisoner", sparked countless debates in intellectual and non-intellectual circles alike. "Hirbet Hiz'ah" (1949) describes one day at the end of the war when the narrating hero and his fellows are ordered to burn and blow up an Arab village and to expel its inhabitants. Of the two groups - the tough Israeli soldiers inured to the suffering of the Arabs, and the victims who do not comprehend the cruel fate that has suddenly been thrust on them - the narrator identifies with the latter. For him it is the Arabs, not his own peers, who have the values on which he was nurtured.

The progress of Israeli literature of the sixties is actually the story of the consequences of "Hirbet Hiz'ah". There, in Yizhar's village, those who fought the War of Independence severed all meaningful ties with essential values. The open spaces of this country, the eternal cycle of sowing and harvest, memories of a meaningful historical past, the biblical God who commands his prophets to foretell comfort or destruction, the traditional Jewish values of justice and morality - all these and not only the narrator's sympathy, pass over to the expelled Arab villagers. At the end of the story the narrator goes searching among the assembled Arabs:

> I passed among them all, among those crying aloud and those gnashing their teeth in silence, regarding themselves and their possessions, among those fighting their fate and those submitting to it mutely, among those shamed by themselves and their disgrace, and among those already making plans to get by somehow. Among those weeping over fields that will be laid waste and among those silenced by weariness, gnawed at by hunger and fright. I wanted to find out whether among all these there wasn't also one somber and blazing Jeremiah, forging a rage here within his heart, calling in a choked voice to an old God from the waggons of exile ...

Small wonder, then, that the Israeli writer of the next generation wakes up on the morning after "Hirbet Hiz'ah" to discover that lo and behold everything that matters has moved to the other side: history, space, nature, meaningful time, social morality and divine force - all are now in the mountains, with the Arabs and the jackals, waiting for revenge.

However, while Yizhar's hero lives in the world of the social Zionist values and his writing accords with the contemporary style, an anti-establishment political group known as Cana'anites was using an altogether different type of writing (with modernistic forms) to give expression to a marginal and oppositional vision of the world.

The central vehicle of this literature is parody, attacking the stereotypes of the period by presenting the exploits, the heroes, the poems and the songs of that generation in a ridiculous light.

For example, in a story by Eitan Notev, "The Battle of Fort Williams" (1950), a skirmish that had actually taken place in the War of Independence is compared to all the great heroic battles in which the hero participated as a child. "From the Jewish revolt against the Romans to Genghis Khan's invasion of Europe, from the Hundred-Year War to the Chmielnicki uprising, from the conquest of the Wild West to the war between the North and the South". Clearly, when compared to all these historic battles the skirmish in the War of Independence is minor and paltry and even the hero's possible death in this war is only an unnecessary addition to his most staggering defeat by "more serious" enemies: the Indians.

This story was in advance of his generation in that for the first time it shattered the illusion of literary reality. This reality, which was so secure among Notev's contemporaries, here becomes a mere game, a fantasy. It was before its time also in its parodic treatment of the invincible Israeli hero.

Another way this marginal group challenged accepted literary conventions was by breaking chronological causal time relations. In contrast to the narrative of the contemporary writers in which past actions influence the present, and present actions determine the future, the writing of the Cana'anite group plays arbitrarily with time. Amos Kenan's story, "His Big Brother" (1950), is a short monologue about a big brother who has left for distant places with a rifle over his shoulder. The monologue confounds three temporalities until it becomes unclear whether the big brother really existed, whether he exists now or whether he is tomorrow's daydream. This amalgamation of times breaks the reality of which the other writers of this generation were so confident.

In this regard the differences between the three types of writing are clear enough. The writers of the first generation begin their stories in the heart of the action. The hero is presented to us in the present. Immediately thereafter the narrative goes back in time and presents the problem he will confront. Once that is done the hero begins to grapple with the problem and sets out to solve it. The following generation shatters this kind of plot structure and employs an assemblage of analogous situations or a circular plot in which the beginning is the end and everything that the hero does merely brings him back to his point of departure or to destruction. The Cana'anite authors break time - and plot - structures (as well as the figure of the hero) much more radically. In their stories, the end comes before the beginning. The shattering of times and plots matches the world vision of these stories, in which the great hope and dream were not distorted in reality (like in the stories of their predecessors) but were transformed while they were still only a dream. Behind this is the political vision of marginal authors who fought in the War of Independence, but already then viewed events with a sharply critical eye. In the subsequent generation, in the sixties and the seventies, social criticism became a feature of the literature of the centre. This literature expresses the feeling that the Zionist dream has been realized in a distorted and destructive way. As this literature becomes more political and realistic, this is revealed more clearly. The protagonists set out towards a lofty goal, to their Jerusalem, and on the way the goal is perverted, their humaneness thwarted, their inner world laid waste and the external world destroyed (Amos Oz, "Until Death"). They remain alone, beneath empty silent skies.

Since Pascal, of course, the sky has been silent for all mankind, Israelis and non-Israelis alike. But in Israeli literature not only are the skies silent and empty, they also threaten to collapse on us and in so doing to destroy all earthly existence. Are these only Israeli skies, or literary skies, or is it the objective sky? That we'll know when the time comes, if we are still around.

SELECTED BIBLIOGRAPHY

Althusser, Louis, 1971, *Lenin and Philosophy and other Essays* (London: New Left Books).

Barthes, Roland, 1953, *Le dégre zéro de l'écriture* (Paris: Edition du Seuil).

Bennett, Tony, 1979, *Formalism and Marxism* (London: Methuen).

Eagleton, T., 1976, *Criticism and Ideology* (London: New Left Books).

Even-Zohar, Itamar, 1978, *Papers in Historical Poetics* (Tel-Aviv: Tel-Aviv University).

Goldmann, Lucien, 1966, *Pour une sociologie du roman* (Paris: Gallimard).

Kristeva, Julia, 1976, *Le texte du roman* (Paris: Mouton).

Lotman, Yury, 1977, "The Dynamic Model of a Semiotic System", *Semiotica* 21, 314, 193-210.

Lukács, Georges, 1963 [1920], *La théorie du roman* (Paris: Editions Gonthier).

Macherey, P., 1978, *A Theory of Literary Production* (London: Routledge & Kegan Paul).

Voloshinov, V. N., 1977, *Le Marxisme et la philosophie du langage* (Paris: Les Editions de Minuit).

CRISIS, INSTITUTIONS AND THE UNCONSCIOUS

David Punter

1. Introductory

This year the Essex Conference committee, in the pre-conference literature, made a distinction between 'papers' and 'workshops'. I designed a workshop under the above title, and this is therefore a report on a small fragment of educational experience rather than a formal paper; and it is divided into various different sections because various different things took place.

I began the workshop by giving a brief account of what the structure was to be, and of the factors I had tried to take into account in designing it. Or rather, in re-designing it; because one of the most significant factors was that I had found myself, during the conference, changing my mind about what would be most useful in the light of proceedings thus far. Principally, it seemed to me that something had come adrift between text and subtext: between the overall title of the conference series ('Sociology of Literature') and the immediate title of this conference ('Confronting the Crisis'). Most of the work which was going on at the conference, it seemed to me, had indeed to do with confronting the crisis, or rather, with confronting *a* crisis; but there appeared to be an unwillingness to examine or value the specificity of literary writing within the constellation of textuality. And, of course, this can be read as symptomatic of difficulties in the contemporary plight of literary academics, and of the problem of 'centring' our subject in a time of accelerating anti-culturalism and enforced discriminatory financial stringency.

It also seemed to me that there was a difficulty in the conference about identifying what the crisis was. Were we dealing in national or international economic and political movements; or in the reduction of educational provision at local or national levels; or in personal or group feelings of despair, tedium or excitement as responses to environing factors? Or, of course, all of those things; but the problem might still be one of experiential identification, of discovering for ourselves, as radical literary academics, some purchase on the slow slide into oblivion.

I said, then, that I started from these problems; and from the premise that the most valuable kind of workshop might be one which, in however faulty and fleeting a way, attempted to mobilise areas of feeling and response which are normally suppressed in everyday academe. In other words, that we might discover something about the crisis in relation to ourselves by attending to some of the fantasies about crisis which are actually around. My attempt in the workshop would be to move into these areas via some ways of imagining the future; my hypothesis was that by moving ourselves into the hoped or feared future, we might get hold of some of the ways in which we are imminently expecting change, whether or not these ways accord with what we might theoretically expect from a late stage of capitalism.

I then outlined the structure of the workshop. I would begin by in various ways trying to provide some examples of the imagining of the future from literary and filmic texts. (1) My demonstration and analysis of these texts is given here as Sections 2-5. I would then try to make a connection between these texts and the possibilities for experiential work on the future (Section 6). I would then invite the members to work together in terms of certain specific small-scale exercises in writing and reflection (here described in Section 7).

Section 8 of this report gives an account of the actual work which was produced under these conditions; and Section 9 offers some of my own reflections on what the overall process might have been saying about crisis, institutions and the unconscious. These last, of course, are highly personal; but then, the evasion of the personal seems to me to be precisely one of the problems which we face. As a theoretical aside, I would say that the theory of the construction of the subject is, like most powerful insights, liable to ideological abuse; and if it entails an insistence that, in fact, we are not creatures with choice, then it seems to me that it plays entirely into the hands of that political will which is, after all, trying precisely to persuade us that there are no alternatives.

2. Invisible Cities

In Calvino's text, Kublai Khan ceases to be concerned with the veracity of Marco Polo's reports on distant cities, and becomes instead fascinated by cities of the imagination. One of the cities which Marco Polo thus offers him is called Thekla.

> Those who arrive at Thekla can see little of the city, beyond the plank fences, the sackcloth screens, the scaffolding, the metal armatures, the wooden catwalks hanging from ropes or supported by saw-horses, the ladders, the trestles. If you ask, 'Why is Thekla's construction taking such a long time?' the inhabitants continue hoisting sacks, lowering leaded strings, moving long brushes up and down, as they answer, 'So that its destruction cannot begin'. And if asked whether they fear that, once the scaffolding is removed, the city may begin to crumble and fall to pieces, they add hastily, in a whisper, 'Not only the city'.
>
> If, dissatisfied with the answer, someone puts his eye to a crack in the fence, he sees cranes pulling up other cranes, scaffolding that embraces other scaffolding, beams that prop up other beams. 'What meaning does your construction have?' he asks. 'What is the aim of a city under construction unless it is a city? Where is the plan you are following, the blueprint?'
>
> 'We will show it to you as soon as the working day is over; we cannot interrupt our work now', they answer.
>
> Work stops at sunset. Darkness falls over the building site. The sky is filled with stars. 'There is the blueprint', they say. (2)

This is not a text of the future; but it defines a set of problems about the nature of 'future', the concept of tense, the myths of teleology and origin. It also images the operations of the armoured ego, continuing from Blake's analysis of Urizenic labour, his visionary connection between the inner and outer forms of industry. It thus describes the 'site' of fantasy, the drive towards interpretation and representation;

in redefining 'meaning' as 'plan', it moves us towards the articulation
of the future onto the gaps in the present, and opens onto a field of
writing.

3. The Balloon

In Barthelme's story, a huge balloon settles over the city, and
becomes the floating objective correlative which begins to provide fragmented fantasy answers to Calvino's implicit question about meaning.

> The private character of these wishes, of their origins,
> deeply buried and unknown, was such that they were not much
> spoken of; yet there is evidence that they were widespread.
> It was also argued that what was important was what you felt
> when you stood under the balloon; some people claimed that
> they felt sheltered, warmed, as never before, while enemies
> of the balloon felt, or reported feeling, constrained, a
> 'heavy' feeling.

Thus the oldest of the 'inventions' returns, that scientific development
which in the West first provoked the extension of a myriad lines into
the future. (3) In its original incarnations, the balloon was instant
communication, harbinger of a fully global economy, transcender of social
division, pathway to the stars: by its form the intricate patterns of
controlled space were relativised and negated, from its balcony the
track of empires could be followed and knowledge could be totalised and
placed in the hands of that cadre who were later to become Wells' beneficent aviators. (4) But here, the transformation of space is itself
transformed into a discourse about projection and fantasy: 'the balloon,
I said, is a spontaneous autobiographical disclosure, having to do with
the unease I felt at your absence, and with sexual deprivation ...'.
Yet this attempted closure is not presented as absolute; in the detail
of the reactions to the balloon we can trace the lineaments of a paranoiac subjectivity, and of a form of surveillance so close that its contours follow exactly the geography of the 'lower' world. 'Each intersection was crucial, meeting of balloon and building, meeting of balloon
and man, meeting of balloon and balloon', because those numerous meetings
reflect the shapes of acceptance and rejection, the contortions to be
adopted by the body in response to an overarching knowledge which itself
repels investigation: 'it was suggested that what was admired about the
balloon was finally this: that it was not limited, or defined'.

The trajectory of the narrative is from agency, through a common
experience of subjection, to a fantasised agency offered merely as provisional, a hypothesis about relatedness. Thus the history of the
encounter between balloon and city replicates the history of a more
massive encounter with power: from the happy consciousness, for which the
agencies of the state are securely within human control, through the
deflating mystery of a seepage of power from individual to apparatus,
into that realm where reality-testing is abandoned and we lay ironic
claim to a power and knowledge from which we are, in fact, irrevocably
alienated. And within this matrix is situated the whole complex of discourses of desire, as the population of the city offers its various
attempts at accommodation with an inexplicable dominance: 'one man might
consider that the balloon had to do with the notion "sullied", as in the
sentence, "The big balloon sullied the otherwise clear and radiant
Manhattan sky" ... Another man might say, "Without the example of ---,
it is doubtful that --- would exist today in its present form"'. What is
clear throughout this profusion of 'exempla' is that the genesis of these
discourses is bound at root to an accommodation with power: that without

the context of a suddenly mirrored world, syntax could not emerge, for syntax is a way of shaping the shapeless, of rendering the indeterminate outline of the balloon in some way conformable with the shapes of the known city beneath.

Thus the desire is not to remove domination but to adjust our perception so that it becomes acceptable, which involves a multiplication of invented functions and uses for the balloon, and simultaneously a multiplication of the points at which the balloon (power) touches the regular shapes of life:

> Once knowledge can be analysed in terms of region, domain, implantation, displacement, transposition, one is able to capture the process by which knowledge functions as a form of power and disseminates the effects of power. There is an administration of knowledge, a politics of knowledge, relations of power which pass via knowledge and which, if one tries to transcribe them, lead one to consider forms of domination designated by such notions as field, region and territory. And the politico-strategic term is an indication of how the military and the administration actually come to inscribe themselves both on a material soil and within forms of discourse. (5)

Just so each of the formations of knowledge deployed by the city's population is bound up with a deepening capitulation in the balloon's unjustifiable and ineffable power: the very shapes of knowledge conform to the interpretations which the properties of the balloon allow. And even the form of Foucault's prose is mirrored in the discourse of the story:

> The upper surface was so structured that a 'landscape' was presented, small valleys as well as slight knolls, or mounds ... Sometimes a bulge, blister, or sub-section would carry all the way east to the river on its own initiative, in the manner of an army's movements on a map, as seen in a headquarters remote from the fighting.

What is proffered is a doubling back of the techniques of surveillance: as the balloon shapes itself to the terrain, so we assume for ourselves the function of producing meaning from its random movements; we come to know it under the impulse of the fear that it might be getting to know *us*, and accommodate our lives to the tightening interface between the material of the city and the group fantasies and myths which are shown performing ideological operations on the balloon's surface.

It is barely the case, of course, that in 'The Balloon' we are confronted with a discourse of the future; or rather, here the invention of the future is telescoped into the single arbitrary event which tests out as in a laboratory the tracks of knowledge along which we shall seek to understand the new world, and thus the processes by which, as with all modes of knowledge, we shall seek to suck the balloon back into ourselves, to reabsorb the threatening presence and to succumb to the illusion that the threat of superior power is merely the materialisation of an intelligible desire. On this surface, marked by a 'deliberate lack of finish', our strategies for coping with the unexpected can be mapped with the precision of a diorama: the power of the balloon can be illusorily dissipated by the apparent allowing of a plurality of interpretations which ends by asserting that none of these accounts has any *specific* validity; that all our imaginings and plans are only a sequence of attempts to give shape to a power which is, in any case, irreducibly *there*.

4. Concrete Island

>   Near the intersection of three giant motorways a speeding
>   Jaguar has a tyre blow-out. As a result Maitland, the
>   driver, finds himself completely marooned on a patch of
>   wasteland, an island in a sea of hostile tarmac and high-
>   speed metal. Here he must learn to survive with minimal
>   resources, fighting for them with the island's other
>   human denizens ... (6)

On Ballard's concrete island, the promise of global knowledge proffered
by the balloon is reversed, and the ego ('Maitland' encapsulates the
lost 'I') is hemmed in by a desolate pubic triangle. He has to convert
the rusted exhaust pipes and tangled metal into use-value, but this
happens only dreamily: in fact, nothing on the island is really any use,
for the subject has ceased to be able to think of any uses to which
things might be put. There is no knowledge, and in the end the experience of constant and surrounding surveillance is itself converted into
comfort: the endlessly speeding cars at least guarantee an end to
striving, a closure of the task of discovery.

>   As well as this new-found physical confidence, Maitland
>   noticed a mood of quiet exultation coming over him. He
>   lay calmly in the doorway of his pavilion, realising that
>   he was truly alone on the island. He would stay there
>   until he could escape by his own efforts. Maitland tore
>   away the remains of his ragged shirt, and lay bare-chested
>   in the warm air, the bright sunlight picking out the
>   sticks of his ribs. In some ways the task he had set
>   himself was meaningless. Already he felt no real need to
>   leave the island, and this alone confirmed that he had
>   established his dominion over it. (7)

Concrete Island continues from the ending of 'The Balloon', after the
series of attempts at the production of meaning from unyielding surfaces
had been shown to fail. 'Pavilioned in splendour', the ego can now abandon its shaping task: the only shape that matters is already given, and
its edges cannot be changed. At the end, a police car goes by, searching,
but Maitland is no longer interested: he 'thought of Catherine and his
son. He would be seeing them soon. When he had eaten it would be time
to rest, and to plan his escape from the island', (8) but we know that
this state of preparation will be perpetual, an endless recitation of a
notion of movement and progress that no longer has any grasp on the
Real.

Out there in the wild and the dark, Maitland does not grow savage,
for he experiences no real opposition, only a continuous adjustment and
scaling down of needs. He presages a wider decline: if he is to see his
wife and son, it will be when they, and the rest of the species, 'join'
him in parallel isolations, retreat into the spaces left between the
lines of communication. The points of intersection between balloon and
world are no longer accessible, but have paradoxically frozen into the
shapes of speed, the patterns left by moving lights. It no longer
matters to Maitland who or what is inside the cars: the species has
divided into those who merely inhabit their machines, and those for whom
machinery has become rubbish, a set of hieroglyphs which cannot be
deciphered.

>   He gave up, unable to decipher his own writing. The grass
>   swayed reassuringly, beckoning this fever-wracked scarecrow
>   into its interior. The blades swirled around him, opening

a dozen pathways, each of which would carry him to some
paradisial arbour. Knowing that unless he reached the
shelter of the Jaguar he would not survive the night,
Maitland set his course for the breaker's yard, but
after a few minutes he followed the grass passively as
it wove its spiral patterns around him. (9)

In this future, the grass provides a continuous production and erasure
of meaning, a maze which really requires no interpreting effort since
its patterns do not endure. There is a mirroring of 'joining and
parting lines': (10) the unassailable fixity of the motorways and the
incomprehensible motion of the grass.

As readers, we experience first a frustration at the apparent
sparseness of Maitland's attempts at escape, his difference from Crusoe;
we are then brought to realise, as he is, that what bounds the deserted
space is not fact but wish, that the island provides the perfect
setting in which to evade competitive demands and to share in a different
kind of struggle, a struggle of adjustment. The power of escape becomes
seen instead as a threatened return to the powerlessness of societal
membership: only here at the still point can the subject experience real
diversity, conjure unreal Others from the shadows, form the waving
shapes into satisfactory adjuvants to the narrative of the heroic self.
There is nothing further to be known by gazing outwards, for all the
cars are the same: like sub-atomic particles, even their existence can
only be inferred by the continuous tensed pattern they describe. Instead,
we are brought to gaze in, into the 'arbours', although it is not that
Maitland has any faith in an ability to make this dross and refuse into
the habitable environment of earlier economic fantasies. He becomes
instead the advance guard of passivity, and runs out of words (ceases to
conjure up addressees).

The concrete island symbolises a renunciation of the impulse
towards the ideal society, and replaces it with a wish for abdication,
yet in the act of that abdication the self reasserts a useless sovereignty, free from all surveillance but free also from location in discourse. Stuffed back into the womb, Maitland represents an end to dif-
ferentiation, and thus himself mirrors the identical passing cars; a
Genet of the machine, he weaves a texture for the world out of himself,
covers the walls of his prison with images, yet these images are not of
opposition and escape but of capitulation. His happiness comes to consist not in setting himself against the universal condition, but in
seeing the universal condition contained in miniature within himself.

5. Close Encounters of the Third Kind

The shape of the film is a trajectory from panic caused by technological overload, through an attempt to find salvation through the primitive and the excremental, to a ritual purification. Visually: from
the jagged and diagonal images of air traffic control, through the dirt
and rough edges of mountain-building, to the order and symmetry of the
final controlled and built encounter. In sound: from the interplay of
jerry-built jargon, through obsessional monologue, to the simplicity of
melody. Thus what is apparently demonstrated is a putting away of the
things of childhood and an achievement of maturity for the species.

But something darker is present in silhouette against this clearing
sky. The fantasised future species, for instance, is one from which
reproduction appears to be exiled, the home of a kind of gender apartheid.
The male 'spirit of adventure' is validated and transformed into an
experience of new worlds, while the female condemns herself to mundanity

several times over: the wife is left behind in the male race for approval from 'parental' aliens, and the female fellow-initiate who replaces her resigns her place in the hereafter.

In fact, adjuvants have a hard time in this fantasy: the hero progressively strips himself of contact, to the point where he and he only, the pure and isolated ego, is capable of travel. Otherwise, only the magus is saved from oblivion; but, played by a real film director, he is one step removed from the action, a benign creator whose role is to admire the indomitable competitivity of his chosen son, and to construct the backdrop of design against which the hero's fate may be most aesthetically played out.

It is, in one sense, the film of the eternal golden braid: (11) Gödel, Escher, Bach, mathematics, visual illusion and music are offered as the guarantee of permanence, a permanence which seems to imply the absolute disappearance of the body and a traditionally Pauline form of resurrection: Pauline also in its suppression of the possibility of women with vision. Where our hero sees the contours of the sun, his companion is merely blinded; where he is offered life eternal, she is rewarded with the return of what is already hers, her child, and must be grateful.

According to the film, this traditional version of spirituality is not incompatible with the military. Soldiers may huff and puff, even be a little rough in their manners, but in the end they are not only benign but, incredibly, fully adequate to the task in hand: to the shape brought from the stars, they can bring an answering shape in a beautified dialogue of invaders; a ritual dance from which the female is excluded.

Many flowers offer their rich visual patterning as guidance for fertilisation, and in this sense the brilliantly lit runway offers itself up to the landing of the strange craft. But the runway is not public, it is hidden, and it is on the far side of the mountain, the mountain which we have been shown as a model in faeces. The sexual act described is not genital but anal, and at that not fully achieved, a fluttering contact undertaken in secrecy. Domesticity and marriage are semiotically opposed to this meeting of males in the scene where the hero throws refuse through his kitchen window, to the accompaniment of traumatised silence on the part of his neighbours.

The aliens arrive, not with a message of change, but with confirmation, in the shape of the returning lost, that the aspirations of the West are in tune with cosmic design. It is through war and speed that these have found their vision; small wonder that their return is into a pool of sentiment, for the American ideal has been sent for hallmarking and has come back having passed its test. Out there, the purity of metal and electronics has found a like national mind.

More than this: a theory of capitalist cycles (Britain/nineteenth century/engineering, U.S./early twentieth century/cars and aircraft, Japan/late twentieth century/electronics) is thus adjusted to counteract the supersession of the American dream, for these aliens are unmistakably orientals. The brief episode of the black guard demonstrates the exclusion of inferior races from that nirvana; in this peaceful rerun of Pearl Harbour, only master-races need speak. For, at one level, only they are capable of the full intercourse symbolised in the 'third' kind, however mechanically aided that intercourse may turn out to be.

The 'hands across the Pacific' scenario is accompanied, again through Truffaut, by a gesture of allegiance towards the 'old West' of Europe: prohibited, through economic stringency, from full participation in the ideal union, we may nonetheless put our ancient wisdom to use, and teach the glass bead game to those with enough money to buy the equipment.

The threat from disaffected youth has also been overcome in this fantasy of American stability and maturity: represented in the ageing hippie who makes a fool of himself and his cause in the presence of a galaxy of air marshals, the culture of dream is revealed as insufficiently disciplined to qualify for the obsessiveness necessary for survival. True, the police are stupid enough to drive off the end of the road; but their plight is also represented as tragic, for they too participate in the drama of uniformed authority.

It is perhaps not surprising, in view of science's failure of image, that such fables should be produced to lure the young into technological jobs, or that multilingual translation should be included among them. After all, so the film says, an old frame cottage is an unsafe place to be, where ventilators rise unbidden out of the ground and a cat-door is large enough to permit the Alice-like escape of a child. Our hero's artistry and sculpture are useless as sources of revelation until validated by television; just as good intentions cannot achieve penetration without the assistance of the technical and skilled.

We are thus in a paradox about adjuvancy: for we are allowed to take, in our sympathies, the path of service, and to see ourselves, not as ego, but as part of the fuel which will propel that ego to the stars. How, in a class-divided society, could it be otherwise? Equality of opportunity has no place in this refined world, although our masters will see to it that nobody is sufficiently ill-informed to intrude between the participants in the final council; men in white coats, representatives of the intelligentsia, are accustomed to scuttling for shelter, lest what they inappropriately see drives them to terror.

The wish hidden, then, in our hero's long narrative is to maintain divisions unquestioned; to connive at the preservation of WASP superiority. It is thus also to avoid questioning the wisdom of the adult, parodically reinforced in the nonsensical precision of the closing 'son et lumière', even if that wisdom appears to include a taboo on sexual activity. After all, such activity is unnecessary in a state of grace: which the aliens manifest by effortlessly cloning the absent boy, and announcing this immaculate conception, or series of conceptions, with the trumpets of Revelation.

6. Fascination

I offered to the workshop, then, these images of the future as spurs to the imagination, and as implicit statements on the nature of catastrophe. But it was not, immediately, the nature of the representations themselves with which I was concerned. In an as yet unpublished essay, 'Narrative, Acceleration, History - Towards a Theory of Fascination', Thomas Elsasser begins from the following argument - although his concerns are, more explicitly than mine here, to do with the representation and reception of sexuality, and with the 'technical' constraints on our reception:

> What very rarely seems to get mentioned in the current debate about subjectivity and sexuality in literature or the media are the temporal and spatial dimensions that, mostly unperceived, inflect and condition the value which the individual attributes to his or her experiences. Because the debate so strongly focusses on representations, images, words, point

of view and mode of address, the critical discourses tend
to apply leverage by demanding a change in these representations and modalities, and they scan the cultural
field for alternative practices. ... I'm more interested
in asking myself what gives the dominant representations
of our literary and visual culture their fascination and
appeal, or, if you like, what imaginary fastens itself to
the words and images people actually consume? For it seems
to me that the status and function of fantasy - verbal,
visual, 'private' - has considerably changed in recent
decades, and any investigation of the literary (outside
its economic or professional manipulations by authors,
publishers and literary critics) has to take account of
the force-field and context of fantasy and the imaginary
in our society, as it provides the medium for individuals
to live their sexuality, their experiences and subjectivity. (12)

My purpose in offering this connecting text was related to the context
of the conference; that, as Marxists, we tend to focus our attention and
our great strength, our grasp on theory, on texts and text-like
materials, but that the questions Elsasser mentions still remain. And
it was my hypothesis that the way of getting at these questions can only
be via our own 'imaginary'; and that the most fruitful way for literary
academics would be through the translation into text itself, in other
words, through writing.

7.   Structure

I therefore asked members of the workshop to do a series of structured exercises. First, I invited them to write something brief and
imagistic about the immediate past. The point of this is to try to begin
a freeing process; to try to allow some of the imagery which we customarily build around experience to escape the censor, but in an area where
there is relative safety. (13) I then asked them to read their brief
piece of work to each other, in pairs. Structured exercises in writing
can be seen as having a double function: on the one hand, the apparent
formality provides a safety net within which the imagination can be
allowed to function (the reverse situation being, for example, asking
students to write a poem, which generally and predictably produces
nothing); and on the other, the experience of writing together has been
shown to be a useful way of producing some kind of group awareness, a
sharing of experience which can be helpful in the processes of seminar
formation. Of course, there need to be ground-rules for such exercises,
the most important of which is that individuals take their own choices,
particularly about whether they wish to share what they have written.

I then invited members to write a brief fantasy about the future,
suggesting the year 1988 as a lynch-pin, and then to share those; and
in sharing them, to try to listen attentively to what the other person
was reading. I then invited them to consider, still in pairs or small
groups, a question: If that is the future, then, looking back, what *was*
the crisis? After a short discussion in groups, I suggested that we
tried to share what we had done so far, not by a general discussion but
in a slightly structured way, by pulling out of the discourse so far
any words or phrases which seemed central. (14) These were written on
the blackboard; they came to constitute what I would call a group text
of the future. (15)

8. Content

That text was as follows:

red and green	resolute	tired stone
independent	cliffhanger	dancing a mazurka
normal	disappearance	broken-backed
the solitary ego	interminable	hanging about
days of inaction	bulldozer	battle of power
privatisation	reabsorption	disaffected
energy	Guatemala City	(16)

I also asked members, if they wanted to, to give me the writings they had done during the session; and received a ritual, a fantasy of bureaucracy, and an image.

The ritual:

There was a circle, a cool circle of dry wood, continuous, a ring of seats.

Overhead and surrounding the circle was stone and light.

But the light was dim, blocked by tangled creepers shadowing, oppressing the circle. The creepers were very tired.

The seats were occupied. Old, tired.

From time to time in the middle of the ring would arise a grey-robed figure, one after another.

For some moments each figure would remain, changing slowly in colour - towards a deeper grey or a brighter, whiter shade. Then each figure would slowly slide again below the ground.

The others sat on in the seats, getting ever more tired.

The fantasy of bureaucracy:

1988; British Rail; Kings Cross.

The weekly public sector train to Edinburgh will depart Tuesday 0930 platform 3. It is expected to arrive Wednesday 2335. Security checks will be held at Peterboro', Doncaster, York, Newcastle, with prolonged border security interrogation procedures at Berwick. Passengers are asked to have all baggage ready for examination at platform entrance. Tickets are on sale on presentation of required permits at your local police station and must be applied for before 1200 on Monday. Number of passengers limited to 950. Bedding and foodstuffs not allowed on journey though drinking-water containers may be carried.

The image:

A broken-backed man driving towards a cliff unaware that what he thinks are sensations in his feet are just 'noise' issuing from the cut nerves in his spine.

9. Reflection

It is clear that the problems these texts were mediating were ones of power and impotence. Kafka was mentioned during the workshop; and it would be into the canon of writers under the dominance of bureaucracy - Kafka, Chekhov, Lu Xun - that the texts would fall. There is a preoccupation with time, and with the incompatibilities between attempts at personal temporal organisation and the imposed time-scales of power. What, in effect, is the scheme of history? To put it in more immediate terms: how can we, while holding on to at least the vestiges of a revolutionary, crisis-oriented theory of history, adjust to a consideration of the devices which are being deployed for endless postponement? Confronting the crisis appears as shadow-boxing: the enemy has already moved on, to a place of even greater obscurity, while we see only the shadows of decline.

In other places, of course, there is crisis - and war, and even rejoicing at wars past. But here, there is only waiting, an empty space, a stone circle where the phantasms of power behave in ways which remain incomprehensible to us. And, of course, the 'here' is Britain, as we wait for the moment when some imagined limit might eventually be passed - some limit, for example, on the number of unemployed who will continue to vote for the resolute approach. But it also seems to me that the 'here' is higher education, where the illusion of a 'natural' timescale has now been forcibly discontinued and replaced by the mechanical transfusion imaged so powerfully in the discourse of 'new blood'. And the problematic is also specifically related to the role of the literary, and thus to our own roles as the interpreters of societal symbolism: cut off from resources, are we correspondingly also cut off from the real sounds, the real forms of the outside world, so that we end up in an echo chamber of our own devising, where the signals we receive are merely amplified versions of the isolation which has become the bedrock of our work, a natural successor to the individualism on which literary studies were founded?

In *The Hitch-Hiker's Guide to the Galaxy*, clearly a satisfying fantasy on many levels, the Earth is indeed cleared away by a cosmic bulldozer five minutes before it reaches a kind of apotheosis; although that apotheosis itself would also have been beyond our control, since it would only have consisted in the solution to a problem which was in any case not of our own devising. Under such circumstances, the question of 'confronting' the crisis appears merely as an ironised hubris; Arthur Dent lying down in front of a real bulldozer, but moving away as soon as he is convinced to do so by the superior wit and wisdom of a galactic messenger. (17)

In terms of fascination, the motifs seem to be those of endurance, of lasting through a spell of dryness, cold, a degree zero; but towards what future? Perhaps the point is indeed simply in the 'hanging on', yet this may also be the source of a fatal compromise, whereby the values of co-operative work and critical stance are obliterated in the half-hidden processes of privatisation and reabsorption. Our skills are based in an assumption of critical distance, in a consciousness of the ever-present danger of being again immersed in the object, in the force-field of ideology; (18) yet the problem is of perceiving when that distance turns into remoteness and we find that the disappearance of the object and the disappearance of the 'profession', in the widest sense, are coterminous.

These reflections on the text can, of course, be linked to developments in theory, and particularly, I would say, to the emergence in Derrida and the deconstructionists of a version of theory which does indeed deal in the interminable, does indeed proffer an account of discourse which decisively severs it from revolutionary practice. And such reflections take us directly back to the 'moment' of the conference itself, to the fear that, precisely at the moment when the crisis might be confronted, a large part of the previously available energy has been deflected into the softer channels of Derrida's machine for endless and pointless productivity. In this respect, the Derridean universe seems to me also to be the universe of Flann O'Brien's paradisial underworld, where the machines are geared to provide you with anything you want. The catch is that to get back from this realm you have to use a lift; and the lift is finely tuned to make sure that you come back with nothing more than you originally had. (19)

No doubt this may seem to be making rather a lot out of a small and fragmentary episode; no doubt also there are other, and better, ways of trying to get at the content of our fantasies. But I would nevertheless say that the images we actually generate in practice are the home of signification; and that the very ignoring of them can be the mark of a hollowness, of a now prolonged uncertainty about the actual theories to which we nominally subscribe and of a failure to think through the experiential implications of 'praxis' as it might be specifically applied to the study of literature and discourse. Before the workshop began, I handed out some sheets on which were a few quotations which appear to me to be ones we might bear in mind as we search for a new practice which will be able to gain a purchase on the empty space we apparently inhabit; and some of them seem to me to be still relevant.

> No work is just a result ... but first and foremost genesis, a work that is in progress.

> The streamers of my consciousness waver out and are perpetually torn and distressed by their disorder. I cannot therefore concentrate on my dinner.

> Sit on my arse and take the sick, that's all I'm good for. Forty-fucking-two and that's my lot. Gets you down, you know, it really fucking does. ... Oh Christ, I get so fucking fed up I can't tell you, I can't put it into words.

> ... the very etymology of the word 'text': it is a tissue, something woven. But whereas criticism ... hitherto unanimously placed the emphasis upon the finished 'fabric' (the text being a 'veil' behind which the truth, the real message, in a word the 'meaning', had to be sought), the current theory of the text turns away from the text as veil and tries to perceive the fabric in its texture ... in the midst of which the subject places himself and is undone, like a spider that comes to dissolve itself into its own web.

> Interest in the active process of making is suppressed in favour of the more negotiable activity of responding to an object ... I believe that the emphasis on practice is now crucial and that neglect of practice is a contributory factor to our cultural crisis ... (20)

FOOTNOTES

1. My four instances were a passage from Italo Calvino, *Invisible Cities*, trans. W. Weaver (London, 1974) (on which I did not comment); Donald Barthelme, 'The Balloon', *The New Yorker* (16th April 1966), pp. 46-48; J. G. Ballard, *Concrete Island* (London, 1974); and Steven Spielberg's film, *Close Encounters of the Third Kind* (1977).

2. Calvino, *Invisible Cities*, p.101.

3. See I. F. Clarke, *The Pattern of Expectation 1644-2001* (London, 1979), pp.29-34.

4. See H. G. Wells, *Things to Come* (London, 1935), e.g., pp.102-106.

5. Michel Foucault, 'Questions on Geography', in *Power/Knowledge: Selected Interviews and Other Writings 1972-1977*, ed. C. Gordon (Brighton, 1980), p.69.

6. Sleeve-note to paperback edition of Ballard, *Concrete Island*.

7. Ballard, *Concrete Island*, pp.175-176.

8. Ballard, *Concrete Island*, p.176.

9. Ballard, *Concrete Island*, p.74.

10. Philip Larkin, 'Dockery and Son', in *The Whitsun Weddings* (London, 1964), p.37.

11. The reference is primarily to Douglas Hofstadter, *Gödel, Escher, Bach: An Eternal Golden Braid* (Brighton, 1979).

12. Elsasser, 'Narrative, Acceleration, History', p.1.

13. I am referring back to the psychoanalytic theory in, e.g., Melanie Klein, 'The Psycho-Analytic Play Technique: its History and Significance', in *Envy and Gratitude, and Other Works 1946-1963* (London, 1975), pp.122-140.

14. For reservations about the ideological concept 'discussion', see, e.g., Elizabeth Richardson, *Group Study for Teachers* (London, 1967).

15. Robert Clark, whom I had asked to write a brief report on the workshop, referred to it as a 'lexicon'; and, to anticipate, one which 'spoke of a hidden collective concern with immobile tension'.

16. I am aware that it was I who separated the full phrase, 'red and green flags over Guatemala City'; perhaps I had an investment in the negation and severance of hope.

17. See Douglas Adams, *The Hitch-Hiker's Guide to the Galaxy* (London, 1979), pp.9-20.

18. See, e.g., Theodor Adorno, 'Cultural Criticism and Society', in *Prisms*, trans. S. and S. Weber (London, 1967), pp.17-34.

19. See Flann O'Brien, *The Third Policeman* (London, 1967), p.121.

20. Paul Klee, *The Thinking Eye*, ed. J. Spiller (London, 1961), p.267; Virginia Woolf, *The Waves* (London, 1943), p.67; Tony Parker, *The People of Providence: A Housing Estate and Some of its Inhabitants* (London, 1983), p.74; Roland Barthes, 'Theory of the Text', in *Untying the Text: A Post-Structuralist Reader*, ed. R. Young (London, 1981), p.39; Raymond Williams, 'Literature in Society', in *Contemporary Approaches to English Studies*, ed. H. Schiff (London, 1977), p.102.

"WHY I WROTE A BOOK ON THE YORKSHIRE RIPPER"*

Nicole Ward Jouve

I. Fascination

Like all women living in Yorkshire at the time of the "Ripper" murders, (1) I was fascinated. When you are "fascinated", you just can't help looking at the very thing you don't *want* to look at. It's got under your skin, in some way. Even when you close your eyes, won't read the papers "about it", refuse to discuss "it", to join in the wave of indignation and fear that follows announcement of each new murder, "it" still materializes on the screen of your lids. Inside the chambers of your brain. I remember being haunted by an image, after the body of the second or third victim was discovered. The papers spoke of a derelict blind alley, where "such women" go. I "saw" a woman lying on a mound of dirt. (2) The mound "became" a mound of coal dust. Later, when the last few women were killed, and panic had really set in, and in Yorkshire universities relays of buses and cars had been organized to see all female students home at night, and you didn't dare let your daughter go to the fair or even cross the village street in the dark, my particular fear focused on having to fetch coke from the shed after sundown. I "thought" that somebody was prowling round there, ready to bash me on the head: as I bent to shovel coke into the spout of my bucket, my back and nape bristled. Black on black mound, black in black. Coal in the dark, the most unseeable thing there is. Taking a torch didn't help: it simply made *me* more visible.

As chance had it, three or four times, professional or administrative duties took me to Leeds or Bradford or through Huddersfield and Manchester almost straight after a murder. It was as if my own life insisted on mixing me up with "it". It altered my way of looking at all that urban waste, the signs of the recession everywhere. You couldn't help wondering what connection there was between the social/economic dereliction which much of the geography "expressed", and the type of violence which was at work in the nooks and crannies of those landscapes. I felt personally affronted: I, a French woman, had "settled" in Yorkshire, because myths like the Brontes, spaces like the moors, had appealed to me as deeply nurturing to femininity. As promising freedom and scope. Now, other places and a new myth that were uncomfortably close to those I had loved, were threatening murder. The place was spelling death to me *as a woman*. It was willing you dead. My back and skull knew it.

And I couldn't let it happen. I had to fight it.

One of the things that were worst about "it" was that, instead of feeling (as you should have done if the police publicity campaign or the high tone of indignation of the papers were anything to go by), self-righteous, full of the spirit of legitimate self-defence, you felt ...

───────────────────────

* *Un Homme nommé Zapolski*, Paris, Editions des Femmes, 1983, 2nd edition.

guilty. Apologetic. About going out in the dark. About wearing attractive clothes. Being out in the street. Almost, about being a woman. Being a woman meant that you were murderable. And it was wrong of you so to be. In order to make up for it, you had to be specially "good". Stay indoors, not wander away from the protective side of a man: your man. No other was safe (and even he, perhaps???). A year after the trial of Sutcliffe, round Malton, the area where I live, the police mounted a huge manhunt for a certain Barry Prudhom: disappointed in his ambition to become an SAS agent, in the wake of the Falklands campaign, the man started shooting at policemen. He killed two, wounded one; had also killed a householder, a postmaster, I think: his targets were male figures or symbols of authority, order. As the manhunt proceeded, a vigilante spirit overtook the male population of the district. The travelling greengrocer told me he'd get his old rifle out and shoot at anyone who came to his door that night. A gentle neighbour who lives in a fairly isolated farm patrolled the grounds with his shotgun, protecting the wife and kids. A courteous old solicitor kept his loaded army pistol in the top drawer of his Malton office. Not to mention the police, complete with helicopters, dogs and survival-in-the-wilderness expert: they ended up shooting their prey full of holes. Barry Prudhom died of more than twenty bullet wounds. The police were cleared in the enquiry that followed, as would probably have been any male householder if he'd shot Prudhom. Every form of support, every sense of legitimacy that society could produce was with them. But the Leeds women who walked with a can of spray paint in their handbags were accused of illegitimately carrying weapons about themselves ... Can you even *imagine* a well-organized group of prostitutes trapping and shooting the Ripper in self-defence? Can you imagine the kind of support "people" would give to a vigilante squad of prostitutes? While the Ripper operated, twelve Leeds women were arrested for picketing the entrance of a cinema that was showing *The Rape of the Bitch*.

Why was it that when men, men in a position of social or domestic authority, were targets, they turned into the righteous defenders of order; when women were targets, they became guilty victims?

When the trial was on, I began to have nightmares. About "it". About "him". At that point I knew I had to do "something about it". Get it out of my system. Stare it out. It was the only way of ridding myself of a fascination that had become far too internalized for my own peace of mind.

It was dangerous to counter-attack. I felt that. For there was protection in anonymity. As long as you were part of the crowd, the chances of your being spotted were very small. I knew, because I had experienced the "guilt" there was in being a woman; knew that the Ripper somehow was on the side of what makes "Society" tick. What would happen if I put myself forward, gave myself to be seen, joined the side of prostitution? This is where being foreign came to be of use. (3) My Frenchness, writing in French for a foreign, detached readership, would keep the thing at one remove. It would also be fitting in that it would place me exactly where I was: still a foreigner in England, observing landscapes and social phenomena from a de-centred position. I had no "inside" knowledge of it all; had no English childhood, none of those instincts which act as an implicit form of understanding. I did not belong, either, to the "classes" from which the Ripper had sprung. I did not even inhabit "his" landscapes; lived East of them: my prow was rightly turned towards the morning sun. A proper church, my door of death was west. West Yorkshire, west of me.

Yet it was also clear that, because I loved those landscapes, because I had "chosen" to live in Yorkshire, because the "thing" had become internalized for me, and because I knew it was of concern to me as a woman, I was also in it; of it. It was in me.

Where I was, then, was where I should be: half in, half out. Half of it, half not. Half foreign, half English. And "it" had to do with intermediary states. "It" belonged to no man's land, and yet to man's land, like the pieces of waste ground. This was the terrain where the battle had to be fought. No one seemed to have seen that. Everyone had conspired to agree with the murderer that waste ground was the place where *dead* women's bodies belonged. He had need to believe that. (Because he could not accept that no man's land should be where he, in fact, was?) And everyone had condoned him in his belief.

But I knew something about no man's land. I knew I was in it. And I wasn't dead. And I was damned if I was going to let myself be killed.

II.   Identifications

How "I" came into "it".

1.   The cultural

Insofar as I was qualified to deal with the Ripper case, culture was the equipment I had. It would have to show what it could do for me, in an emergency. It would have to save me, instead of rendering its usual suspect services, as when I wrote fiction; of loading for me the dice of theory. It would have to save me, by urgently making sense. Much of the book therefore is taken up by culture's attempt to deal with raw social data. And culture helped. Through its formality, the processings things had already had at the hands of myth or art or thought, it diffused, it refracted, it made bearable the unbearable. Culture was my oven gloves.

Here are some examples of what happened.

a)   Roland Barthes was positively inspirational. I had always found his *S/Z* a superb book. It is the detailed account of *Sarrasine*, a short story by Balzac. Sarrasine, the character who gives its title to the story, is an eighteenth century French sculptor who goes to Venice and falls in love with a beautiful opera singer called Zambinella. He hears her at the opera, is penetrated by the splendour of her voice, makes a statue of her imagined body which is his ideal of womanhood. She strangely evades his amorous pursuit. And he, finally, discovers that Zambinella is in fact a castratum, one of those young boys whom the Republic processed and trained to produce lovely female singing voices. The story of Sarrasine's love for Zambinella is told, sixty years later, to a young and beautiful woman, by the narrator of the tale. The narrator had hoped to seduce her: his expectations are disappointed. Rather like Sarrasine's love for Zambinella had been disappointed. At the heart of the tale lies a meditation upon the nature and origins (or lack of visible origins) of wealth in Parisian society under the July Monarchy: the beginnings of "capital" in France. Zambinella made a great fortune as both singer and prized courtesan. The family, at whose house ball the story begins to be told, are his descendants. Zambinella is the source of their wealth. A wizened old man, he now haunts their brilliant "salons" like a ghost.

Barthes uses the Balzac story to do and say a multiplicity of things. That which concerns me, is the way he unfolds how *Sarrasine* revolves around castration. Castration as both contagious and deadly.

There are incipiently "feminine" traits in Sarrasine the sculptor. He's been his mother's darling, is shy, a loner, has been over-protected. When he falls in love with Zambinella, he is suffused, "penetrated" by her voice: much like Endymion, in the picture that now hangs in the house of Zambinella's wealthy descendants, and for which Zambinella posed as a nude model, by Diana's moonlight. The discovery that his feminine ideal is a "man", and a castrated man at that, symbolically castrates Sarrasine: he will never be able to love a woman again; he has, in fact, never loved a woman: Zambinella was his first love. It kills him: ruffians in the pay of a cardinal, Zambinella's powerful lover, murder Sarrasine soon after he's found out who Zambinella really is. It is as if (Barthes says) the castration which has been inflicted upon Zambinella passes on to Sarrasine as a contagious disease. Even the lettering of the names expresses this. Zambinella has the "a" ending of Italian feminine nouns, but the harsh Z sound, the sound of the whip, marks him: both as male/hard and as castrated/castrator. The name Sarrasine is also full of ambiguity. The word does not exist in French. There is "sarrazin", masculine, with a "z", which means a cereal, and a Saracen. The "ine" ending (as in Delphine or Corrinne) connotes a feminine name (yet it is the sculptor's surname). The "z" of "sarrazin" has been replaced by an "s": the sign of Sarrasine's secretly "feminine" nature, as is the "ine" ending of his name, but also already the sign of castration to come. It is as if the "z" had mutated to the name of Zambinella; as if the name Zambinella lashed at Sarrasine, inflicted a feminine "s" (an inversion, a mirror image of z) upon him.

Of course, it is not (I hasten to say this because this type of speculation causes a lot of difficulty for some English people I have spoken to) as if these mutations of "s" into "z" and vice versa functioned automatically and always. But within the complex of the story they do, most convincingly. It is as if "masculine" and "feminine" signs, endings of nouns, individual letters, were caught in processes of travelling and mutation: the marks of a world in which sexual identity has been profoundly disturbed. Where indeterminacy, lethal mistakes as to gender, prevail. Above all, it is a world in which "woman" turns out to be a male suffering from lack - a castrated male. Where, as a result, the male in love with the "woman" suffers "lack" - castration - in his turn.

Testifying at his trial in May 1981, Sutcliffe said that he heard the "voice of God" for the first time while he was working as a gravedigger in Bingley cemetery. He was some five feet underground, digging a grave. He heard a voice. He climbed out, went up the hill, and after some investigation found that the voice came from a tomb in the Polish part of the cemetery. "It was the tomb of a man called Zapolski".

The Times I was reading reported this testimony in detail. But either the reporters misspelt the name (though a photograph of the tomb, with the name: *Bronislaw Za*polski, clearly legible on it, was reproduced at the centre of the article) - or the typographer had: it was printed that "They showed Mr. Sutcliffe the photograph of a tomb. It was that of a man called *Stanislaw Zi*polski".

I don't know whether it was the repeated juxtaposition of the names Sutcliffe/Zapolski that struck me, or the fact that the reporters/ typographers had misspelt Mr. Zapolski's name and surname. But it was as if a contagion of misspelling, mis-reading, had passed on from Sutcliffe to the newspaper. On Sutcliffe's own evidence, it looked as if the whole murderous situation had had a lot to do with misunderstanding: the mis-hearing of a voice, the mis-reading of a message; the search for the *written* source of an *aural* hallucination (which is extraordinary, when you come to think about it); the mis-seeing of the tomb (Sutcliffe saw a statue of Christ on top of it; there was a little crucifix stuck on it); the mis-reading of the inscription (none of the mysterious Polish words that Sutcliffe "read" were there to be seen, at least on that tomb). It was as if identity was in a state of wandering (as in the Balzac story): letters were mutating, and so were sounds, signs, from one place or object or sense to another. In particular, there was a mutation of the same letters as in the Balzac, but in the reverse order. It was not a case of "z" becoming "s" (Sarrazin to Sarrasine), but of "s" becoming "z" (and "c" into "k"): the soft, the feminine signs became the hard, the masculine; changed into the lash, the sign of destruction/ castration. *Sutc*liffe had become Zapo*l*ski. Sutcliffe's alter ego was speaking from the *tomb* of a man called Zapolski. A "reading" to account for all the mis-readings was suggesting itself. Here was a man who somehow felt (feared?) that he was "soft", "feminine", threatened by femininity as a "lack" - felt, in a manner of a way, castrated. His aural hallucination - his hearing of the voice of God - followed by his visual identification of the voice as coming from (and eventually written on) a particular gravestone, were the projection of a "hard" self. The self he wanted to be. It was being granted to him by a father-figure, God. A God who called himself by a "hard" name, disguised himself as a *dead, foreign* man - whose monument was an erect gravestone at the top of a hill. It was as if in that "experience" Sutcliffe had been offered (had created for himself) another, wished-for and spatialized self - the topography of erection was manifest in the whole scene. Having heard and identified and understood the voice, Sutcliffe said, he had felt wonderfully happy, important.

Only, that voice happened to be the voice of death. Incipiently, it suggested that death - someone else's death (somebody else, after all, was lying in the tomb from which there rose the voice and the inscription on the gravestone) - was the way to the longed-for sense of sexual identity ...

A great deal followed from there, which the book went on to examine.

b) A major question was why the police took so long in catching the Ripper. They could, after all, be remarkably quick at catching a murderer if they, or alternative figures of authority, were the targets: the Barry Prudhom case had shown it. Seventeen days elapsed between the beginning of the manhunt and Prudhom's death. It took five and a half years to arrest Sutcliffe, and he was only caught by "accident".

Many difficulties intervened in the Ripper enquiry: administrative complexities, overlaps, a mass of data so great that it could not be sifted, the chaotic beginnings of computerization, the false trail laid by the "hoaxer", etc. The fact remains that the police questioned Sutcliffe nine times, the last few times when they had some pretty hard evidence in their possession: and let him go nine times. It was as if they *could not see him*. Thinking this, I was reminded of Poe's story, *The Purloined Letter*, and the analysis Lacan has offered of it.

In *The Purloined Letter*, the King enters the Queen's apartment whilst the Queen is reading a letter. What that letter is, or says, remains unspecified. What matters is that the Queen does not want the King to see it. As the best defence against detection, she casually places the letter in full view, on the piano, wrong side up. The King does not notice the letter, but the Minister who has entered with him, and is the Queen's enemy, (4) sees and understands the Queen's gesture. Casually too, he takes a letter from his own pocket and substitutes it for the Queen's letter, placing his letter also wrong side up. From then on, he is in possession of the Queen's letter, having the power to blackmail her. The Queen, acting secretly still on account of her fear of detection from the King, asks the police to find the stolen letter. Despite an extensive and intensive search of the Minister's apartment and of his office, going through the books of the library page by page and unscrewing the legs of the chairs to see if they are hollow, the police find nothing. Dupin, Poe's Sherlock Holmes, is called to the rescue by the chief of police. He calls on the Minister on some pretext or other. Spots the Queen's letter, turned inside out (yet again), there for all to see, on a letter rack. He arranges another visit during which the Minister's attention is called to the window; and substitutes a fake letter, with outside markings identical, for the stolen one. He then "sells" the Queen's letter to the chief of police.

Well, what with their TV cameras in the Leeds and Bradford red-light districts spotting millions of cars, the forty thousand calls received in answer to the publicizing of the hoaxer's tape, their computers sifting masses of data, and their hundreds of thousands of door-to-door, street-by-street enquiries, it was as if the police, in the Ripper case as in the Poe, had searched every inch of the ground - gone through the books of the library page by page, as it were - but had failed to see the evidence, the inverted letter, even when it was in full display. Sutcliffe, at his trial, told how he once was questioned by a policeman who held a photograph of a bootprint found by or on two of the bodies; and then climbed back into the cabin of his lorry, putting the soles of the very same boots right under the policeman's nose - and the policeman (like the King, like the police searching the Minister's office) did not *see* them.

In his "Séminaire" on the Poe, Lacan stresses a number of things. The letter is "pur-loined", pro-longed. Like the signifier (you never know what its "signified" might be: what the letter actually is, says, why it is compromising), it *travels* from one person to another in the course of the story. From Queen to Minister, from Minister to Dupin, from Dupin to the chief of police. The signifier is movable. It repeats its effects: possession of it affects the holder. The holder turns out to be in a feminine, a passive position. Like the Queen before him, the Minister, once he *has* the letter, is vulnerable: to theft, to "having it done" to him. Dupin parts with the letter for a large sum of money, Lacan suggests, in order not to become "feminized" in his turn. Rather in the way the psychoanalyst gets paid a handsome fee, so as not to be infected by what he has come into contact with. Money breaks the spell which the letter passes on. The letter *is* femininity: contagious, like the castration which passes from Zambinella to Sarrasine in the Balzac.

When I thought about the police search, and what they were after, in the light of the Poe story, it looked yet again as if one was dealing, not with what is normally regarded as "male violence", but with the "feminine" as a movable and dangerous "signifier" (and a resulting hatred for, need to destroy, femininity). The evidence from Sutcliffe's interviews with psychiatrists, from his own testimony, from what is known of his childhood and youth, suggests that he felt "castrated": haunted by fear of his own impotence, of the "feminine" elements in his character. It also looked as if the police, like the police in their search of the Minister's premises, *could not see* the evidence which, (like the Medusa stare?), was "inverted" femininity. They could not see in the smallish, polite, soft-spoken, respectable man with a good job and a mortgage and a nice house in a nice area, the mad "male" killer, the Public Enemy No. 1, the embodiment of working-class/underprivileged/anti-Establishment Evil which they, as representatives of "order", were trained to seek. They were looking for a male sign. They were dealing with a female (inverted) signifier. Whose only way of "signifying" was the way it killed and projected, *inscribed* obscenity.

Sutcliffe was killing according to the codes "Society" had set. Which the police are paid to uphold. Sutcliffe only killed "bad" women. His hatred for femininity was a hatred of the feminine in himself. He was threatened by it. He could not get rid of it. Any more than the Minister, once he is in possession of the Queen's letter, can get out of the situation which the letter creates: vulnerability to theft, the need for concealment by a combination of inversion and display. Only, instead of blackmailing, Sutcliffe killed. *Black-mailed* the feminine, inscribing obscenity upon it, by means of murder.

The danger which the letter represented was that it could be purloined. That it could pass on from women to men. Prostitutes, Sutcliffe had found in his first encounter with one, could make you into a "woman": castrate you, make you impotent. As Sutcliffe could become Zapolski, Z could become, or re-become, S. His own wife, Sonia Sutcliffe, had after all once been called Oksana Szurma. Letters did travel. The only way Sutcliffe knew of making himself "Z" (and it had to be repeated again and again) was to lash at the feminine in his turn. Kill those prostitutes who had mocked and robbed him. Kill those women who had children when his own wife couldn't. Mark them as obscene. Know erection through death. Someone else's death.

The tombstone on the hill-top had shown the way.

c) What all this suggested, ominously, confirmed my initial sense of "guilt". The Ripper was not *against* Society, he was very much "with" it. It's not just that he thought he was. The way the whole thing was perceived (as by the police) helped confirm the sense he had of things.

The murder and desecration of the victims had the effect of placing them "fuori le mura". Outside the walls of the city. Outside culture. And outside nature: their sexuality, derided and useless.

I thought of Antigone.

Polynices has been left to lie unburied outside the walls of Thebes. Antigone goes and buries him. So he can find peace.

Sutcliffe's victims had been placed outside culture, not just by the way he killed them, but by the way in which the murders had been "read". Described, used, publicized, by the papers, the authors of books on the "Ripper", the police, the judiciary. At the trial, the attorney-general, brandishing the screwdriver used to perforate the uterus of one of the victims, made that uterus "speak". Declare that there had been a "sexual" dimension, etc. against the suggestion by the psychiatrists that there hadn't. *Hysteria* had been already inflicted on the murdered women by the way their murderer had killed them, silenced their voices, made their bodies "speak" of obscenity by displaying them in "obscene" fashion. But everyone who wrote about them (and who spoke, like the attorney-general), *followed his lead*. At least, until some of the mothers counter-attacked, denouncing cheque-book journalism; until some prostitutes with placards reminded those who attended the Old Bailey proceedings that they were mothers too. But it was the perception that a consensus had been at work which made me decide to "un-read". To work, like Antigone, against the law: the (largely implicit) laws of interpretation. To place the violence and mutilations back where they belonged, inside a consciousness that would make sense. That of Sutcliffe. I decided to read the "signs" as *deeds*, not as inscriptions. To stop playing the role devised for us, it seemed, by Sutcliffe: one which everyone seemed quite pleased to play. To stop obeying the dictates of a supposed voice of God-the-Father which was in fact the voice of the Tempter. "You will be like Gods. All the kingdoms of the earth will belong to you, my son, if you prostrate yourself before me and worship me. Worship me, Death." A gravestone, with an inscription on it.

d) One question above all emerged from these, and related, "cultural" interpretations. Why can a man like Sutcliffe think of murder as a way of asserting his *malehood* - of laying down the *law* - of making *sense*? Why can the murdering of *women* be thought of as a way of inscribing what is allowed and what is not allowed? For we are dealing here with a specifically male type of murder. With a hatred for the feminine shared by a whole society. Bound up in it, consciously or unconsciously, is identification with a cultural order.

What seems to have been at stake in Sutcliffe's killings was the definition of women as either "good" or "bad". The good woman proves her "decency" by being faithful, staying at home (especially in the evenings) and becoming a mother: hence the panic and confusion for Sutcliffe when his own "angelic" mother turned out to be having an affair (with a policeman of all people); when his own wife failed to have children (she miscarried) and threatened to be unfaithful. The bad woman shows, through her behaviour and clothing, that she is "sexed" and circulates: out in the streets at night, way of walking, "coarse" language, etc. It is as if, among other complicated "motives", Sutcliffe, by killing "bad" women and making them look horrible, was defining them *as* bad and therefore cleansing "his" women (mother, wife, girl-friends) from the stain of evil. You cannot reverse the operation: imagine a woman who would kill men to demonstrate that some are Casanovas, others "good", faithful husbands.

The murder of Carmen by Don José, of Thérèse Raquin's husband, of Mr. Verloc by Mrs. Verloc (however complex, metaphysically or socially; and however much each may express the situation of men versus women, or women versus men), imply passions of lust, jealousy, revenge, possessiveness, the drive for freedom, which can be felt by men and women alike. The murders committed by Sutcliffe (possibly also by Jack the Ripper; *and* by Nilsen) are the case of a *man* identifying with the letter of the taboos of a social order, and either believing that they are maintaining that order, or enabling themselves to "function normally", by marking others (women) out, through murder, as the evil party. Also perhaps punishing them for their own propensity, their own desire: but insofar as this is true (it is the pattern of Hitchcock's *Psycho*), one is moving back towards the middle ground, to what can surface in men's and women's experience. I am trying to lay my finger on what makes the "Ripper" type of murder a specifically "male" type of murder.

The "signs" of prostitution: always female, whether a man or a woman are the bearers of them. At a conference at the Sheffield City Polytechnic in September 1983, I heard Cora Kaplan discuss the urgency with which Emily, in *The Mysteries of Udolpho*, as soon as she has escaped from Montoni's clutches, sets upon ... getting hold of a hat. She finally buys a straw hat from a peasant woman. Different types of head gear would connote different classes, mark you out as rich or poor, coquettish or devout. But going hatless meant you were a prostitute. There is no equivalent way in which a male can signal, or fear lest he signal, sex/availability in that way: unless he becomes "female" by becoming a transvestite or acting the homosexual "whore": who is female. In which case (viz. Nilsen) he becomes murderable in that way too. As "evil".

The repeat murder of the prostitute, or the "bad" female: always by a male. When I wrote *Un Homme nommé Zapolski*, I related this type of murder to the violence produced by racism and anti-semitism. Recent discussions have persuaded me that I was wrong to use them both as analogical. It has been pointed out to me, quite persuasively, that the racist regards the "nigger", or the Arab worker, as *naturally* his inferior, as sub-human, "animal". Beating him up is "punishing" him for not having kept his place. Whereas the anti-semite, the Nazi, implicitly acknowledges the "humanity" of the Jew; but decides that he is "evil", must be destroyed, so that a moral, perhaps a metaphysical, certainly a *cultural* order should be saved. Ku Klux Klan men, "Paki-bashers", do not want to "exterminate" their victims. They know it is far too useful to have a sub-proletariat - or whatever. They are "making examples" to assert, in the face of a social and economic threat, who is "master". The Nazi would readily destroy down to the last Jew so that society at large should be purged from a corrupt element. The killer of prostitutes is closer to the anti-semite (as I had tried to show when discussing how Sutcliffe came to believe that "prostitutes were the dregs of the earth", that they "were littering the streets", that he was "only cleaning out a little"). He believes that his mission is moral, is religious. Also, you can tell whether a man is black or white at one glance.* You cannot tell whether he is Jewish or not, unless he is dressed in a particular way: any more than, unless you know him some way, you can tell whether a man is Catholic or Protestant in the streets of Belfast. The signs by which you can tell that a woman is a prostitute are equally tenuous, "mystical", as Sutcliffe's frequent mistakes showed: Jacqueline Hill, a Leeds student, was "condemned" because she turned to adjust her skirt.

There you are: there *is* something specific in the murder of "prostitutes" in that it entails even less the identification of something "real" - be it group, or class, or colour or nationality or sect - than racism or fanaticism or chauvinism or Nazism. And has to do with something far more widespread, which I am hard put to express. Women's sexuality. The way in which the *division* of women, in all sorts of ways, has become the cornerstone of the *definition* of manhood. That division can take a thousand and one shapes. It operates *inside* the home, or between the home and the street. It can wear the face of colour, the face of all the other "isms" that entail the identification of a group as "to be persecuted". Whether as emissary goat or not. Every prostitute is a woman. Every woman is, potentially, a prostitute. If you are "under-privileged", prostitution is a continuous temptation. If you are middle-class, it is doubly your "border". You move close to it whenever you decide to become "sexed"; to attempt to attract, to wear the signs of attractiveness, to engage in sexual encounters outside the bounds of marriage or regular coupling. Conversely, when you are or act "respectable", prostitutes are your counterpart: you can be "decent" *because* they exist. You are their exploiter. They give your men the "satisfaction" your respectability denies them.

― ―

* I realize I am grossly simplifying: there can be a subtle mystique at work wherever an "aristocracy of the skin" prevails, where the "signs" of being "black" or "white" can be as tenuous and arbitrary as those which mark a woman out as a prostitute or not.

How do you define a prostitute? Because of the money? If so, how come that people like Sutcliffe and some of his friends think it is a good joke to "pay" a prostitute in blows? That the Reading police who were filmed by Thames TV questioning a woman who had complained of rape be persuaded that she was "one" because they made her "confess" that she had had sex with more than one man? Is it being a "professional" of the "oldest profession in the world" that defines a woman as a prostitute? Because she does it as a full source of income? Do the "semi-professional", the "occasional", count? Does getting favours, political clout or prestige, a social position, through sex, qualify? There is, in prostitution, something in excess of the merchant system. Something which has to do with the definition of virility by means of a line of demarcation between, inside, women: a line none the less rigid for being a phantom line. Sutcliffe's murders had to do with the inscription of that line.

Like all other women, as a "sexed" being, I was the "prostitutes" ("actual" or not) that were being murdered. As a "respectable" wife-and-mother, I was what was being "protected", "cleansed", by means of the murders. Whichever way I turned, I was "in it". Up to my neck. As you all were, sisters. And brothers.

2. The personal: Ariadne in the Labyrinth

Even while I was working, I felt that some of the "meanings" I made were, however persuasive I found them, tenuous. I couldn't "prove" some of the things I was saying. I was spinning gossamer from my belly. A spider's web. Then it occurred to me that nothing more solid than an Ariadne thread had guided Theseus out of the labyrinth inhabited by the monster. Spiders' webs at least have the advantage that they can travel and hang over voids, where nothing else can. No doubt some strange identifications had taken place.

The "Ripper" operated between 1975 and January 1981. There was an intensification of the killings in 1977-78.

I started writing *L'Entremise* in 1978. It was published by the Editions des Femmes in the autumn of 1980. It is the story of a beautiful woman, a model, Léa, who is pursued by her double. That double always appears from behind. The first view Léa catches of her, after having "heard" a voice from the rear seat of the car she's driving, is in the rear-mirror. As the "double" repeats her appearances, Léa's *back* feels constantly under threat. It is a menace she cannot face up to. Hence for her its particular terror.

I had actually come close to experiencing the hallucination Léa is subject to. It had triggered off the book. But it was only *after* I had written *Un Homme nommé Zapolski*, examining at length the data of the case, in 1981-82, that it occurred to me that perhaps, whilst writing *L'Entremise*, I had displaced a fear of an attack from behind. Such an attack was "in the air", I suppose. Or had reports of these attacks unconsciously fuelled a private neurosis? It must have been "unconscious", because it was not known at the time how the attacks were conducted. It was not known that the killer always struck from behind. When I looked at the evidence, and later thought about Léa, I was struck by the report that Sutcliffe himself had a phobia about being approached from behind: he always stood or sat with his back to the wall. All the surviving victims now live the nightmare of the same exacerbated phobia. Furthermore, Sutcliffe, it seems, suffered from a "Dr. Jekyll and Mr. Hyde" syndrome - had, or cultivated, two interdependent and contradictory personalities. *L'Entremise* is "about" such a syndrome, but as it affects a *woman*. Also, Sutcliffe always "hunted" by car. One of his cars at least (as reported by one of the survivors) had *two* rear-mirrors. One of his most proven tactics was to invite his intended prey to climb into the rear-seat of the car, so he could hit her on the back of the head as she bent to climb in. Had *L'Entremise* by accident(?) hit upon a common neurotic/psychotic complex? How did the transference occur? What did it all mean?

There were other "coincidences". One of the stories from *Le Spectre du gris* (1977), "The Wheel", concerns a man's attempt to escape from the "respectable" pressures exerted upon him by his wife and his mother, by means of his car. He fetishizes it, drives wildly, dangerously. It was evident from all that was said about Sutcliffe's treatment of his cars and lorries that similarly fetishistic, though much more aggressive, transfers had been at work for him.

Another story from the same book (published in translation by Virago in 1981) is called "L'Immaculée Conception". It is about a woman who, sexually and emotionally frustrated, suffering from her repeated failures to have a child, becomes maniacal about house-work. She cleans life out of her house, and herself out of life: dies of exhaustion and despair. Sutcliffe's wife, Sonia, is described by all witnesses as having become, through her marriage, fanatically house-proud. She had suffered miscarriages, had been told she could not have a child. She seems to have suffered from sundry sources of frustration too. Sutcliffe himself was punctiliously clean: signed his riddle poem to the *Sheffield Star* "The Streetcleaner". What was literally hallucinating for me in this "well-known syndrome" was that some of the *details* of what was the life of Sutcliffe and his wife were identical to those I had used, "invented", in my story. So that it was as though, in one respect at least, I had already *written the script* of Sonia's experience.

At another, more comprehensive level, I felt concerned by the case: as it involved a man - and his wife - who were *astride* cultures. Caught between different classes, different modes of being, different languages. Sonia was the daughter of first generation immigrants. Spoke Czech at home, English at school and play. Had two names. Sutcliffe's father and mother were of different "classes", different origins (his mother an impoverished middle-class Irish Catholic, his father working-class). In both families there is a complicated relation to *dumbness*, native or inflicted. Because of temperament, of hitches in his upbringing, sexual definition according to one code or another seems to have been impossible for Sutcliffe. Profound socialsexual crises, which had to do with being found "wanting" by the various systems by which he wanted to be recognised (fathered?), certainly helped to precipitate him into violence. With that I could not (at least consciously) identify. But I could recall mis-readings and mishearings of my own, provoked by the clash between my Frenchness and my Englishness, the several "personalities" which are bound up with one milieu or another, and these were not unlike Sutcliffe's hallucination in Bingley cemetery. Coming back on the north-bound train from London after having stayed in France for some time, and perceiving the talk around me *as* French: only, somehow, I can only understand bits of it, and it's rather tiresome. Were I to find it too tiresome - were my resistance to being back in England, hearing English, just a bit more acute - wouldn't I start "interpreting" what I hear *as* French, a French that would make more coherent sense, would be especially exciting because it was half in code (a Message)? Election (how right the term is: a choice *is* implied) is *the* solution for mongrel beings, half-breed, halfcastes, the illegitimate, the sinners who want to be just and cannot stop themselves either from sinning or from wanting to be justified. I could understand this. I once was horrified at seeing there was a "Ripper" recipe in the *Guardian* Women's Page, until a closer inspection revealed it to no worse than a "Kipper" pâté ...

Indeterminacy, indifferentiation - the mind abhors it. I get away with it by moving fast from one world to the next, as you move your eyes up and down when you're wearing bi-focal glasses, avoiding the blur and sickness of the in-between line. Unlike happy, stable people who enjoy the translating activity, I avoid it: a caustic bath of infinite possibilities lies for me between languages. But if you're *doomed* somehow to the state of suspension - what do you do? Begin to draw a phantom line? The line that goes through women? Isn't it either that, or "doing" the "President Schreiber"? Psychosis, or neurosis?

Whereupon we fall back upon the same question: how is it that murder can be seen as the drawing of a line - the making of sense - the way to "phallic" power? Why is it, how is it, that the "virile economy" has this terrifying connection with death? And not just anybody's death: the death of a female.

III. <u>Out?</u>

There had to be a way out. At least an imaginary way out. Being able to *see* some of what had happened, to ask questions the right way round, was already a relief. It seemed to me that the one way I could go further, in my capacity as a writer, which was the only capacity I had, whatever it was worth, was to try and give the murdered women their voices back. Without "possessing" them. Without inflicting hysteria upon them. Without playing, as Sutcliffe had done as a gravedigger in Bingley cemetery, the ventriloquist with the dead. A piece of "fiction" came out. I called it "An Elegy for a dead prostitute". It was "for" one of the women in particular. I gave her as much as I could of what I was when I wrote it.

Where does all this put me? In the middle I expect. Nowhere clear, nowhere clean. But the only place to choose, when you see what wanting the world to be one thing *or* another can amount to.

<u>FOOTNOTES</u>

1. Between July 1975 and January 1981.

2. Writing this, I remember the Dustman's heap in *Our Mutual Friend* - Stephen Dedalus's vision of the infinity of hell in *The Portrait of The Artist as a Young Man*.

3. It may be important to note that the major article written by a *woman* on the Ripper case is by an *American* working on a research grant - in "foreign" territory; and is centred on Jack the Ripper. See Judith R. Walkowitz, "Jack the Ripper and the Myth of Male Violence", *Feminist Studies*, Vol.8, No.3, Fall 1982. There are otherwise three main studies, discounting Superintendent Gregory's recent revelations: Roger Cross, *The Yorkshire Ripper: The In-Depth Study of a Mass-Killer and his Methods*, Granada, 1981; John Beattie, *The Yorkshire Ripper Story*, a Quartet/Daily Star Publication, 1981; and David A. Yallop, *Deliver Us from Evil*, Macdonald Futura, also 1981.

4. There are interesting repeats of this "triangular" situation in the fiction of the period. The King of France - Queen Anne d'Autriche - Cardinal Richelieu in Dumas's *Les Trois Mousquetaires*; and the Lord

Dedlock - Lady Dedlock - Lawyer Tulkinghorn in Dickens's *Bleak House* - not to mention Balzac's *Ferragus* and probably a host of others.